Globalization and Uncertainty in Latin America

Globalization and Uncertainty in Latin America

Edited by
Fernando López-Alves
and
Diane E. Johnson

GLOBALIZATION AND UNCERTAINTY IN LATIN AMERICA
© Fernando López-Alves and Diane E. Johnson, 2007.

All rights reserved. No part of this book may be used or reproduced in any manner whatsoever without written permission except in the case of brief quotations embodied in critical articles or reviews.

First published in 2007 by
PALGRAVE MACMILLAN™
175 Fifth Avenue, New York, N.Y. 10010 and
Houndmills, Basingstoke, Hampshire, England RG21 6XS
Companies and representatives throughout the world.

PALGRAVE MACMILLAN is the global academic imprint of the Palgrave Macmillan division of St. Martin's Press, LLC and of Palgrave Macmillan Ltd. Macmillan® is a registered trademark in the United States, United Kingdom and other countries. Palgrave is a registered trademark in the European Union and other countries.

ISBN-13: 978–1–4039–7893–6
ISBN-10: 1–4039–7893–X

Library of Congress Cataloging-in-Publication Data

    Globalization and Uncertainty in Latin America / edited by Fernando López-Alves and Diane E. Johnson.
      p. cm.
    Includes bibliographical references and index.
    ISBN 1–4039–7893–X (alk. paper)
    1. Globalization—Political aspects—Latin America. 2. Globalization—Economic aspects—Latin America. 3. Uncertainty—Political aspects—Latin America. 4. Uncertainty—Economic aspects—Latin America.
    I. López-Alves, Fernando. II. Johnson, Diane E. (Diane Elizabeth), 1958–

JZ1318.G57923 2007
303.48'28—dc22
                                                2006049486

A catalogue record for this book is available from the British Library.

Design by Newgen Imaging Systems (P) Ltd., Chennai, India.

First edition: March 2007

10 9 8 7 6 5 4 3 2 1

Printed in the United States of America.

Transferred to digital printing in 2009.

Contents

List of Figures   vii

Notes on Contributors   ix

Introduction: Uncertainty and Globalization   1
Fernando López-Alves and Diane E. Johnson

Part 1   The Uncertainties of Liberalism and Neoliberalism, Past and Present

1. Victorian Globalization in Microcosm: The Rise and Fall of Jabez Spencer Balfour   27
   David Rock

2. Uncertainty, the Construction of the Future, and the Divorce Between Citizens and the State in Latin America   47
   Fernando López-Alves

3. Isomorphic Neoliberalism and the Creation of Inevitability   77
   Miguel Ángel Centeno

4. Can the Backlash Against Globalization Be Contained?   97
   Benjamin J. Cohen

Part 2   Uncertain Relations between the State and Civil Society

5. Globalization and Public Policy in the Americas: Are We Heading Toward Convergence?   117
   Diane E. Johnson

6. Development Assistance, the Environment, and Stakeholder Participation: Toward a New Conditionality?   145
   Jonathan Rosenberg

Part 3 Uncertainties about Human Rights and Justice

7 Globalization and the Modern Conception of Human Rights 179
Steven Cassedy

8 Generating Uncertainty: Globalized Punishment and Crime 205
Thomas Siemsen

Conclusion 227
Diane E. Johnson and Fernando López-Alves

Index 237

List of Figures

2.1	Unemployment and Poverty in Buenos Aires, 1988–2002	57
2.2	Do You Think That You Owe Anything to the State?	64
2.3	Are You Aware of Your Obligations Toward the State?	64
2.4	Survey 2001: Who Do You Think Makes the Decisions That Affect the Future of your Country?	66
2.5	Survey 2002: Who Do You Think Makes the Decisions That Affect the Future of your Country?	66
2.6	Survey 2003: Who Do You Think Makes the Decisions That Affect the Future of Your Country?	66
2.7	Survey 2004: Who Do You Think Makes the Decisions That Affect the Future of Your Country?	67
2.8	Do You Think This Country Got What it Deserves or Is a Victim of International Circumstances?	69
2.9	What Type of Future Do You Favor for This Country?	70
3.1	Government Expenditures	81
3.2	Latin American Government Deficits	82
3.3	Social Expenditures	83
3.4	Government Employment	83
3.5	Growth of Inequality in Latin America	84
3.6	Poverty in Latin America	84
3.7	Urban Unemployment in Latin America	85
3.8	Latin American Inflation	85
3.9	Openness to Trade	86
3.10	Terms of Trade	86
3.11	Share of Global Wealth	87
3.12	U.S. and European Audiovisual Trade (Includes Theatrical Films, Videos, and TV Programs)	89
3.13	Latin American Telephone	90

3.14	Latin American Tourism	90
3.15	Debt Growth	92
3.16	FDI in Latin America	93
3.17	Total FDI	93
3.18	Types of Investment Portfolio/Direct	94
5.1	The Media-State System and Globalization	126

Notes on Contributors

Steven Cassedy is Professor of Slavic and Comparative Literature, Director of Eleanor Roosevelt College's Making of the Modern World, and Associate Dean of Graduate Studies at the University of California, San Diego. His research interests include Russian literature, other western European literatures, intellectual history of the West, and Russian-Jewish and American-Jewish cultural history. He is the author of *Selected Essays of Andrew Bely* (1985), *Flight from Eden: The Rise of Modern Literary Criticism and Theory* (1990), *To the Other Shore: The Russian Jewish Intellectuals Who Came to America* (1997), and *Dostoevsky's Religion* (2005). He has also published articles in *Slavic and East European Journal* and *Russian History*.

Miguel Ángel Centeno is Professor of Sociology and International Affairs and Director of the Princeton Institute for International and Regional Studies. He has published nine books as author or editor including *Democracy within Reason: Technocratic Revolution in Mexico* (2nd ed., 1997), *Blood and Debt: War and Statemaking in Latin America* (2002), *The Other Mirror: Grand Theory and Latin America* (2001), and *Essays in Latin American Military History* (2005). He serves as an editor for several journals including *World Politics*. He has received grants from the Harry Frank Guggenheim Foundation, the National Science Foundation, the National Endowment for the Humanities, and the Woodrow Wilson Foundation. He has been a Fulbright scholar in Russia and Mexico and a visiting professor at Korea University in Seoul.

Benjamin J. Cohen is Louis G. Lancaster Professor of International Political Economy at the University of California, Santa Barbara. He previously taught at Princeton University and the Fletcher School of Law and Diplomacy, Tufts University. His numerous publications have addressed issues of international monetary relations, U.S. foreign economic policy, monetary integration, developing country debt, and theories of economic imperialism. He is the author of ten books, including

The Geography of Money (1998), *The Future of Money* (2004), and *The Future of the Dollar* (2006).

Diane E. Johnson is Assistant Professor of Political Science at Lebanon Valley College (PA). She has published book chapters on the relationship between interest groups and political parties in Argentina, and the democratic impact of the Internet in the United States. She has also presented several papers on the effects of globalization on media-state relations in Latin America, the impact of neoliberal economic reforms on democracy in Argentina, and issues related to freedom of the press in the Southern Cone. She is currently doing research on the reemergence of the left in recent South American elections, and the relationship between neopopulist leaders and the mass media.

Fernando López-Alves is Professor of Sociology and International Studies at the University of California, Santa Barbara. From 1997 to 2001, he directed the University of California Washington Program, and he has served as a member of the boards of several nongovernmental organizations and foundations. He has published several books: *Between the Economy and the River Plate* (1993), *State Formation and Democracy in Latin America* (2000), and *Societies without Future* (2002). He is also coauthor of *The Other Mirror: Grand Theory and Latin America* (2001), and co-editor of *Seven Scenarios for the 21st Century* (2004). His articles on globalization, Latin America, and comparative politics have appeared in *Latin American Research Review*, edited collections, and *Past & Present*. He is presently working on another book, *States, Nations and Futures*.

David Rock is Professor of History at the University of California, Santa Barbara. He is the author of *Politics in Argentina, 1890–1930: The Rise and Fall of Radicalism* (1975), *Argentina 1516–1987: From Spanish Colonization to Raúl Alfonsín* (1987), *Authoritarian Argentina: The National Movement, its History and its Impact* (1993), and *State Building and Political Movements in Argentina, 1860–1916* (2002). He also edited *Argentina in the Twentieth Century* (1975) and *Latin America in the 1940s* (1994), and he has published numerous articles and book reviews in journals including *Latin American Research Review, Cambridge History of Latin America, Past & Present, Hispanic American Historical Review*, and *Journal of Social History*.

Jonathan Rosenberg is Associate Professor of Political Science at the University of Alaska, Fairbanks. He is coauthor of *Comparative*

Environmental Politics (2006) and has authored several papers and book chapters on Cuban political economy, Mexican parties and interest groups, and participatory environmental management in the Eastern Caribbean. His current research evaluates the activities of development assistance agencies, multilateral lending institutions, and nongovernmental organizations as they affect the participation of local stakeholders in environmentally sustainable development projects. His articles have appeared in *Latin American Research Review, Journal of Environmental Management, Global Environmental Politics,* and *Journal of International Wildlife Law and Policy.*

Thomas Siemsen is currently a consultant to several federal government agencies in the areas of government acquisition policy and organizational structuring. He has previously taught at the Defense Acquisition University in Virginia, and the Industrial College of the Armed Forces in Washington, DC, and he has guest lectured at Cranfield University, UK. His previous articles have appeared in *History of Political Thought* and *Acquisition Quarterly Review.*

Introduction: Uncertainty and Globalization

Fernando López-Alves and Diane E. Johnson

Is globalization a novel phenomenon that requires a new academic paradigm, or does it reproduce familiar patterns of capitalist development that we have studied for almost two centuries? As this volume and many others reveal, the definition of globalization varies—and the debate as to whether the concept means too much or anything at all is far from resolved. Like Alice in Wonderland, academics and practitioners traveling through the intricate world of globalization literature at times find realities that turn into fantasy, and fantasies that become tangible facts. It often seems as if our center of gravity shifts so quickly that both the phenomena that we seek to explain and our resulting explanations are caught in a whirlwind.

It would be pretentious or even foolish to claim that the goal of this volume is to offer a secure haven from this, in many ways welcome, storm. We see the ongoing debate about the meaning and scope of globalization, with its different trajectories and levels of analysis, as a very healthy development. We not only believe that the controversy about globalization has contributed to a vigorous revitalization of social science, history, and economic theory without parallel during this and most of the last centuries, but we also believe that it is time to concern ourselves with the unintended consequences produced by this process. We seek to demonstrate that frequent shifts in direction and intent create strong uncertainty among actors and that this in turn can alter the very definition of globalization. At least in Latin America, uncertainty is a feeling shared by both elites and masses. Our objective is to reveal some of the practical consequences of this uncertainty, as well as to contribute to the theoretical debate on globalization that has emerged in the past two decades. A focus on the connection between globalization and uncertainty will shed valuable new light on the important and often radical changes affecting both individual nation-states and the international system of power.

Uncertainty results when the outcome of a situation is not known or fixed, just as the direction and effects of twisting winds are unpredictable. The whirlwind analogy applies to those who aim to construct a theory of globalization, but it also reflects the day-to-day experience—within the framework of different social, institutional, and political contexts—of all those caught up in the global process. Particularly in the developing world, this experience produces uncertainty in the minds and lives of people who see globalization as a force that they cannot control. It also creates some degree of uncertainty among policymakers and financial circles in countries that have been implicitly, or at times explicitly, portrayed as the generators of the rules, institutions, and soft power that promote what we loosely call "globalization."

The liberal reforms that accompanied the process of globalization in Latin America sought, among other things, to eliminate uncertainty. The objective was to wipe away blurred and outdated regulations, to promote transparency in economic transactions, and to impose the rule of law in countries where investors faced considerable uncertainty and risk. International Monetary Fund (IMF) and World Bank packages gave priority to clear rules of competition that would attract foreign direct investment (FDI) and provide new incentives for local entrepreneurship. Although most reformers knew that in the short run major changes in economy and society would bring about higher levels of uncertainty and risk, their long-term goal was to provide a framework for economic development based on clear market rules, international standards of excellence, and transparent regulations. This would ultimately lower uncertainty to a minimum. In the early (or "traditional") literature on globalization disseminated by the World Bank and the IMF, as well as in the manifestos of many governments that quickly adhered to the cause, globalization was conceived as a mixture of fatalism, salvation, and punishment.[1] Yet punishment would be of limited duration, and salvation more than rewarding. The predictions are well known. As states become more efficient and international competition comes to rule the marketplace, national entrepreneurs and groups seek benefits that were hitherto public. In the long run, privatization helps pave the way to prosperity and stable democracy. Thus in the initial phase of global integration, uncertainty is a necessary but temporary evil.

We argue in this volume, however, that after more than 25 years of first- and second-phase liberal reforms, uncertainty in Latin America is far from disappearing. On the contrary, individuals, firms, private and public institutions, as well as other actors, continue to exist in an uncertain and risky environment. Uncertainty has become an integral part of the process of globalization itself. This collection of chapters studies some of consequences of uncertainty in the social, political, and economic context. Economists and other social scientists have long engaged in a debate about the meaning, scope, and consequences of uncertainty.[2] The free enterprise system is, in an often-cited reference to economist Frank H. Knight, strongly linked to risk and uncertainty. According to Knight, uncertainty cannot totally be avoided because it is an intrinsic part of economic transactions. At the same time, however, according to Knight the very development of capitalism reduces its influence both in the material world and in the minds of decision makers. His argument is simple and sound: "capitalization brings about a reduction of uncertainty through consolidation (of capital)," and as the free enterprise system contributes to the "consolidation of capital, indeterminateness becomes less of a problem."[3] Thus, Knight associates the very existence of the free enterprise system with risk and uncertainty. The study of this equation contributes, for Knight and others, to a better explanation for profit, demand for assets, financing, the size of firms, expected utility, investment decisions, and so forth.

Following Knight's reasoning, one could argue that since in most developing societies globalization has not brought about enough capital consolidation, uncertainty is higher. Given the characteristics of mobile capital, shifting international investment flows, and the fact that in most cases national industry faces insolvency rather than prosperity, capital consolidation seems difficult to obtain. The 1996 tequila shock in Mexico, the 1998 Brazilian crisis, and the economic debacles that followed in Argentina and Uruguay, in addition to the high risks incurred by Chile's successful experiment with liberal reform toward the end of the 1990s, spoke more of increasing uncertainty and risk than of order and capital consolidation. Indeed, these financial crises, following nearly two decades of liberal reforms in different countries, produced almost the opposite of what the reform-minded policymakers had predicted. As of mid-2006 these countries and the rest of Latin America continued to experience high levels of both uncertainty and risk. Going back to Knight's argument, dubious capital consolidation in Latin America and the confusing new economic, political, and social rules that accompanied liberal reforms, strengthened uncertainty rather than diminishing it.

Are uncertainty and risk one and the same thing? Many economists, among them Knight, have treated uncertainty and risk as connected phenomena.[4] Yet most of them agree that for analytical purposes, these two concepts should be treated separately.[5] The major difference is that one can theorize better about risk than one can about uncertainty, because under risk situations we can still make a probability distribution of outcomes; under uncertainty, this is almost impossible to achieve.

While it is not our aim to review the economists' debate on uncertainty and risk, the arguments offered in that literature are quite helpful in understanding the connection between globalization and uncertainty as we see it in Latin America. Our meaning and use of the term is broader and more descriptive than the technical definitions used in economic literature, but our use of the concept of uncertainty is close to the definition offered by John Maynard Keynes: a condition that does not allow us even to know what possible outcomes could occur. His argument is that in an uncertain situation we are unable to distinguish what is known from what is probable; it means that when something is uncertain we cannot actually form any calculable probability that would help us predict the outcome. Depending on changes in the social, legal, political, and economic environments, what is uncertain today may be more certain tomorrow. But it is also true that in a situation of uncertainty one finds one's capacity to make decisions about the future seriously diminished. We find this to be a ubiquitous problem in Latin America. Indeed, the economist Kenneth Arrow and others have argued that we cannot even theorize in the face of uncertainty.[6]

What we mean by uncertainty, therefore, connects with the economic debate, but it is perhaps more straightforward. We simply suggest that in the face of rapid change and shifting rules, uncertainty creates an inability to plan ahead. More than a quarter of a century into the most recent wave of globalization, Latin America has gone through unsettling times that have called into question the rationality assumption—that is, that people make the best possible rational decisions when they possess sufficient information, when they are motivated, and when the problems are simple. In the instances studied in this volume, globalization led to an environment that was not conducive to rationality. Unexpected outcomes turned out to be more the rule than the exception.

As some of the chapters show, the old rules of the political and economic game have collapsed, and the new set of rules that was supposed to replace them is often confusing and treacherous. This has caused most citizens to feel uncertain about their environment and to believe that they and their societies are at risk. Numerous factors lead to uncertainty about the present and future: the complexities of the financial market and international competition, the strong presence of foreign investment (or the lack of it when it is wanted badly), radical transformations in state institutions and in the workplace, changes in capital ownership and different labor codes, deregulation, and shrinking welfare systems accompanied by spectacularly high levels of unemployment. This weakens trust. Politicians have been increasingly seen as retailers of public goods for their own benefit. Their reputation as a corrupt group that manipulates public opinion has skyrocketed. Governments are aware that their own agencies have limited power to tackle the problems they face, but the political elites are reluctant to delegate that power to other organizations. The retreat of the welfare state, or simply the elimination of social programs, means that one of the mechanisms for managing insecurity is no longer available. The public expects a quick compensation for the shrinking of public policy, but this generally does not happen. When it does, the new measures only generate further discontent. In sum, in Latin America as elsewhere, changes in the way people think about their social and institutional environment tend to undermine trust in the capacity of both public and private services to handle the consequences of uncertainty.

In this volume, the Argentine case fares prominently. Several of the essays focus on Argentina's experience with liberal reform and globalization. We believe that this is a particularly interesting and telling case regarding the connection between globalization and uncertainty. First, it was considered the "poster child" of neoliberal economic reforms in the early- to-mid 1990s. Therefore, if the reforms should have reduced uncertainty anywhere, we would have expected it here. This did not happen, and we wanted to ask "why"? Second, Argentina is an excellent testing ground for our argument about the integration of *uncertainty* as a variable in the debate about globalization. The country has experienced some of the most drastic social and political changes in the continent in connection with globalization. It has, for instance, undergone one of the major financial crises of Latin America—so critical that it led to the removal from office of an elected president and the shattering of the whole financial system. Third, Argentina provides an example of the political left's advent to power in Latin America in recent years. As at least two of the chapters in this collection show, whether the current Argentine government can be labeled "leftist" or "progressive" remains an open question. We would characterize the current government of Néstor Kirchner as a sort of leftist, progressive-populist government that emerged in part as a reaction to neoliberal reforms and the political fragility they provoked—rather than one with a radical reform agenda. Indeed, while the left has achieved important electoral victories in the region[7] and while some of these countries have embarked on serious social reform, this is not entirely the case in Argentina. Nonetheless, the Kirchner administration has elaborated a leftist-Peronist popular discourse, and has embarked on some social reform. As with other left-leaning governments in the region, Argentina's has tried to find a way to retain the benefits of liberalism while at the same time creating a more progressive regime that could modify and correct the negative social effects of liberal reform. In sum, during the 1990s and the first years of the twenty-first century, Argentina offers an excellent case study to capture the impact of globalization, the full adoption of the liberal reform package, and the drastic social, economic, and political adjustments that followed.

We suspect that globalization by its very nature is accompanied by uncertainty everywhere, and we hope that experts on other countries and regions will engage in this dialog. It is clear at this point that the promises of globalization have not been fulfilled and that the assurance of a better future, central to liberal reform and to the process of globalization, has not materialized. Many hopes have been shattered. By the end of the 1990s, most of the staunchest supporters of globalization faced frustration and discontent. This includes the enthusiastic entrepreneurs who perceived globalization as a golden opportunity for getting ahead, the financiers who believed that liberal reforms could only benefit their business and their countries, the politicians who took liberalism as the backbone of their political strategy and ideology, the producers who hoped for a more profitable export economy and global openness, and the business leaders who took the liberal credo to heart. Moreover, the lower classes also confronted growing frustration. In fact, as we shall see in the following chapters, they encountered even more serious challenges and were more drastically exposed to the ups and downs of uncertainty.

Did the mass public hope that liberal reform would bring about some prosperity and less uncertainty, or were the expectations limited to the political and economic elites in Latin America? We cannot answer this with complete confidence, but important indicators suggest that the bulk of the population initially did view globalization with considerable optimism. During the early 1990s, electoral results throughout the region reflected the expectation that globalization and sound economic reform was the right economic strategy and would very likely bring about tangible prosperity. President Carlos Menem of Argentina won a second term in 1995 precisely because the people of Argentina supported his liberal policies and especially his strategy of pegging the peso to the dollar ("convertability"). In Chile, there is little doubt that people voted for a package of neoliberal reforms with the conviction that economic reform would continue to improve the country's situation.[8] In public opinion surveys in Uruguay in the mid-1990s, respondents identified the government of President Luis Alberto Lacalle de Herrera—the most neoliberal of all presidents since the early 1980s—as the most prosperous government since the return to democracy.

As Kurt Weyland has noted, "a majority of the population, including large numbers of poor people" initially supported the painful economic shock treatments imposed in Argentina by Menem, in Brazil by Fernando Collor de Mello, and in Peru by Alberto Fujimori.[9] In the early 1990s, presidential popularity rose significantly in the weeks following the implementation of the liberal package: Menem enjoyed approval ratings of 85–89 percent, Collor of 74–81 percent, and Fujimori of up to 60 percent.[10] These figures suggest that the level of public trust in economic globalization was relatively high and that the future seemed promising. Today, however, as the chapter by López-Alves argues, it seems almost impossible for the common Latin American citizen to plan for the future with any degree of certitude. Sound economics and the wisdom of the market were supposed to secure the well-being of Latin Americans regardless of social class, ethnicity, or race. By 2006, however, market wisdom had yet to deliver such an outcome. In the late 1980s most of the region's governments trusted the wisdom of global markets and liberalization. The downsizing of the state became a substitute for local development strategies, and officials believed that exposure and competitiveness would achieve what past development plans had not. Today, increasing numbers of economists admit that globalization as a development strategy for Latin America has failed to provide sustained development and stability.[11]

The political benefits of liberal reform also remain elusive. If globalization was supposed to help the economy, it was also supposed to create democracies that, spreading their influence around the world, would secure more stable government structures and offer more opportunities to all. Instead, political instability spread throughout the continent after the early 1990s. From Peru to Ecuador and from Argentina to Bolivia, the political landscape was uncertain. While political instability in Latin America obviously long predates liberal reform, the idea was precisely that liberal reform would resolve the problem. Today, we know that it did not.

Is this the fault of Latin Americans? Has the region failed to take the necessary steps to reap the benefits of neoliberalism and globalization? Has Latin America been too slow to adjust and comply with the new policies? As can be seen in the following chapters, the answer is negative. In fact, it has been the opposite. Moreover, we submit that Latin America's entry into the new global order offers a fascinating opportunity not only to better understand the region but also to construct a different perspective from which to analyze the present evolution of the international system of power. We argue that rather than remaining at the margin of world developments—as some have suggested—Latin America has eagerly responded to globalization, incorporating and transforming some of the components of the theory along the way. In particular, the region offers an intriguing case of reaction and adaptation in the context of strong international pressures and high levels of domestic insecurity.

What makes Latin America particularly valuable as a study for students of globalization is that as a whole, the region's reaction to global forces has not been characterized by the violence and terrorism of the Middle East, nor by fatal fractures in state structures and bloody political wars as in much of Africa. The comparative study and classification—in terms of their explanatory power—of the many contextual factors that separate Latin America from these other regions in regards to globalization can enrich our theorizing about this phenomenon. Indeed, systematic comparisons among these areas in terms of their reaction, adjustment, and innovations in connection to global change and the rise of the United States as the most influential superpower in the international system, would lead to a redefinition of globalization theory itself. Latin America's response to global forces and liberal reform stands out as a fascinating case of adjustment and reaction.

Politically, for instance, unlike other regions most of Latin America today is resisting the influence of the United States both from below and from above. Traditionally, opposition to the United States in Latin America has taken the form of social mobilization and grassroots collective action, including the mobilization of radical political movements against established governments. Today, however, some of these movements have either conquered a share in power, or are in power. Thus, they and others voice their opposition from within the state. We can argue that the left's advent to power in the region, whether in its more radical versions (Venezuela and to an extent Bolivia) or in its milder forms (Uruguay, Argentina, Chile, and Brazil) has led to a new phenomenon: resistance to U.S. influence on the part of democratically elected governments.

The authors whose work is included in this volume suggest that in Latin America and elsewhere, societies have been forced to adopt a variety of new ways to cope with local and global insecurity. Indeed, the creation of new public and financial policies on the part of states, in addition to both organized and spontaneous manifestations of discontent on the part of the populace, are connected to the increasing message of uncertainty that globalization has conveyed—and even promoted—in the developing world. The chapters show that uncertainty extends well beyond concerns about the future of the economy and has started to shape culture, society, and politics.

The chapters by David Rock, Miguel Centeno, and Benjamin Cohen submit that the economic transformations that these societies have endured, either in the first wave of globalization or since the late 1970s, include a strong component of uncertainty. We can also detect the impact of uncertainty at the level of organized groups, culture, and the attitudes of the public. For instance, in his chapter, Fernando López-Alves examines the impact of uncertainty on public opinion and in the way Argentines today conceive of the future. Thomas Siemsen and Steven Cassedy, respectively, consider evolving notions of punishment and human rights that affect institutions, politics, and culture, in the context of increasing global uncertainty. The chapters by Diane Johnson and Jonathan Rosenberg focus on shifts in public policymaking, the former in the area of communication policy and the latter in the area of environmental policy. Cohen, Centeno, and López-Alves also speak to the notion that the adoption of neoliberalism means much more than the implementation of a given economic policy; it means the construction of a new mindset and the incorporation of new ideological and cultural ingredients to better cope with ambiguity and insecurity.

Indeed, our argument that uncertainty shapes behavior is in some ways similar to the claims of those who contend that social discipline shapes behavior. One is compelled to remember Michel Foucault's dictum that "[disciplinary power] . . . introduces . . . the constraint of a conformity that must be achieved."[12] The chapters in this volume, however, suggest that the disciplinary power of globalization and the standards it imposes are still in the making. This is because uncertainty prevents a settled criterion for conformity and triggers unforeseen outcomes. People in Latin America have had to adjust to a hierarchy imposed by neoliberal reforms, superpower foreign policies, transformations in international norms and jurisdictions, increasing U.S. soft power, and changing agendas of state reform. This volume suggests that all such adjustments have created uncertainty and have been implemented in the context of increasing insecurity. This, we argue, has influenced the social, economic, and political costs for

Latin American societies, as well as the sort of political and institutional solutions (or compromises) that they have finally adopted. In addition, many of the outcomes have been unexpected in the sense that they differed from the objectives contained in the original agendas of first- and second-phase liberal reforms. We assert that scholars need to focus not only on the norms imposed by globalization but also on how the subsequent levels of uncertainty have shaped outcomes. Again, we believe that only by bringing uncertainty as a variable to the equation will scholars be able to develop an adequate theory of the consequences, scope, and future of globalization in Latin America.

Overall, the following chapters contend that the region is the byproduct of an unsettled environment in which standards and disciplinary norms are quite unclear. Uncertainty regarding outcomes and procedures contributes to a confusing milieu in which, among other things, elites seem unable to articulate a clear and coherent picture of what is right or wrong, and what is feasible or attainable. Political elites seem, as the chapter by López-Alves suggests, incapable of elaborating a view of "the nation" that combines the works of the market with the works of government. States and markets seem to act separately under different logics and divergent sets of rules; despite the "return" of the state depicted in some recent scholarly literature, the state in some ways seems to have less control over society than it did in the past. The legitimacy of the democratic systems that emerged (or reemerged) in the 1980s and early 1990s is at stake, and most citizens in Latin America think that their countries are not on the right track.[13] We argue that globalization has created great uncertainty at both the individual and state levels and that this uncertainty is now one of the most noticeable aspects of globalization in Latin America.

THE PLACE OF LATIN AMERICA IN THE GLOBALIZATION LITERATURE

Latin America has occupied a marginal place in most of the mainstream theorizing on globalization. With the exception of some work by economists or humanists, the literature on globalization offers few systematic references to the region. Economists have written about the effects of globalization on tax reform and economic policy in Latin America, usually with the goal of prescribing economic policy.[14] Scholars in the humanities and social sciences have contributed equally useful analyses of the cultural and social transformations affecting the region.[15] In addition, a host of valuable work has come from Marxists and neo-Marxists,[16] and from authors who have attempted to place Latin America in the context of globalization literature from other theoretical perspectives.[17] All in all, however, Latin America is largely absent from the mainstream comparative and theoretical literature on global transformation. One of our chief objectives with this volume is to help remedy this deficiency.

Asia, Europe, and of course the United States dominate scholarly attention and furnish most of the data used to prove or disprove the power of globalization. Discussions about the evolution of global capital, its impact on culture, institutions, and markets, typically do not include Latin America. Despite the many crises of neoliberalism, the readjustments undergone by the South American trading bloc MERCOSUR, the interesting political and economic history of the North American Free Trade Agreement (NAFTA), and the advent of leftist governments in many countries during the past years, Latin America has received far less attention than western Europe, the Asian "tigers," China, or even Russia.[18]

Curiously enough, the current literature on the creation of empire also largely ignores Latin America. The theoretical work on empire has understandably concentrated on whether the United States is entering a phase of empire, and whether this will mean substantial changes for different regions of the world. Yet Latin America, the region closest to the United States and one of the soundest historical examples of U.S. intervention and influence, is hardly considered in this literature.[19] Nor has the scholarship coming from Latin America addressed the role that the region would play in a new world order if, as some have argued, an age of empire is effectively on the rise.[20] This lacuna is more striking given the strong tradition in Latin American scholarly literature of stressing international factors such as imperialism and U.S. influence to explain the region's economics and politics. The legacy of those who once wrote extensively about Latin America and its transformations in the context of empire, militarism, imperialism, and capitalist expansion, apparently has not motivated today's scholars to do research about the region in the context of changing globalization.[21] Thus, much work still needs to be done.

One reason why Latin America has not been fully incorporated into the conventional theoretical discussion about globalization, and why Latin American cases do not figure prominently in this literature, is that many observers believe that the region has remained rather dormant while others have reacted quickly to the incentives offered by globalization. Contrary to the striking evidence offered by countries such as Argentina, Brazil, Chile, Ecuador, Bolivia, Venezuela, and Peru, the picture that emerged of Latin America during the decade of the 1990s and early 2000s was one of sluggish and leisurely adaptation to the demands of global markets.[22] Moreover, the region mainly has been portrayed as a "globalization receiver," rather than a "globalization generator." Latin America's limited participation in world trade seems to have contributed to its meager role in the construction of theory about globalization or empire. Of course, the lethargic integration of Latin America into the world economy, if that were the case, could itself provide solid justification for incorporating the region into the debate on globalization. Slow integration or the lack of it appears as puzzling as quick integration. Yet most literature has concentrated primarily on the superpowers and those countries in Asia and Europe that "reacted" quickly and as expected.

Neoliberalism and Integration

For many years, the discussion about globalization and the adoption of neoliberal policies in Latin America has been confined largely to the study of regional trade agreements such as NAFTA and MERCOSUR, as well as the economic consequences of neoliberalism and the "rescue" packages imposed by the IMF and World Bank. Attention has now been turned toward the consolidation of the 34-nation Free Trade Area of the Americas (FTAA) that was supposed to be completed in 2005.[23] A debate on economic and commercial integration is always welcome, and we do not deny the importance of these developments. But the debate on globalization and neoliberal reform in Latin America cannot stop there. The key question, for instance, of why neoliberalism was accepted so rapidly and became a dominant policy for the most important financial agents of globalization (e.g., the IMF and World Bank) has not been a central part of this debate. This is an important issue and serves as the topic of Miguel Centeno's chapter in this collection. Given its centrality to the debate on globalization and integration, most of the chapters in this volume focus in one way or another on neoliberalism and its consequences for Latin America.

Integration has of course been seen as a response to globalization, but as some of the authors suggest, one can also conceive it as a move *against* globalization. After all, we have heard sound arguments that regional free trade should not be confused with global free trade. Agreements such as MERCOSUR may in reality stand in opposition to the creation of a global market, and its goal may be to shelter members from global competitiveness. One gets this impression from the rise of new governments in Venezuela, Argentina, Brazil, and

Uruguay that seem to be looking for new ways to consolidate integration while at the same time offering an alternative to U.S. dominance in the region, as well as selectively protecting their markets from foreign competition (as much as this can be possible).

Historically, Latin America has collectively lacked the will to act as a trading bloc. Yet today we may be seeing serious attempts at regional integration. This push toward integration has been provoked by opposition to U.S. policies and the FTAA's prescription for regional integration. This is especially true in the context of MERCOSUR. A leftist MERCOSUR, or at least a MERCOSUR that seeks not to play by the rules of the United States, is one unintended consequence of the adoption of neoliberal policies. Broken promises of economic prosperity in tandem with the declining appeal of the traditional political parties opened the way for the return of the left.

This may mark an important policy shift in regards to integration and postneoliberal economic planning. This is an initiative of integration that originated in the region while a number of previous efforts were led by North America. The FTAA is mainly a U.S. initiative and so is NAFTA. If one goes back to Latin American strategies for regional integration in the nineteenth and twentieth centuries, the picture that emerges is one of disarray and frustration. Long before the beginning of the postwar wave of globalization, governments in the region talked about integration and made grandiose plans for Latin American solidarity and trade cooperation. In reality, they made very little concrete progress. One can cite the Central American Common Market as an example: a great struggle that rendered little. Almost the same argument can be made about the Andean Pact, which likewise accomplished more on paper than in practice.[24] Although the traditional rivalry between Argentina and Brazil may jeopardize the process, it is possible that we are witnessing a very different move toward integration today. And as we suggest later in this chapter, Chinese policies toward the area may provide a further incentive to integrate.

Globalization and Democracy

For more than two decades the prominent—in fact, nearly dominant—theme in the social science literature on Latin America has been democratization. Scholars have analyzed transitions to democracy, democratization, redemocratization, and democratic consolidation. This has created a strong theoretical base for the interpretation of democratization elsewhere.[25] Curiously enough, however, it has not provoked a serious discussion about the relationship between democratization and globalization. Some observers have remarked, of course, that globalization has not delivered its promise of democracy and that the region has failed to achieve political stability. In some ways, we can argue that a major part of Latin America is worse today than it was just a few years ago. The most frequently noted examples include a severely unequal distribution of wealth, poor economic performance, discriminatory public policy, and political unrest.

Thus, assurances that globalization would lead to deepening democracy, enhanced security, and fuller employment have not materialized. Instead, financial crises in 1995 and 1998—and a third in December 2001 in Argentina—revealed Latin America's political and economic vulnerability. Therefore, the message of democratic consolidation under globalization is, at best, mixed. Most opinion polls indicate that while a number of people in the region still prefer democracy to more authoritarian systems of government, their dissatisfaction with the former is rising significantly.[26] And the influence of the United States has been constantly challenged. Some countries followed the path predicted by liberal reform and democratized their political systems in the image of liberal democracy. But these are exceptions. Liberal democracy in Latin America has not necessarily strengthened ties with the United States.

Mexico appears to have followed the pattern predicted by those who saw globalization as beneficial, at least in the sense that it did evolve into a more competitive political system. There, a centralized political system broke down in 2000 with the victory of the opposition candidate Vicente Fox in the first truly open presidential elections in seven decades. His administration was friendly to the United States, but this was clearly to a great extent a consequence of NAFTA. Yet in Brazil, which for more than a decade has shown a solid and clean election record, a different type of leadership emerged. In 2002, Brazilians elected Luiz Inácio Lula da Silva, a former left-winger who, although shifting toward the middle of the political spectrum, has tried to stand up against U.S. interests. In Venezuela, the antiglobalization and anti-U.S. President Hugo Chávez gained office by an ample majority in 1998 and was reelected in 2000. Bolivia under the new President Evo Morales is not very likely to be friendly to the United States, and in Chile the government has adopted an approach to public policy and the role of the state that starts to differ more and more from neoliberal prescriptions. In neighboring Argentina, the social democrat and Peronist Kirchner won the 2003 presidential election and in Uruguay, socialist Tabaré Vázquez assumed the presidency in March 2005. Regarding the establishing of democracy, therefore, as in anything else, we have seen a number of unexpected developments.

The role of the middle class in these democracies is another intriguing development. The middle class traditionally has been considered a necessary ingredient of democracy; yet the processes of democratization in the region have gone hand-in-hand with the decline of the middle class. Argentina is an extreme case that provides the worst possible news: from January 2002 to the time of this writing, more than 5 million middle-class Argentines have fallen below the poverty line. In Uruguay, the numbers are not as high, but they could reach a similarly terrifying level if the financial situation does not quickly change for the better. Peru, Venezuela, Ecuador, and Colombia are encountering the same problem, and most of Central America remains unable to produce a significant middle class. One of the defining features of these democracies is that they have consolidated and transformed in a context of increasing uncertainty. This has clear implications for the quality of democracy. We stress that increasing uncertainty has been a mark of the times for Latin America during the past two decades and that it has forced people and governments to create new ways to cope with change, and to construct different forms of interaction with the domestic and international environments.

Conclusions: One Claim and Some Suggestions

The chapters in this book advance one claim and some suggestions. We qualify them as "suggestions" because the chapters herein touch upon them only lightly; they are stated as ideas for future research rather than as part of this volume's findings.

Our central claim is that Latin America has rapidly assimilated and responded to the message of uncertainty contained in the very process of globalization. It has done so at the political, cultural, and institutional levels. It seems that the rapid transformations we detect in this volume all are characterized by a strong drive to cope with uncertainty. Different conceptions of public policy, the evolution of notions of punishment and crime, changes in the relations between civil society and the state, the transformation in the ways that people act collectively at the local and global levels, and, in particular, the local assimilation of these changes by Latin American elites and masses alike, reflect attempts to cope with uncertainty. This uncertainty in part derives from structural economic changes associated with the logic of free markets; unemployment, for instance, is a great generator of uncertainty. But it has also been the result of a restructuring of civil society, the role of the state, and collective action that has taken on a life of its own as people in the region have sought in various ways to adjust to neoliberalism. We believe that the incorporation of uncertainty as a causal factor in explaining globalization will contribute to our understanding of a number of unexpected outcomes—unexpected at least by the liberal reformers in the late 1980s and early 1990s. We do not want to be misinterpreted. We are not denying the enormous and predictable impact of global markets, communications, or international financial institutions upon the region. Who could? Rather, we argue that the array of community and institutional responses do not necessarily follow the expected character, goals, and pace of reform.

One of our suggestions is that Latin America has been responsive to the logic of free markets and the expansion of global capital but has been so unevenly and in fascinating and varied ways that need to be incorporated into mainstream social science literature on globalization and empire. Some chapters in this volume offer a contribution in that direction. It is precisely because Latin America does not compare to the Asian and European experiences (overall considered successful cases) or to the Middle East and Africa (overall considered unsuccessful cases) that it presents a superb opportunity to rethink the impact of global capital on developing societies and the emerging cultures of globalization. During the reign of modernization theory and again under the supremacy of globalization theory, Latin America has offered fascinating lessons not yet fully understood or used in comparative analysis.

Another suggestion is that the relationship between globalization and uncertainty opens new avenues for future research. We give two examples here. First, the correlation between institutions and regimes in the framework of global capital needs to be seriously revisited in light of Latin American examples, especially the rise of leftist governments through elections. While for many years Chile under Salvador Allende stood as the exception in having elected a socialist government, today the exceptions may very well become a rule. Second, we need to examine the role of the state and its relationship to civil society in contexts of uncertainty. How are states responding to the spread of global cultural parameters? Diane Johnson's chapter about the relations between the state and the media under globalization suggests that these cultural transformations are indeed taking place. This is tied to the question of social collective action under conditions that are far from certain and where actors cannot guess outcomes with any degree of certitude. Whether these practices are creating a "cultural revolution" with visible social and political consequences in a number of countries is still to be seen. Yet we suggest that different scenarios promoting that kind of "revolution" are developing in the area. From very different perspectives, the chapters by Miguel Centeno and Fernando López-Alves offer a similar proposal.

A last suggestion is that Latin America should be seen as an actor of globalization and not simply as a passive respondent to global forces. The new partnership of South American countries with China, for instance, indicates a strong sense of initiative on the part of Latin American governments (at least in South America) that may signify a shift from the Atlantic to the Pacific in terms of favorite trade routes and foci of development. This may accomplish what responses to global plans for integration generated outside the area have not. In fact, some have argued that China may play a role in South America reminiscent of the so-called informal British Empire of the nineteenth century, when Britain controlled many of the trade routes of the Southern Cone and established a structure of trade based on the Atlantic.[27] China may try to construct an informal empire with the full partnership and initiative of the MERCOSUR partners and the quick incorporation of Venezuela and other South American nations into the agreement. Argentina is planning to ship goods over the Andean mountains into Chile in order to reach the Pacific and, in turn, China; Valparaiso would be the port of choice. Likewise, Uruguay seems very interested in going along with such an opportunity. This would definitely bring Chile into the MERCOSUR agreement and consolidate its role as a trade and political partner. Brazil, not surprisingly, is trying to play the leading part in these new ventures between China and South America, and several agreements with China were signed in 2003 and 2004. In short, these developments would alter the traditional relations between South America, the European Union, and the United States.

THE ORGANIZATION OF THE BOOK

At first glance, the selection of chapters may seem unlikely. The variation in approach, focus, and method was intentional, however; indeed, we see this as one of the volume's greatest strengths. One of our central assertions is that the debate about globalization will be much more fruitful if we acknowledge and embrace the eclectic nature of the phenomenon. There is not, as these chapters clearly demonstrate, a single meaning of globalization. In fact, there are numerous types of globalization, with widespread implications for history, politics, economics, and society. The book brings together works by scholars from political science, history, sociology, and language.

Given the interdisciplinary nature of the collection, it is not surprising that our methodological approaches vary as well. Individual authors focus on aspects of globalization as different as changes in the economy or the redefinition of theoretical notions such as justice, human rights, punishment, and discipline. The authors explore the modification of travel and consumption patterns, public policy, the media, transformations in political and religious attitudes, as well as collective action, ideology, and notions of "duty" toward the state and community.

Finally, we differ in our views regarding the normative implications of globalization. Some see globalization as essentially positive, while others see it as essentially negative, and there are still others who are implicitly or explicitly split in their assessment. All of this helps to demonstrate the multifaceted nature of globalization and the variety of possible responses to it. The complexity of the phenomenon is in fact one of the reasons that it has led to such great uncertainty: the expectations can vary depending on one's understanding of globalization and the combinations of different aspects of the phenomenon.

In part 1 of the volume, the authors suggest that the adoption of economic liberalism (and neoliberalism) raises the level of uncertainty among both citizens and policymakers. This uncertainty to a large degree defines circumstances for most people living in Latin America today. Moreover, there is no compelling theoretical reason to think this uncertainty should be unique to the current wave of globalization that began in the mid-1970s. For this reason, we begin part 1 with a historical chapter by David Rock that examines the uncertainties unleashed or exacerbated by globalization between the late 1800s and World War I. Through his telling of the story of Jabez Spencer Balfour, a British politician, businessman, and adventurer, Rock assesses both the individual and collective impact of globalization upon people living in Argentina and Britain during that period.

In chapter 2, Fernando López-Alves contends that globalization has bred a popular pessimism among Argentine citizens who sense that local elites have relinquished their control to the international economic institutions. In addition, neoliberalism has not been able to create a social mystique that could compensate for uncertainty, leading citizens to create their own new conception of the future. Miguel Centeno in the following chapter argues that economic policymaking is now shaped by macroeconomic goals rather than by political reasoning, and that neoliberalism represents the triumph of an "imperial vision."

While neoliberalism first brought about hope and trust in science and efficiency, this has given way to uncertainty. But despite this, Latin American policymakers saw no real alternative to its adoption if they wanted to receive much-needed international resources.

In the final chapter of part 1, Benjamin J. Cohen also focuses on the popular response to globalization in Latin America, providing evidence of a growing backlash among the "losers" of the game. He argues that policymakers must respond effectively to the legitimate concerns of globalization's critics regarding the effects of open markets and the uncertainty that this has created.

In part 2, we discuss the relations between state and civil society. Our focus on global uncertainty and modifications in routine social practices raises important questions about public policymaking, the role of civil society in a democracy, and community activism. Economic and cultural globalization has led to the replacement of old rules and the uncertainty of what will follow for the policymakers themselves and for the corporations, organizations, and individuals that perceive a stake in the policy outcome. In this section, we consider the impact on the different sides of the complex relations that evolve between the state and society.

In her chapter (chapter 5), Diane Johnson analyzes the degree to which public policy in Latin America is becoming homogenized, specifically in the area of policy regarding ownership of the mass media. She argues that changes resulting from deregulation and internationalization swept both policymakers and the media themselves into unfamiliar and uncertain territory, with outcomes that vary somewhat from state to state. In the following chapter, Jonathan Rosenberg examines the effects of globalization on environmental policy in light of the conditions imposed by international lending agencies and banks. In recent years, recipient governments and communities found themselves faced with a new set of conditions that could affect economic growth and empower new groups. This in part reflects the uncertain course of a rapidly changing world.

Finally in part 3 of the volume, we address globalization and uncertainty as it pertains to justice and human rights. These are topics that have been little explored by scholars, and they help to illustrate the broad range of areas that are affected by globalization. The two chapters (chapters 7 and 8) in this section suggest that globalization has led to uncertainty about conventional understandings and about what the future holds. In a long-term comparative view, Steven Cassedy asserts that both the nineteenth- and twentieth-century waves of globalization contributed to the alteration of our understanding of human rights and their relationship to nationalism. Likewise, in the final chapter of the book, Thomas Siemsen claims that crime and punishment have taken on new meanings in light of globalization. Global markets seek to exert a disciplinary function by identifying "crimes" and punishing offenders. This in turn necessitates the creation of new norms.

Thus in distinctive but complementary ways, each of the authors in this volume contributes to our understanding of how globalization is shaping (or reshaping) contemporary Latin America: from its worldview, ideas and attitudes, to the character of its public policy, civil society, and popular discourse. In each case, it is clear both that globalization has led to uncertainty, and that uncertainty has to some extent influenced the various responses to globalization. The outcome is still unfolding. But it is, we believe, a crucial dimension to our study of the effects of globalization—and we hope that we have raised important questions and contributed something that will prove valuable in the ongoing debate about globalization as it evolves in the early twenty-first century.

Notes

1. For further analysis, see John Ralston Saul, "The Collapse of Globalization and the Rebirth of Nationalism," *Harper's Magazine*, March 2004.
2. One of the most important sources for this debate is the 1921 treatise of Frank H. Knight, *Risk, Uncertainty, and Profit* (New York: Kelley & Millman, Inc., 1957). Others contributors to the debate include John Hicks, John Maynard Keynes, Oscar Lange, and Douglass North. For their part, sociologists, political scientists, and anthropologists have linked uncertainty to trust, ethics, justice, and culture. See, e.g., Sean Watson and Anthony Moran, eds., *Trust, Risk, and Uncertainty* (New York: Palgrave-Macmillan, 2005) and Tomas Hellström and Merle Jacob, *Policy Uncertainty and Risk: Conceptual Developments and Approaches* (Boston: Kluwer Academic Publishers, 2001).
3. Knight, *Risk, Uncertainty, and Profit*, 333.
4. The economic literature on uncertainty and risk includes multiple debates and a wide array of subjects, from lottery games and pure mathematical modeling on randomness to the construction of expected utility models, not to mention serious considerations of ontological and epistemological problems.
5. See, among many other well-known sources, John Maynard Keynes, *A Treatise on Probability* (London: Macmillan, 1921); David Newbery and Joseph Stiglitz, *A Theory of Commodity Price Stabilization: A Study in the Economics of Risk* (Oxford: Clarendon Press, 1981); John Von Neumann and Oskar Morgensteur, *Theory of Games and Economic Behavior*

(Princeton: Princeton University Press, 1947); Gerhard Tintner, *Econometrics* (New York: Willey, 1952); and Paul Davison, *International Money and the Real World* (New York: Wiley, 1982).
6. Among other books by Kenneth Arrow, see *Essays on the Theory of Risk Bearing* (Chicago: Markham Publishers, 1971).
7. Since the late 1990s, the Left has experienced electoral victories in Uruguay, Brazil, Bolivia, Venezuela, and, depending on one's perspective, Chile.
8. The chapter by Miguel Centeno in this collection demonstrates the popularity of liberal strategies.
9. Kurt Weyland, "Populism in the Age of Neoliberalism," in *Populism in Latin America*, ed. Michael L. Conniff (Tuscaloosa and London: University of Alabama Press, 1999).
10. Ibid.
11. For a review of the literature and a good assessment of the economic performance of Latin America under globalization, see Omar Sanchez, "Globalization as a Development Strategy in Latin America?," *World Development*, 12 (December 2003): 1977–1995.
12. Michel Foucault, *Discipline and Punish: The Birth of the Prison*, trans. Alan Sheridan (New York: Vintage Books, 1977).
13. When asked whether they think that their countries are going in the right direction, only in four countries did an average of 40% of citizens respond positively (Argentina, Chile, Colombia, and Brazil); in all the rest, an overwhelming majority of citizens responded negatively. Extreme cases are Peru and Ecuador: in both, 92% of the population believes that their country is not on the right track. Curiously enough, despite NAFTA, 84% of Mexicans believe the same. Latin American Barometer, "Una Decada de Mediciones," Santiago de Chile (August 2004): 37.
14. An exception is Benjamin J. Cohen's chapter in this collection. For a more traditional view of global Latin America from an economic point of view, see Albert Fishlow, "Latin America in the 21 Century," in *Economic and Social Development in the 21 Century*, ed. Lewis Emmerij (Washington, DC: Inter-American Development Bank, 1997); Dani Rodrik, *Making Openness Work: The New Global Economy and the Developing Countries* (Washington, DC: Overseas Development Council, 1999); and J. Ramos, "Policy Directions for the New Economic Model in Latin America," *World Development*, 28, special issue (2000).
15. See, e.g., G. M. Joseph Catherine LeGrand, and Ricardo Donato Salvatore, eds., *Close Encounters of Empire: Writing the Cultural History of U.S.–Latin American Relations* (Durham: Duke University Press, 1999).
16. A substantial part of this work has followed a Marxist or neo-Marxist line of analysis. A few examples are Richard Harris, "Resistance and Alternatives to Globalization in Latin American and the Caribbean," *Latin American Perspectives*, 29 (November 2002): 136–151; William Robinson, *Transnational Conflicts: Central America, Social Change, and Globalization* (New York: Verso Editors, 2003); Atilio Boron, *El Buho de*

Minerva (Buenos Aires: Fondo de Cultura Económica, 2000); and Richard Harris, "Globalization and Globalism in Latin America: Contending Perspectives," *Latin American Perspectives*, 29 (2002): 5–23.

17. For some examples, see Fernando López-Alves, "Globalization and Its Ideologues: Lessons from the Beginning of the 21st Century," in *Cuba, el Caribe y la Globalización*, ed. Andrés Serbín and Carlos Oliva (São Paulo: Universidad Estadual Paulista, 2003), 80–105; Andrés Serbín, "What Do We Mean by Globalization?: Consequences for Latin America and the Caribbean," in *Foro Abierto*, vol. 1, no. 3 (Buenos Aires: Universidad Abierta Interamericana, 2003); William C. Smith and Roberto Patricio Korzeniewicz, eds., *Politics, Social Change, and Economic Restructuring in Latin America* (Boulder, CO: North-South Center Press and Lynne Reinner Books, 1997); and Fernando López-Alves, *Sociedades sin Destino: America Latina Tiene lo que se Merece?* (Buenos Aires and Madrid: Taurus-Santillana, 2002).

18. MERCOSUR (Mercado Común del Sur) in Spanish, or MERCOSUL (Mercado Comum do Sul) in Portuguese, is a trading zone among Brazil, Argentina, Uruguay, Venezuela, and Paraguay. Established in 1994, its purpose is to "promote free trade and the movement of money, goods, skills and people." MERCOSUR, if anything, has run behind in the accomplishment of all these objectives and its dynamics are bound to change as a result of the election to power of the left in Brazil, Argentina, and Uruguay.

19. See e.g., Zbigniew Brzezinski, *The Choice: Global Domination or Global Leadership* (New York: Basic Books, 2004); Michael Hardt and Antonio Negri, *Empire* (Cambridge MA: Harvard University Press, 2000); Benjamin Barber, *Fear's Empire: Wars, Terrorism, and Democracy* (New York: Norton, 2003); Emmanuel Todd, *After the Empire* (New York: Columbia University Press, 2004); Chalmers Johnson, *The Sorrows of Empire* (New York: Metropolitan Books, 2004); Niall Ferguson, *Colossus: The Price of American Empire* (New York: Penguin Press, 2004); Michael Mann, *Incoherent Empire* (New York: Verso, 2003); and Jim Garrison, *America As Empire: Global Leader or Rogue Power?* (San Francisco: Berret-Koehler Publishers, 2004).

20. Only a very few scholarly books and articles have been written by Latin Americans connecting the changing landscape of the region to globalization and empire. See e.g., Serbín and Oliva, eds., *Cuba, el Caribe y la Globalización*; Atilio Boron, *Imperio y Imperialismo: Una Lectura Critica de Michael Hardt y Antonio Negri* (Buenos Aires: CLACSO, 2002); and some of the contributions made by Latin Americans in *Siete Escenarios para el Siglo XXI*, ed. Fernando López–Alves and Daniel Dessein (Editorial Sudamericana, 2004).

21. During the 1960s and 1970s, and even the early 1980s, a host of Latin American authors offered different theoretical perspectives about the insertion of the region into the international system. Some of their contributions stand today as serious foundations of our thinking about

Latin America. The conceptualization of Latin America offered by dependency theory, or the debates on modernization and bureaucratic authoritarianism, for instance, continue to serve as important analytical tools. One can argue that most of them still offer a solid foundation for new interpretations of the role of Latin America in an age of globalization or empire.

22. Evidence of this "slowness" is of course erratic, and ignores the quick adaptation to, or reaction against, globalization experienced by many countries. Venezuela has challenged U.S.-led globalization and Bolivia is doing the same; Argentina underwent one of the most orthodox adoptions of neoliberalism during the 1990s; Brazil implemented financial, social, and economic reforms; Uruguay resisted rapid reform; and Chile today remains a centerpiece of discussions on the successful and quick adoption of neoliberalism in the region.

23. See, e.g., José Manuel Salazar X. and Maryse Robert, eds., *Toward Free Trade in the Americas* (Washington, DC: Brookings Institution Press Organization of American States, 2001); Ambler Moss, "Toward a Free Trade Area of the Americas: Progress and Prospects," in *The Challenge of Change in Latin America and the Caribbean*, ed. Jeffrey Stark (Coral Gables; Boulder: University of Miami, North-South Center Press, 2001); Paulo S. Wrobel, "A Free Trade Area of the Americas in 2005?," in *Trade Politics: International, Domestic, and Regional Perspectives*, ed. Brian Hocking and Steven McGuire (London; New York: Routledge, 1999); and Ricardo Mosquera Mesa, *Globalización & ALCA: América para los Americanos* (Bogotá: Universidad Nacional de Colombia, Facultad de Ciencias Económicas, 2002).

24. Guatemala, El Salvador, Honduras, and Nicaragua formed the Central American Common Market in 1960; Costa Rica joined three years later. The organization collapsed in 1969 following the Football War between Honduras and El Salvador, but it was reinstated in 1991. The Andean Pact is also a customs union, originally formed in 1969 by Bolivia, Colombia, Ecuador, Peru, and Chile. Venezuela joined in 1973; Chile withdrew in 1976. For further information on the successes and failures of these organizations, see the edited volumes by Roberto Bouzas and Jaime Ros, *Economic Integration in the Western Hemisphere* (Notre Dame: University of Notre Dame Press, 1994); Irma Tirado de Alonso, *Trade, Industrialization, and Integration in Twentieth-century Central America* (Westport: Praeger, 1994); and Ana Julia Jatar-Hausmann and Sidney Weintraub, *Integrating the Hemisphere: Perspectives from Latin America and the Caribbean* (Washington, DC: Inter-American Dialogue, 1997).

25. Some of the best examples of this work are found in edited volumes: Guillermo A. O'Donnell, Philippe C. Schmitter, and Laurence Whitehead, *Transitions from Authoritarian Rule, Latin America* (Baltimore: Johns Hopkins University Press, 1986); Roderic Ai Camp, ed., *Democracy in Latin America: Patterns and Cycles*

(Wilmington, DL: SR Books, 1996); and Felipe Agüero and Jeffrey Stark, eds., *Fault Lines of Democracy in Post-Transition Latin America* (Coral Gables and Boulder: North-South Center Press/University of Miami, 1998). See also Guillermo O'Donnell, *Counterpoints: Selected Essays on Authoritarianism and Democratization* (Notre Dame: University of Notre Dame Press, 1999).

26. Latin American Barometer is the most cited source on dissatisfaction with democracy. See especially, Latinobarometro, "Una Decada de Mediciones," Santiago de Chile (August 2004): 22–27.

27. Vitor Hugo Molina, "China y la Argentina en el 2004," paper presented at the conference "New Partners: MERCOSUR and China in the 21st Century," Universidad Abierta Interamericana, Buenos Aires, Argentina, October 22–24, 2004.

Part 1

The Uncertainties of Liberalism and Neoliberalism, Past and Present

One of the most widely discussed aspects of globalization is the extensive adoption of promarket economic policies. Liberalism is nothing new in much of Latin America, of course; some states began to adopt it in the late nineteenth century. However, liberal—and more currently, neoliberal—economic policies were most prominent during the periods from approximately 1880 to 1914, and from the 1970s to the present.

Each of the four chapters in this section focuses on how liberal economic reforms have in some way and to some degree increased levels of uncertainty among both elites and citizens. The chapters by David Rock and Fernando López-Alves serve as "bookends" for the Argentine case. Rock describes how dramatic technological, economic, and political changes during the first wave of globalization created uncertainty in Argentine society, and for individuals such as the adventurer Jabez Spencer Balfour. Fernando López-Alves fast-forwards to Argentina at the dawn of the twenty-first century. He argues that neoliberalism has greatly exacerbated existing uncertainties in the region, leading to a worrying divorce between citizens and state. Moreover, the neoliberal project failed to construct a positive vision of the future.

Likewise in chapter 3, Miguel Centeno argues that the early optimism in Latin America about liberal economic reforms has eventually given way to uncertainty; but policymakers saw no real alternative to their adoption if they wanted to receive much needed international resources. At the end of the section, Benjamin Cohen discusses the growing backlash against neoliberal policies, in part caused by the uncertainty they engendered, and asks whether globalization can—or should—be stopped.

1

VICTORIAN GLOBALIZATION IN MICROCOSM: THE RISE AND FALL OF JABEZ SPENCER BALFOUR

David Rock

As a backbench member of Parliament during the late Victorian era, Jabez Spencer Balfour ranked as a very "minor" British politician. Contemporaries knew him far better for his scandalous business and real estate dealings. He led the Liberator Permanent Benefit Building Society, which in its day became the largest entity of its kind in Great Britain. In September 1892, the collapse of the Liberator and several related companies caused heavy losses among many small investors and creditors. To evade prosecution for fraud, Balfour fled to Argentina, a country that at the time had no extradition treaty with Britain and eventually found his way to the small northwestern city of Salta. He chose a destination at the terminus of the Argentine railroad as the farthest he could find from his pursuers, believing he had reached a safe refuge. But as his victims at home demanded retribution, the British authorities tracked him down and finally secured his return to stand trial. In April 1895, more than two years after his flight, Balfour traveled in custody from Salta to Buenos Aires by train and then embarked on board a ship for England. Following his trial and conviction, he received a sentence of 14 years imprisonment.[1]

A century or so later, Balfour's story first catches the eye as burlesque. He appeared the archetypal bounder—a charming, manipulative, and unscrupulous crook. Alongside deceitfulness, hypocrisy stood out as his most glaring personal flaw. He made a fortune through the Liberator by standing up as a man of religious principle. He appealed to the powerful Temperance Movement, attracting straitlaced Nonconformists and those who took the pledge to abstain from drink, and he used clerics to advertise his companies. When the British authorities caught up with him in Salta, however, they found him immersed in the business of a brewery. He was living in "sultanic luxury" with Lucy Freeman, a young Englishwoman, who was the daughter of one of his former business associates. In 1895, British officials recounted the melodrama as they sought to transport Balfour from Salta to Buenos Aires. They had to bribe local officials and to contract a special train for the journey. Eventually they won the assistance of the governor of Salta, but he inconveniently insisted that Lucy Freeman accompany the party and her presence, they suspected, added to the risk of an attempt to free Balfour by force. Indeed, as his captors tugged and pushed him aboard the train, a band of horsemen ("a rabble high on oaths and exchanging the most foul language") swept along the platform to free him. Barely accelerating beyond its pursuers, the train then sped southward on its long journey to the Argentine capital.

Balfour's business practices embodied the type of fraud known today in the United States as a Ponzi scheme: the money paid into his companies in new deposits drained out almost instantaneously to pay dividends to previous investors. Fraudulent accounting and auditing created illusions of large company profits.[2] From another perspective, his career also illustrated Victorian forms of globalization—the extensive connections between different parts of the world established by trade, investment, and technology. His rise and fall were closely related to the interlinked domestic and overseas expansion of the British economy. His fate bore witness to the Victorian revolutions in communications and transportation, which enabled the British authorities to discover and to expose the fugitive and to bring him home.

As a man who began his business career in a humble local building society and ended as a real estate tycoon in central London, Balfour encapsulated some of the expansive and dynamic attributes of nascent global capitalism. He embodied the values of Victorian free enterprise; his companies exemplified the growing complexity of corporate organizations and the late nineteenth-century trend toward big business.[3] Similarly, his political career began on a local stage in Croydon, a developing London suburb and progressed to national politics as a member of Parliament. The existence of a global mass market obtruded continually in the Balfour case. The press brought the issue before a national and international readership. Newspapers campaigned for Balfour's prosecution on behalf of creditors scattered throughout Britain and titillated a mass public with the scurrilous tale of Lucy Freeman. In some respects too, the Balfour case illustrated the limits to globalization. In the 1890s, a high-water mark of imperialism, Britain possessed great economic power in Argentina, but its political influence remained limited. To extricate Balfour, the British could not rely on bribes alone. They had to observe legal procedure and to respect the nuances of Argentine politics. Protracted judicial proceedings underlined the differences between the legal systems of Britain and Argentina. The chief limits to globalization thus became visible in the power of local authorities and local institutions in Salta, and in divergent legal traditions between the two countries.

THE RISE OF A LIBERAL TYCOON

Born in 1843, Balfour grew up in an upwardly mobile middle-class family, typical of the successful Nonconformists of mid-Victorian Britain. Clara Lucas Balfour, his mother, became a distinguished public speaker and a popular writer whose subjects included the rights of women, the virtues of teetotalism, and "self-help," which was one of the great precepts of the Victorian era.[4] A woman of style, flair, and enthusiasm, Clara Balfour became a major influence on her son, cultivating his entrepreneurial energies, his persuasiveness, and his willingness to speak out on public issues. As Balfour's parents advanced socially, they provided exceptional opportunities for all their children. One of his brothers became a colliery owner and one a stockbroker, while Balfour himself enjoyed a privileged education in continental Europe.

He began his business career in the Liberator, a company founded in 1868 by Nonconformist financiers in the City of London. Incorporated in 1874 under the motto *Libera Sedes Liberum Facit* (A Free House Makes a Free Man), the company originally financed the construction of chapels as well as provided mortgages to householders.[5] The title Liberator indicated a link with the Liberation Society, an association founded in the 1850s to oppose lingering discriminatory barriers against Nonconformists.[6] During the company's early years, Balfour came to be known as "a psalm-singing Dissenter, who opened his board meetings with a prayer."[7] By the mid-1870s, he had a preponderant role in three companies that became the foundation of his business empire: the Liberator, the Lands Allotment Company, and the House and Land Investment Trust. He prospered as a young man. By 1880 he lived in his own mansion and educated his son in one of the most prestigious schools in England. The single blight on his life stemmed from the incurable mental illness of his wife.

Clara Lucas Balfour had developed close ties with influential Nonconformists led by Jabez Burns from whom Balfour inherited his unusual biblical forename. Burns, a leading figure in the Liberation Society, belonged to the General Baptist New Connexion, one of the most radical Nonconformist groups.[8] The links between the two families grew closer when Balfour's sister married Dawson Burns, the son of Jabez Burns. For 35 years, the younger Burns served as the chief London representative of the United Kingdom Alliance, the largest antidrink association in Britain. In the mid-1870s, he published *Christendom and the Drink Curse: An Appeal to the Christian World for Efficient Action against the Causes of Intemperance*. He campaigned for the "Local Option," namely the right of local authorities to close public houses in their own jurisdictions.[9] By employing members of the clergy as its recruiting agents, the United Kingdom Alliance provided the Liberator with a model to conduct business. Balfour and Dawson Burns became close associates. Burns provided Balfour with a readymade market among the teetotalers and the Nonconformists; Balfour provided Burns with an income to support his campaigns for moral reform.

Balfour's Nonconformist background shaped his political activities. His political career began in Croydon south of London, an expanding suburban town currently outgrowing its archaic system of local government based on the parish council.[10] The Croydon Nonconformists were demanding broader representation to give them better access to local charities and educational funds. As chairman of the Croydon School Board, Balfour led campaigns to provide Nonconformist schoolchildren with the same financial support as the privileged Anglicans, who were the members of the established church. He led the movement for the incorporation of Croydon as a borough, which would allow the council to fund local public services like the streetcar company in which he and other Nonconformist businessmen had a financial interest. When Parliament passed an Act of Incorporation in 1883, the councilors of Croydon elected him the first mayor of the borough. His business ambitions were already drawing him into a larger political arena. He became a Liberal Party member of Parliament in 1880 in the Tamworth constituency in the English Midlands, where his brother owned the colliery. In 1885, he ran for Parliament in the new constituency in Croydon but lost that election against an exceptionally strong Conservative Party opponent. In 1889, he reentered the House of Commons as the member for Burnley, a town in northern England close to the heartland of the Lancashire cotton textile industry. His adoption in Burnley, so far from his base in Croydon, reflected, above all, his financial contributions to the liberals.

Balfour defined himself as a "sincere, thorough, and hearty Liberal ... a man who had given much of his time, some of his substance, and all his energy to promote the Liberal cause."[11] Like many Nonconformists, he identified with the radical wing of the party and endorsed nearly all the progressive causes of the day. He took up Home Rule for Ireland to support the Catholic majority against the Protestant landed classes and the Ulster sectarians.[12] He supported the Married Woman's Property Act, declaring that before the Act, "the condition of women in England was worse than the condition of a Negro in America."[13] He extolled social reform benefiting labor. He wanted working people to own their homes "free of the tyranny of landlordism."[14] He denounced privilege and tradition as barriers to the expansion of markets and consumption, in which his interests lay as a businessman. In his memoirs, he detailed his credentials as a progressive landowner. In 1887, he bought a large country house and several farms in Oxfordshire. As the local squire, he provided a village hall for community activities and tore down some old thatched cottages as relics of the past and incubators of disease.[15] His business activities grew increasingly diverse. He attracted a group of associates, mostly Nonconformists from Croydon, who helped him to extend into large-scale building projects in central London. His companies constructed several large hotels and an edifice on the River Thames Embankment known as Whitehall Court that later became the National Liberal Club. As an investor, he developed a global outlook. He bought land in Wichita, Kansas, and participated in a suburban railway scheme in Rome. He joined the boards of numerous corporations throughout Britain.[16]

Balfour veered into misrepresentation and fraud around 1880 as he gradually switched from household mortgages to financing construction. At the time, the law directed that funds deposited in a building society like the Liberator could be applied only to buy and not to construct or to develop real property. To surmount this obstacle, he created subsidiary companies that borrowed money from the Liberator as mortgages but employed it to finance construction. Originally, the loans from the Liberator became first mortgages but as the borrowings increased, the early loans became relegated to second and even third mortgages. Ultimately, when the depositors of longest standing sought to withdraw their funds from the Liberator, they found themselves at the tail end of a long list of creditors. Throughout, Balfour misled shareholders in the Liberator into believing that the company was lending to small homebuyers, but in reality conventional mortgages represented only 7 percent of its outlays: instead, he was using some of his money to finance new construction or to pay earlier investors. In early 1892, Balfour claimed that "they had avoided the speculative builder. They had written over the door [of the Liberator] 'No Speculator need apply.' "[17] On the contrary, he and his associates speculated recklessly. Covertly, they used the subsidiary real estate companies and funds from the Liberator to sell properties back and forth among themselves at fictitious profits. In one notorious case, two directors of the Liberator bought an estate for £17,000, and they then sold it to another of Balfour's companies for £34,000. They used funds from the Liberator and pocketed the difference between the purchase and sales prices.[18] Balfour strengthened the illusion that real profits were being made by employing his cronies to conduct false audits.[19] He also reported these so-called profits to his shareholders in the company annual general meetings to encourage depositors to provide new funds. Whenever shareholders received dividends, they were deriving them not from company earnings but from new deposits. His companies thus ended up with enormous liabilities and with a few grossly overvalued assets that were mortgaged several times over. Reform imposed by the Building Societies Act of 1894 designed to prevent such secret internal transactions highlighted some of Balfour's practices. This act required the use of professional accountants in audits; for the first time, it permitted members of a building society to inspect the books and to call meetings; and it obliged building societies to make public all their loans over £5,000.[20]

Fraud in a Global Context

Balfour's career as a real estate financier lasted for more than a decade. He promoted some legitimate ventures that turned a genuine profit when real estate prices in London rose during the 1880s. He juggled funds between his companies, managing to persuade his creditors and depositors of the soundness and profitability of his business. After his bankruptcy, his enemies pointed to his exploitation of gullible Nonconformists, typically widows or retired clerics, as another principal feature of his business methods and some therefore blamed Dawson Burns, whom they had followed and trusted, for their misfortunes, as well as Balfour.[21] The bankruptcy proceedings, however, illustrated that Balfour's companies dealt with investors from a broad cross section of British society, "every calling in the middle and working classes," in addition to the Nonconformists.[22] His companies were successful for a while not only because of the network of clerics they employed and their links with the teetotalers and Nonconformists, but more likely because they paid slightly higher dividends than their competitors. At root, Balfour owed his temporary success in the 1880s to his ability to tap into a supply of surplus capital held by many ordinary people; when the surplus disappeared or became diverted into different channels in the early 1890s, his empire collapsed.

In the 1880s, national income in Britain rose sharply to a late nineteenth-century peak at the end of the decade. Economic expansion in and around London prompted the growth of middle-class suburbs like Croydon and rising real estate prices in central areas of the city.[23] The expansion of the real estate market that expanded Balfour along with it was closely linked to the growth of British trade and capital exports.[24] In light of Balfour's later experiences, it proved an ironic coincidence that in the 1880s Britain developed exceptionally close commercial and financial ties with Argentina. The boost to Anglo-Argentine trade resulted in part from falling shipping freights as improved marine engines reduced the consumption of coal by steamships. Of the exceptionally large British capital exports to Argentina in the late 1880s, around one-third flowed into the Argentine railroads; the expansion of railroads transformed the Argentine pampas into a major exporter of grains and livestock. British investment in Argentina reached a highpoint in 1887–1889, rising from £45 million in 1885 to £174 million in 1890.[25]

Bankruptcy and Flight

Policies in Argentina encouraged the boom. The administration of Miguel Juárez Celman, which took office in late 1886, represented a new type of Latin American government obsessed with economic development in ways more typical of the twentieth century than the nineteenth. In an effort to develop fringe areas of the pampas, Juárez Celman encouraged provincial governments to establish new banks, allowing them to issue their own paper currency. Artificial, inflationary expansion proved unsustainable. When the inflow of British investment ended around late 1889, the Argentine economy crashed. Economic depression then rebounded from Argentina to Britain. As a contemporary noted, "The great fall in South American stocks in 1890 reacted upon the best European stocks.... The general want of confidence created high rates of interest and a dearth of money for new ventures."[26]

By late 1891, the downturn was affecting the British real estate market. As a result, Balfour's grossly unsound companies faced mounting difficulties. As interest rates rose, his sources of funding melted away. Sensing disaster, in March 1892 he placed some of his property in trust on behalf of his wife.[27] In midyear, he fought successfully to retain his parliamentary seat in a general election, but then he had to devote all his efforts to saving his business. To shore up investors' confidence, he sought to set himself apart from the downward trends in the international economy. "The fluctuations and vicissitudes of the Stock Exchange [would not affect him]. He was glad to think [his own business] did not depend on the state of trade with the Argentine Republic. . . . His business was one of an extremely home character, dealing with home securities."[28] While making these assertions, he was borrowing at rates as high as 17 percent to staunch the outpouring of funds from his companies. In the first half of 1892, the outflow from the Liberator climbed to around £500,000.

On September 2, 1892, the London and General Bank suspended payments. Days later, the Liberator crashed, followed domino-like by Balfour's other companies. During the dying days of the House and Land Investment Trust, one of the original flagship companies, the depositors withdrew £700,000.[29] Following the plunge, a chorus of angry questions filled the press. Where were the assets of Balfour's companies? Why did the Liberator hold so many third mortgages? How could he have claimed so recently that his companies were profitable? The Liberator shareholders clamored for a public meeting, but with 20,000 aggrieved people, there was "no building in London in which such a meeting could be held."[30] In vain, the company directors appealed for new capital.[31] Fifteen years later, Balfour's memoirs recalled these cataclysmic days but blamed anyone but himself for what had happened. He had tried to save his companies but "predatory hosts who were determined to drive the companies into liquidation [forced him] to slaughter their assets. Should the history of that liquidation ever be written, it will reveal [utter] recklessness in dealing with the assets."[32]

As his excuses were ignored, he became a target for revenge. En masse, his shareholders and depositors demanded that he resign from Parliament.[33] Balfour then consulted a member of a "famous legal firm [who urged me to] leave England that very day. . . . It was impossible that I could obtain a fair trial in view of the natural indignation of the thousands of small investors, who had, together with myself, lost their all."[34] He resigned his parliamentary seat, abandoned his country mansion, and vanished. On the advice of the lawyers, he was en route to Argentina, currently a favorite destination for British fugitives. Recently, Britain and Argentina had negotiated an extradition treaty, but as yet neither country had ratified it.

Balfour had protected his wife by means of the trust but he left James Balfour, his 23-year-old son, to face his creditors. When the official receiver convened a meeting on the Liberator, James Balfour was "greeted with a storm of groans and cries of execration, some of the audience shaking their fists at him." That meeting revealed another trail of deception and malfeasance. In the company's annual report for 1891, the directors claimed that the deposits had risen by £200,000 and the reserves by £5,000 to £95,000, allowing a 5 percent dividend to the shareholders. As all were now well aware, however, the dividend came from borrowed money.[35] Another bankruptcy meeting on behalf of the 13,000 depositors in the House and Land Investment Trust exposed more of Balfour's business methods. The Trust held the deeds of some of his largest properties in central London. It had recently mortgaged Whitehall Court for £569,000, but in the current market the property was worth less than half that amount. The directors had assigned inflated values to the other properties of the Trust, while rewarding themselves with generous fees. Balfour had always depicted this company in glowing terms. He had never mentioned that "no profits had been earned or that fictitious sums were being charged for interest on the various properties."[36]

The Liberator Relief Fund was formed to assist those smitten by the crash. *The Times* reported that "the entire savings of many thousands of people in narrow circumstances have been wrecked. . . . The mere announcement of a fund for their relief has brought in over one thousand applications giving heartrending details: widows, orphans, old people, persons in ill health and others, more or less helpless, have been deprived of their all."[37] Fifty-one thousand people claimed losses from the collapse of the Balfour group, but they received scant support. Over the next several years, the fund raised scarcely half its targeted figure of £100,000. It assisted only 5 percent of the creditors, some 2,629 people, of whom many were women over the age of 60.[38] The effort to drum up relief funds illustrated not only the kind of ordinary people who became investors in Britain in the 1880s but also the "global" outlook they represented. A reporter quoted the case of a clergyman's daughter as typical of Balfour's victims. "In 1891 she lost the greater part of a small independence by the Argentine failure, and immediately after came the Liberator crash."[39]

In December 1892, the police arrested some of Balfour's associates on charges that included money laundering, false accounting, and using Liberator funds for the fraudulent sale and purchase of real estate.[40] They were tried at London's Central Criminal Court, the Old Bailey. In half an hour, the jury returned guilty verdicts on almost all charges. Two men received sentences of 20 years hard labor, and a third man imprisonment for 5 years.[41] The convictions failed to satisfy the demand for retribution, since "the biggest scoundrel of the lot has evaded justice, and prepared himself a very comfortable existence in foreign parts." Foreign Secretary Sir Edward Grey promised that he would spare no effort to bring the fugitive to justice.[42]

Argentina

In mid-1892 Balfour had crossed the English Channel, taken a train to Genoa, and joined a boatload of Italian harvest workers on the four-week voyage to Buenos Aires. He arrived with limited funds—he had lost nearly all his own fortune in the crash. His brief sojourn in Buenos Aires illustrated the extensive web of connections between Britain and Argentina and, by the standards of the day, the sophistication of transatlantic communications. The tellers in a British bank in Buenos Aires recognized the fugitive almost the moment he arrived to cash a check; journalists of *The Times of Argentina* swiftly relayed the news to London. Within weeks, plans were afoot to bring him back. Leaders of the Liberator Relief Fund proposed to kidnap him but abandoned the idea when the Argentine government made it known that it would prevent abduction.[43] The Foreign Office advised waiting until the British parliament and the Argentine congress ratified the pending extradition treaty.

Fearing kidnap, Balfour first set up guards outside his residence but soon fled once more into the Argentine interior. He was now keeping a diary and once he felt safe, he began sending extracts of his writings to his son. To raise some money, James Balfour arranged to publish the diary in the tabloid-style *Pall Mall Gazette*. (It was then reprinted in British provincial newspapers.) The "strain of buoyant cheerfulness" of the diary infuriated Balfour's enemies, particularly when they discovered he had become a partner in a local brewery.[44] As an unschooled and idiosyncratic description of the Argentine interior, however, the diary had some fascinating features. Balfour wrote a lyrical account of his journey across the prairies of the pampas and through the old city of Córdoba. From here, he had continued northwest into Tucumán, the site of a sugarcane industry. Sultry Tucumán would have been an attractive final destination but Balfour feared betrayal by the resident British population. He pushed on farther north to the dry upland town of Salta.

"With its numerous religious edifices and a college," and its colonial atmosphere, Salta appeared to lie far beyond the frontiers of globalization and untouched by the economic tribulations of recent years.[45] The area had very a small European population, and the British contingent amounted to scarcely a dozen. Mule breeding, which began during the colonial era more than 200 years before, still connected the region with Bolivia to the north. The landed gentry dominated the province, controlling the peasants through debt peonage and enforced deference.[46] Local politics consisted of competition for offices and patronage as the gentry vied for control over the provincial budget.[47] From his Nonconformist perspective, Balfour regarded the religious customs of the local population as degraded and superstitious. He disliked the way young women remained under tight parental control, although, as he admitted, the chaperones avoided the spectacles back home since "the philandering of our lanes and fields is never seen here." He betrayed a paternalistic regard for the poor and lamented the sharp class distinctions in Salta. He called debt peonage "a species of domestic slavery."[48]

Balfour's core beliefs included limited government, free independent associations, and "self-help." From this viewpoint, he found the town of Salta (as opposed to its unprogressive rural areas) quite attractive. It appeared "truly and to my thinking, delightfully Democratic. . . . Some very rich people are quite outsiders and some very poor people are welcomed among the best families. The draper and the grocer have just as much consideration as the lawyer and the doctor." He struck up an acquaintance with Antonio Díaz, who as the chief minister stood second in the local administration after the governor. As "a plain man of business with many irons in the fire," Díaz resembled Balfour. Despite these positive features in Salta, he noted a striking difference in the role of government compared with what he was used to. As a radical liberal, he sympathized with social reform to curb the exploitation of labor but had no time for government meddling. In his opinion, the Government of Salta did too little for the poor but was far too willing to play the game of favors, dispensations, and handouts. Reform that led to "the restriction of the Government to its proper and legitimate functions" would convert Argentina "into one of the richest and happiest countries in the world."

Balfour arrived in Salta toward mid-1893 at a time of intense disputes that stemmed from the economic collapse in Argentina of 1890. Despite first appearances, the far interior of Argentina too was experiencing some of the shocks of globalization through a contraction of credit and a reduction in revenues. The depression weakened ties with the federal government in Buenos Aires, which could afford fewer subsidies, and encouraged the provincial governments to adopt a more independent line. Throughout the country, the economic depression had provoked deep political splits between factions of conservatives supporting the national and local governments and the rebellious members of the Unión Cívica Radical, the so-called radicals. From his remote location, Balfour witnessed the political crisis that gripped Argentina in July–August 1893 when the radicals attempted to overthrow the incumbent regimes in several provinces, including Salta. He noted the stir of agitation as the local radical newspaper intensified its antigovernment propaganda. The rebels attempted to disrupt the rail links to the south to which the administration responded by dragging them off and "anyone who resisted willy-nilly to the cantonments" where they were forcibly drafted. After a brief stand off, the radicals surrendered. At that point, "the band played and the cannons sounded."

Extradition

In his impoverished place of exile, Balfour had no difficulty in working himself into an apparently secure position. He was soon dabbling in several local businesses, including the brewery. Rumor that he possessed extraordinary wealth made him a figure of awe in Salta. *El Pueblo*, the local newspaper, predicted "he will make Salta famous" because he had brought £1 million with him.[49] In truth, Balfour came to Argentina with £500, which by the end of 1893 had dwindled to around £200. Two women, who had followed him out to Argentina, were helping him. Lucy Freeman posed as "Miss Ferguson," and her sister Ethel as "Miss Baker."[50] British diplomats identified Lucy Freeman as Balfour's mistress, "his enamorada, who was formally living with him."[51]

Throughout 1893, the British government attempted to conclude the extradition treaty with the Argentine Republic. At the end of the year, as a degree of political stability was restored, the Argentine congress ratified the long-delayed treaty. Early in 1894, Ronald Bridgett, the British consul in Buenos Aires, traveled to Salta bearing an authorization from President Luis Sáenz Peña to arrest Balfour. Bridgett accosted Balfour in the street and persuaded the police to commit him to jail, but his actions stirred controversy. Some Argentines were adopting a tone of defensive nationalism and opposed handing over Balfour on the grounds of the "honor of the Argentine Nation."[52] Several newspapers in Buenos Aires and in Salta accused the British of high-handed behavior and demanded Balfour's release.[53] Following Bridgett's arrival, Balfour was kept for a time in the awful town jail but at Freeman's instigation, the Salta criminal judge allowed him to return to his "wife."

Hopes of taking Balfour back to Buenos Aires failed. He filed a writ of habeas corpus and appealed to stay in Salta. Henceforward, the extradition faced numerous obstacles. They included the issue of jurisdiction over the case between the federal authorities in Buenos Aires and the provincial courts in Salta. Under the Argentine federal system, the president of the Republic could authorize the British consul to proceed to Salta where he could appeal to the local authorities to carry out an arrest. The president could not empower the consul to remove Balfour from the jurisdiction of the Salta authorities, or allow him to be sent abroad in foreign custody. The judiciary in Salta had to settle these issues.

The stage was set for a prolonged battle in the courts. In London, an expert described many other legal obstacles now in play. The Argentine federal system and the division of powers imitated the United States, creating a relationship between the executive power and the judiciary quite different from that in western Europe. In Britain, the authority of Parliament overruled that of the courts; in Argentina (as in the United States) the reverse prevailed. "The lawyer is supreme in the Republic," observed a legal expert. "As a consequence the willingness of the Argentine Executive to surrender the accused is of no effect, except to allow the process to commence in the Federal Courts." Another crucial issue concerned extradition for crimes committed before the treaty came into effect—so-called retroactive extradition. In "respectable" nations, no law could be applied to offenses committed before the law existed: that principle represented a fundamental protection against tyranny. As yet another basic principle, an accused person could be considered for extradition only on the charges mentioned in the petition of extradition. Further, under Argentine law, a person accused of crimes in Argentina had to be tried on those charges first, and if convicted suffer the penalties, before an extradition could be allowed. The penalty abroad for a specific crime could not be greater than in Argentina. Lastly, Balfour's purchase of property in Argentina (namely the brewery) gave him grounds to apply for Argentine citizenship, which if granted would become yet another barrier to extradition.[54] In the view of the *Law Journal*, the British government's case was very weak.[55]

As the case commenced, the British grew exasperated at the long delays resulting from local legal procedure. As a survival from Spanish colonial practice, under Argentine law all deponents presented written evidence. The case dragged on for several months as Balfour's lawyer deployed some telling arguments on his behalf. He noted that the British were requesting a retroactive extradition, which Great Britain itself had never granted. Surprisingly, Balfour suddenly had to return to jail but with strong hints that the British were bribing the judge.[56] Balfour's memoirs claimed that at this point he was offered a deal to escape extradition. Using a gun smuggled into the jail, he would shoot an unsuspecting convict placed by his cell and serve only six years for murder. He had to pay £1,000 to the organizers of this scheme, who included the public prosecutor and the chief of police.[57] Instead, he appealed his case to the Supreme Court in Buenos Aires, where his lawyer fought the case once more chiefly on the issue of retroactive extradition. In Buenos Aires, the fulcrum of British business interests, the British had a far easier task than in Salta and in late 1894, the Supreme Court declared against Balfour unanimously.[58]

The decision of the Supreme Court merely sent the whole case back to Salta, where Balfour tried a new ploy. He would escape extradition if convicted of the same crime in Argentina, namely fraud, of which he was accused in Britain. He persuaded a confederate named Otto Klix to file a fraud charge on the grounds that he had never paid for his share in the brewery. A second fraud charge (to which the accusation of bigamy was appended) came from Louis Borthwick, an Englishman from Buenos Aires whom Balfour had enticed to Salta with the promise of business opportunities. Balfour and Borthwick made little attempt to hide the bogus nature of the allegation. When they appeared in court, "the public took note of the cordial relationship between the accuser and the accused, who chatted with one another in the friendliest terms."[59] In January 1895, British officials in Salta paid Klix and Borthwick to drop their charges. Klix then filed another suit prompting the British to offer him another ex gratia payment. At length, probably after yet another bribe, the Salta judge dismissed Klix's latest suit, leaving Balfour's appeals exhausted. The judge, however, failed to inform the federal authorities who would become responsible for his transportation to Buenos Aires that the appeal had concluded. British officials suspected the omission was intended to allow yet another suit to be filed, leading to yet more extortion.[60]

The British appealed to Delfín Leguizamón, governor of Salta, who ordered that Balfour be placed under federal authority and allowed the British to act as proxy custodians. He authorized them to remove Balfour from jail and to arrange his transport to Buenos Aires with the only proviso that "*la señora de Balfour*," namely Lucy Freeman, accompany the party to Buenos Aires. The farce of Balfour's departure from Salta followed. As British officials placed him aboard the train, the posse headed by Borthwick, which included several police officers under orders from the judge, galloped along the platform to release him.

"It seems that no less than five trumped charges were being got ready," reported a British official, "a piece of rascality which was happily foiled."[61] With Balfour in custody, the train drove at full steam, running over and killing a horseman on its two-day journey to Buenos Aires. There, the British feared another legal wrangle as the Salta judiciary tried to reclaim jurisdiction. When the Salta prosecutor telegraphed orders to return Balfour into his custody, the federal government ignored them and handed Balfour over to the British, enabling his embarkation for England. At length, a brief ceremony took place on the dock in Buenos Aires when a Scotland Yard officer formally took charge of the prisoner. As Balfour sailed from Buenos Aires on the *Tartar Prince*, Lucy Freeman returned home alone.

As they pursued Balfour, the British received the cooperation of the government in Buenos Aires but numerous obstructions in Salta, which illustrated the weakness of federal authority in the provinces during the early 1890s. Until the last moment, Leguizamón had played no part in the affair. His belated intervention followed a request to the Argentine government by Francis Pakenham, the British minister in Buenos Aires, to secure the governor's cooperation.[62] Pakenham had made this request several times before but to no avail until late March 1895. Leguizamón's shift from inertia on the Balfour issue to supporting the British reflected the currents of Argentine politics. In essence, the prolonged weakness of the federal government after the 1890 crash had created an "intense sensitiveness of the National Government as to interfering with Provincial Authorities."[63] In early 1895, conditions changed when President Sáenz Peña resigned in favor of Vice President José E. Uriburu, a scion of the Salta landed gentry, whose promotion immediately strengthened the national government. Henceforth, the governors became more subservient and responsive to central dictates. The Uriburu administration signified a strengthening of the pro-British faction in Argentina led by ex-President Julio A. Roca, the great local architect of expanding Anglo-Argentine ties in the early 1880s. The denouement of the Balfour saga thus became one small illustration that by 1895 Argentina was emerging from the disruptions of the early 1890s and attempting to restore close relations with Britain.

Trial And Retribution

The *Pall Mall Gazette* lampooned Balfour's departure from Buenos Aires in hymnal verse titled "The Coming of Jabez." "Bring him back, O gallant vessel / Bring him safely, we implore! / With the stormy billows wrestle / 'Til thou land'st him our shore."[64] A large crowd gathered when Balfour arrived at the port of Southampton. Journalists tracked his movements until London where a magistrate remanded him to Holloway Prison. Balfour traveled across the city in the police conveyance known as the Black Maria alongside the "refuse of the London police courts."[65] Six months later, he faced trial in the High Court of Justice. The case against him comprised two relatively minor charges, namely absconding from debts and taking an illegal commission, which enabled the prosecutors to comply with the terms of the extradition agreement. During the trial, they exposed the full scope of Balfour's fraud. His companies had collapsed with liabilities of £8.3 million and suffered a net loss of £5.5 million. In defense, his counsel acknowledged his "stupendous act of folly" in fleeing from Britain but depicted him as a victim of a financial depression. Having dismissed that claim and directed the jury to return guilty verdicts, the judge imposed the maximum penalties, namely seven years imprisonment on each charge.[66]

The British press had mocked Balfour during his absence and displayed no sympathy for him during his trial. *The Times* declared that his "plausibility, his fecund ingenuity, his specious profession of religion, philanthropy, and political earnestness [had] assured the success of one of the most impudent swindles on record."[67] Balfour's few apologists claimed that he was feckless rather than criminal. A Croydon businessman found him as "vain as a peacock but a perfectly upright and straight man," whose errors and fate stemmed from becoming involved in "speculative enterprises."[68] Balfour spent 11 years in prison. In 1906, good behavior earned him an early release. In the interval, he caught a glimpse of the outside world only once during a transfer from one prison to another when he saw a newspaper billboard announcing the war of 1898 between the United States and Spain. He remained the committed supporter of progressive capitalism, referring to the Spanish defeat and the American victory in 1898 as "two substantial steps in the path of human progress."[69] Emerging from prison in his early sixties, he wrote *My Prison Life*, his lugubriously titled memoirs that were intended principally to aid the cause of prison reform. He died ten years later having returned from supervising a mine in Burma.[70]

In Balfour's career, the strands of progressive liberalism and early globalization became closely combined. He surged forward with the expansion of the domestic British market during the 1880s and fell during its downturn early in the following decade. Despite his denials, his career as a real estate financier became closely tied to the overseas development of the British economy. Specifically, his life and fate became closely linked to the ties between Britain and Argentina—a classic late nineteenth century example of the evolving global economy.

Notes

1. For an outline narrative account of the Balfour story, see David Rock, "A Fraud Abroad. The Flight and Extradition of Jabez Spencer Balfour," *History Today*, 49 (8) (August 1999): 27–35. For this paper, John Titford supplied me with numerous documents relevant to Balfour's career. For a book-length account of Balfour's career in Britain, see David McKie, *Jabez. The Rise and Fall of a Victorian Rogue* (London: Atlantic Books, 2004).
2. Balfour's methods recurred on a massive scale, for example, in Enron, the giant U.S. firm, which collapsed in 2001.
3. Trends in corporate organization encouraged new forms of crime. See George Robb, *White-collar Crime in Modern England. Financial Fraud and Business Morality, 1845–1929* (Cambridge: Cambridge University Press, 1992), 1.
4. As examples of her writings, see Clara Lucas Balfour, *The Trials and Triumphs of the Great and Good* (London: Houlston and Storeman, 1846) and *Working Women of the Last Half-Century. The Reason for Their Lives* (London: W. and G. F. Cash, 1854).
5. Seymour J. Price, *Building Societies. Their Origin and History* (London: Franey, 1958), 286.
6. In 1853, the British Anti-State Church Association became the Society for the Liberation of Religion from State Patronage and Control (the Liberation Society).
7. H. Osborne O'Hagan, *Leaves from My Life* (London: Bodley Head Ltd., 1929), 1: 142.
8. On Burns, see Brian Harrison, *Dictionary of the British Temperance Society* (Coventry, University of Warwick: Society for the Study of Labour History, 1973), 18.
9. W. S. Caine, MP, William Hoyle, FRS, and Reverend Dawson Burns, *Local Options* (London: Swan Sonnenschein, 1885).
10. J. N. Morris, *Religion and Urban Change. Croydon, 1840–1914* (Woodbridge: Royal Historical Society, 1992), 175.
11. *Tamworth Herald*, March 20, 1880.
12. In the election campaign of 1892, Balfour spoke out strongly on the Irish question. He described the opponents of W. E. Gladstone's proposed measure as "Ulster bigots [who] more than absurd [are] contemptible and hateful. [Their attitude] arises out of a bad spirit of ascendancy, and the equally despicable spirit of race hatred and superstitious (it would be wrong to call it religious) malignity." (*Burnley Gazette*, June 20, 1892).
13. *Tamworth Herald*, March 10, 1883.
14. Price, *Building Societies*, 293.

15. J. S. Balfour, *My Prison Life* (London: Chapman and Hall, Ltd., 1907), 4.
16. See Thomas Skinner, *The Directory of Directors for 1892* (London: Royal Exchange Buildings), 28.
17. *Manchester Guardian*, December 21, 1892.
18. Price, *Building Societies*, 298. The practice of inflating real estate values resulted in the resignation of Leonard Balfour Burns, Balfour's nephew and Dawson Burns' son, from his post in the Liberator in 1890. According to *The Times*, "Bogus transactions, in which hundreds and thousands of pounds were involved, were brought about by the interchange of cheques among the three principal concerns. . . . The result of the methods adopted by the Liberator group was that the companies, which were supposed to be prosperous, had actually lost their capital, had incurred vast liabilities, and had overmortgaged their assets." (*Times*, February 25, 1916, in Balfour's obituary).
19. During a liquidation hearing in 1893, a former Congregational minister and agent for the Liberator admitted having served as an auditor to the company until January 1891 despite having no training in accountancy. "He could not explain how it was his name appeared in the prospectuses with the title 'Reverend' prefixed after he had retired from his ministerial duties. It was not done by his authority." (*Manchester Guardian*, March 28, 1893).
20. On the legislation, see Robb, *White-Collar Crime*, 141. On specific complaints against the existing Act of 1874 that allowed the incorporation of building societies, see *Daily Telegraph*, November 17, 1892.
21. A victim of the bankruptcy recalled that "we knew nothing and thought nothing of Balfour. But we did know, and often have applauded, the Reverend Dr. Dawson Burns and critics on the Drink Bill, and it was his name that inspired us with a sense of security." (*Pall Mall Gazette*, January 31, 1894).
22. *The Times*, September 21, 1892.
23. On construction see Brinley Thomas, "Demographic Determinants of British and American Building Cycles, 1870–1913," in *Essays on a Mature Economy: Britain after 1840*, ed. Donald N. McCloskey (Princeton: Princeton University Press, 1971), 39–79.
24. General descriptions of the British economy include Derek Aldcroft and Harry W. Richardson, *The British Economy, 1870–1939* (London: Macmillan, 1969).
25. Ibid., 41–48. On British exports, see *The Economist*, August 2, 1890.
26. *Bankers' Magazine*, 1892, 53: 411.
27. *Manchester Guardian*, December 29, 1892.
28. *The Times*, September 10, 1892.
29. *Daily Telegraph*, October 25, 1892.
30. *Manchester Guardian*, September 16, 1892.
31. *Manchester Guardian*, November 5, 1892.
32. Balfour, *My Prison Life*, 6.

33. *Manchester Guardian*, November 5, 1892.
34. Balfour, *My Prison Life*, 6.
35. *Manchester Guardian*, December 21, 1893.
36. *Daily Telegraph*, March 28 and 29, 1893.
37. *The Times*, January 26, 1893.
38. *The Times*, October 20, 1893; *Manchester Guardian*, November 29, 1895.
39. *Daily News*, March 29, 1893.
40. *Daily Telegraph*, December 9 and 17, 1892; *Banker's Magazine*, 1893, 761.
41. *Manchester Guardian*, March 28, 1893.
42. *Manchester Guardian*, May 30, 1893.
43. For discussion, see FO 6–445, July 5, 1893.
44. The extracts appeared in the *Pall Mall Gazette*, August 24 and 29, September 17, and October 3, 1894.
45. *Burnley Express and Advertiser*, January 21, 1894.
46. Balfour described this system as follows: "The police here interfere in the disputes between employers and employed in a manner which is quite unknown in England. . . . Any labourer, who, without good cause, absents himself from his work, is liable to fall into the hands of the police. One reason for this practice is undoubtedly the custom which universally prevails here of making payments to labourers in advance. . . . This leads to frequent disputes, and certainly puts the workman very much in the power of his employer. For this debt can be recovered criminally . . . that is to say, no new master is allowed to employ a man who is thus indebted to another employer. . . . Until that debt is discharged the labourer is not free to take employment elsewhere." (*Pall Mall Gazette*, September 17, 1894).
47. On Argentine politics, see David Rock, *State Building and Political Movements in Argentina, 1860–1916* (Stanford: Stanford University Press, 2002).
48. *Pall Mall Gazette*, May 6, 1895.
49. Quoted in *Burnley Express and Advertiser*, February 28, 1894.
50. For details, see *Pall Mall Gazette*, January 25, February 12 and 27, 1894; *La Nación*, February 27, 1894.
51. FO 6–446, April 15, 1894.
52. British observers noted that Balfour's imprisonment in Salta, apparently on the orders of the British consul, "aroused the national amour propre, the idea being that a powerful nation is exercising an undue pressure on a weak one." (*Burnley Express and Advertiser*, March 24, 1894). In March 1895, a newspaper in Buenos Aires objected to comments in the British Parliament where "we were compared with Turkey and other countries in which justice exists at the level of Barbary or Manchuria." (*El Diario*, March 11, 1895).
53. *El Diario*, March 7, 1894.
54. *The Times*, February 5 and 13, 1894.
55. *Law Journal*, quoted in *The Times*, January 21, 1894.
56. An officer from Scotland Yard sent to apprehend Balfour claimed "the only way to get a matter expedited is to bribe every official from the

doorkeeper to the Minister" (enclosed in Pakenham to Rosebery, FO 6–446, July 2, 1894).
57. Balfour, *My Prison Life*.
58. Pakenham to FO, FO 6–446, May 29, August 17 and 22, October 4, November 3, 1894.
59. *La Prensa*, March 17, 1895.
60. Gastrill to Pakenham, FO 6–446, April 5, 1895.
61. Ibid.
62. Ibid. Gastrill reported from Salta that Leguizamón's current political weakness in the province forced him to defer to requests made by the federal government in order to enlist its support against his local opponents.
63. Pakenham to Rosebery, FO 6–446, April 23, 1894.
64. *Pall Mall Gazette*, April 10, 1895.
65. Balfour, *My Prison Life*, 13.
66. *Manchester Guardian*, October 26 and November 14, 1895.
67. *The Times*, November 29, 1895.
68. O'Hagan, *My Life*, 143.
69. Balfour, *My Prison Life*, 144.
70. *The Times*, February 26, 1916.

2

UNCERTAINTY, THE CONSTRUCTION OF THE FUTURE, AND THE DIVORCE BETWEEN CITIZENS AND THE STATE IN LATIN AMERICA

Fernando López-Alves

We live in an uncertain world. The bipolar system with its equilibrium is gone, drastic changes in state structures and political systems all over the world keep surprising observers and scholars, nuclear rearmament has become an unwelcome reality, new nations have renewed their claims for independence and sovereignty, alliances among countries seem rather unstable, and terrorism seems today more damaging and difficult to control than ever before. These, and other developments, make for a more unstable and uncertain global scenario. Of all of these factors, many have argued that terrorism and the war on terror, especially after September 11, 2001, is the variable contributing most to insecurity. When it comes to Latin America and other parts of the developing world, however, the visible impact of all these factors is not so clear and acquires a different intensity; in particular, the importance of terrorism as the main factor contributing to instability and insecurity is a dubious proposition. Other factors, typically associated with globalization, have provoked more uncertainty than terrorism.

At least in the Southern Cone, uncertainty goes back to the early 1990s and is directly related to the adoption of neoliberal policies as contained in the packages promoted by the International Monetary Fund (IMF), the World Bank, or the Inter-American Development Bank. As we shall see, while the Southern Cone has a long history of uncertainty and while Latin Americans have traditionally declared pessimism about the short- and long-term future, the adoption of neoliberalism has provoked unprecedented levels of insecurity that, in turn, have negatively affected political legitimacy and obligation. Unlike in other parts of the world where increasing uncertainty (especially associated with security) is closely linked to the era that started on September 11, uncertainty in Latin America has long constituted part of the landscape of globalization, with negative consequences for politics and democracy.

First, I propose that the adoption of neoliberalism in the late 1980s and early 1990s has substantially increased existing levels of uncertainty in the region with dreadful consequences for democracy. The citizens of Latin America have historically suffered from disquieting levels of insecurity about markets, economic development, inflation, unemployment, education, and political stability. These have led to an unsure picture of their short- and long-term future. But when during the 1990s neoliberalism changed the rules of the economic and political game offering little in the way of a concrete recognizable plan for the future of country and nation, uncertainty became exasperatingly ubiquitous and permeated more than ever the lives of individuals and communities. Planning for the short- and long-term future turned out to be more and more difficult. Investments, savings, retirement plans, and jobs became more volatile. In addition, state institutions appeared feebler than ever. Financial systems became more unreliable; in fact, they collapsed in 1998 in Brazil and in Argentina and Uruguay in 2001–2002. In short, most evidence from opinion polls indicates that since the early 1990s, and especially after the middle of this decade in the Southern Cone, Latin Americans have felt much more uncertain about their personal future and that of their countries than ever before.

What were the consequences of these rising levels of uncertainty? This chapter suggests that among other things, higher levels of uncertainty have caused a serious breakdown of political obligation and a growing divorce between the citizen and the state. Such a gap translates into a strong blow to democracy and political stability that has further decreased Latin Americans' scarce faith in their political institutions. Uncertainty has encouraged more corruption among the rulers, the strengthening of local mafias, increasing crime rates, and the progressive erosion of legitimacy and authority. In an atmosphere of political instability, many members of the legislature and at times even presidents, assuming that their days in office are numbered, have opted for short-term gains and corrupt practices.

This chapter focuses on Argentina and draws empirical evidence from the city of Buenos Aires during the 1980s, 1990s, and the first five years of the twenty-first century.[1] The reason that Argentina is an excellent case study is simple: since the early 1990s, this country incarnated the most radical application of neoliberalism in the region and provided the best example of a harmonious partnership among the IMF, the World Bank, and the national government.[2] It also represents an instance in which uncertainty affected the everyday life of most of the population and triggered a virulent grassroots reaction against neoliberalism as a doctrine. In addition, Argentina shared with other countries in the Southern Cone a wave of optimism about the future and democracy during the 1980s after the fall of the military regimes. Therefore, Argentina offers a good comparison between a preneoliberal period in which trust in the future of the country was stronger, and the neoliberal period in which this trust, I argue, was lost. As is the case with the postneoliberal period in other countries, Argentina suggests that theories of globalization should factor in uncertainty as an independent variable to better account for the most drastic transformations that Latin American societies have experienced due to globalization.

The Southern Cone in the Post-September 11 World

For those who emphasize terrorism as the main cause of rising uncertainty in the world, globalization appears divided into two very different phases: before and after September 11. The former would represent a more secure and certain world, the latter a period riddled by insecurity. It seems reasonable to argue that in the United States, Britain, and most of Europe, or in the Middle East and parts of Africa, terrorism (and the war against terror, however conceived) topped all other factors of globalization as a creator of uncertainty. Latin America, and especially the Southern Cone, however, is perhaps the area where the terrorist threat and the war on terror have had a lesser impact. Citizens, at least in urban areas, do not see terrorism as a major factor creating insecurity. While personal security is a big worry especially in large urban centers, massive terrorist attacks like the ones experienced in the United States, Britain, or Spain, are not.[3]

In Southern Cone countries, the war on terror has not triggered substantial changes in terms of domestic or international policy. And when one looks at national security and defense, the two areas that have changed the most in the U.S. and Europe, the contrast with Latin American countries is striking. Security and defense have experienced slow and predictable transformations that do not respond to the war on terror.[4] Major changes in U.S. military expansion that characterized the post-September 11 period have not affected the region in any substantive way either. The inclination of the United States to go "solo" in international affairs as part of the war on terror, for instance, comes as no news to Latin America.[5] Prior to the war on terror Latin American countries had long experienced the effects of a "solo" policy on the part of the superpower. The war against Afghanistan, the invasion of Iraq, and other U.S. military ventures provoked neither surprise nor fundamental changes in Latin America domestic, foreign, or military policy. The region tasted U.S. unilateralism long ago; for all the novelty and profuse writing that the unilateral policies of the United States have provoked, it is known that the propensity of the U.S. to conduct an aggressive foreign policy along these lines can be tracked back to John Quincy Adams, the most influential American political strategist of the nineteenth century.[6]

The United States and the Southern Cone

The question of whether the United States is becoming a new type of empire would seem to be of relevance to Latin America.[7] This does not seem to matter very much to the Southern Cone, however, because the superpower's traditional approach to the area has changed little. Interventionism, aggressive or indifferent foreign policy, and imperialism (if we decide to label it that way) are well-known characteristics of the traditional policy of the United States toward the region. Thus, during the last decade and a half, Southern Cone countries and the region in general have not experienced important shifts in U.S. foreign policy.[8]

This is an important point simply because in the early 1990s, a close commercial partnership with the United States raised hopes of prosperity and the belief that the superpower's policy toward Latin America was changing; after all, this was supposed to be a part of the neoliberal package of reforms. Yet this has not become a reality. Rather, what we see are growing tensions and instability in relations as a result of the absence of a coherent (imperial or otherwise), long-term U.S. policy toward Latin America. The commitment to democracy as the only blueprint of U.S. policy in the region has failed to create support among Latin Americans. Tellingly, Latin Americans today perceive the United States as they have in the past for the most part. They are often at a loss when asked about U.S. policies toward their countries, except for historically rooted perceptions of exploitation, mistrust, and dependency. A good measure of the strength of a particular foreign policy is whether that policy is reflected in the public opinion of the country or region to which it applies. As some have argued, public diplomacy matters not only within U.S. borders but also abroad.[9] In Latin America, the United States has failed miserably on this count.

Recent survey data suggest that at least in the Southern Cone, the connection between U.S. foreign policy and the pursuit of democracy remains far from established. In recent surveys conducted in the capital cities of Buenos Aires, Montevideo and Santiago, an overwhelming majority of respondents did not in fact see such a connection.[10] Forty-four percent thought that if needed the United States would, again as in the past, use military force to achieve its goals. Only 12 percent of those interviewed thought that the promotion of democracy was part of the U.S. agenda in Latin America, but they were not really sure what that meant or how it would affect their own country. Moreover, of those who did make the connection, only a few (3 percent) said that the United States had actually done something to promote "imperfect democracy." They thought the impact of the U.S. commitment to democracy on their country might likely be negative just because the United States was behind it.[11] It seems likely that similar surveys in other countries would render similar results.

In sum, like his predecessors, George W. Bush has offered scarce innovation in his policy toward Latin America. Following a pattern established by previous administrations, the Bush White House has offered a few grandiose statements, pronounced warnings, and made scattered promises about financial assistance. Yet when the administration has taken action, this action has often been ill timed and contradictory. For example, former Secretary of State Colin Powell in 2001 signed the Inter-American Democratic Charter in Lima; the following year, the Bush administration supported a coup d'etat against Hugo Chávez, the democratically elected president of Venezuela. In Bolivia and El Salvador, U.S. ambassadors have taken sides in presidential elections. And as in the past, the United States has antagonized democratically elected leaders if they happen to be anti-American. None of these initiatives surprise the Latin Americans. If this is a new empire, it acts exactly the same as the old one of the cold war era.

Asia and the Southern Cone

It is not surprising that major post-September 11 developments have not affected the Southern Cone. From the point of view of the region, much of its future still depends upon the same group of powerful countries that have dominated the political and economic scene almost since the end of World War II. The big revolution in commercial and international relations experienced by South America has nothing to do with the war on terror but more to do with the dynamics of a global process that started long before September 11. This revolution is to a great extent related to the advent of the left to power, changes in relations among the countries involved in MERCOSUR, the position of different countries with regards to the proposed Free Trade Area of the Americas (FTAA), and last but not least, the forceful commercial policy of China.

Chinese interests in the area, and its aggressive and effective diplomacy, have altered Latin America's foreign policy initiatives. While Chile, Brazil, Uruguay, and Argentina have long courted China, South Korea, and Japan as possible commercial partners, since 2002 Argentina, Uruguay, Chile, Bolivia, Peru, and Brazil have been able to start important accords with China that have transformed (for better or worse) the prospects of the region. Indeed, China's ambitions with respect to Taiwan and its economic expansion beyond Asia and Europe, especially into Africa and Latin America, are great changes brought about by globalization.[12] China's growing need for energy has driven it to consolidate agreements with places that had not been a priority in the past, particularly Africa and Latin America.[13] Especially since July 2004, MERCOSUR countries started to strengthen agreements with China that, if they were to consolidate, would very likely shift the Atlantic-based trade to the Pacific.[14] Future Chinese influence in South America can be compared to nineteenth-century British control of trade under the so-called informal empire.[15]

Even if things do not change much, in about five years China will replace the United States as South America's major trading partner in primary commodities, especially in mining. China has initiated trade deals with Chile and has gained possession of copper, and China has now displaced the United States as the leading market for Chilean exports. In Brazil, bauxite and iron ore and zinc are part of an expanding Chinese investment. Brazilian and Argentinean soybeans are included in a trading package that also contains agreements on the exploitation of iron, precious metals, and steel. Therefore, Chinese industrial expansion is cementing a rapidly developing affiliation between Latin America and Asia.[16] According to a recent testimony before a U.S. congressional subcommittee, "Hu Jintao's vision of greater economic, financial, trade, and technology ties was precisely the sort of engagement that Latin America has long wanted from Washington."[17]

Globalization and Uncertainty

The prospects of a new partnership with Asia, in addition to important changes in politics and government, are no doubt important developments associated with globalization that are new to the Southern Cone. Uncertainty, while not new to the region, stems from factors that are associated with the general process of globalization. Globalization has created uncertainty about how countries would fare in a more competitive world, about the future of welfare policies and social security, about a less orderly or at least less familiar international and commercial environment, and about different rules of engagement, diplomacy, and war.

Globalization has changed the established rules of the economic and political game by imposing free-market policies and new rules for international competition. It diminished—at least in its first phases—the power of the state, imposed new cultural parameters, and concentrated power in fewer hands. Yet it offered little in terms of clear new rules of the game. In fact, to the bulk of the population the new world seemed one in which there were no guarantees or protection: individuals were left with the impression that an abstract concept completely out of their control (the "market") could run their lives. Survival started to depend on knowing something that for the common citizen remained a mystery: the hidden designs the market had in store for individuals, their income, the economy, and the country in general. The market was not a concrete visible actor, neither was it incarnated in any particular leader or institution. People could protest specific policies and demonstrate against their leaders but could not hope to affect the market. All of this contributed to a feeling of insecurity about the short- and long-term future.

Thus, while globalization created wonderful new opportunities, it simultaneously created societies that look at a future with less hope and greater distrust.[18] The uncertainty affecting the developed world as a consequence of terrorism and the uncertainty that Latin America faces are different: in the former, there is still optimism about the future; in the latter, the future keeps looking unpredictable and full of unpleasant surprises. Moreover, despite the brutality and frequency of terrorist attacks in more developed societies, the uncertainty created by terrorism appears shorter-lived. At least if one looks at the behavior of the stock market and the popular support that most of these governments have been able to secure from their constituencies, levels of uncertainty appear to have been much less damaging. Why? My suggestion is that, among many other factors, the construction of the future (i.e., the way most people perceive the future) is a very important variable that differentiates Latin America from the core countries. Unlike in Latin America, in most of the developed world the future seems to hold promises similar to those it offered prior to September 11.

Rising levels of uncertainty in Latin America have provoked outcomes unforeseen by the enthusiastic neoliberals who, in the late 1980s and early 1990s, pushed for free markets and state reform. Some outcomes were easy to predict: the weakening of state authority, the shrinking of social programs, the fall of real wages for the lower earners in the economy, the weakening of reliable retirement systems and pensions, and growing unemployment in the face of the decline of national industry. These remain today perhaps the most damaging outcomes for the social and political fiber of these nations.[19] Other damaging outcomes, however, were unforeseen. Market forces did not allocate resources in the expected way; the image of politicians under neoliberal democracy deteriorated deeper and faster than ever expected; and the gap between government and the governed kept widening with damaging consequences for political obligation, legitimacy, and the performance of citizen duties toward the state. Thus the silent—and not so silent—citizen rebellion that we see in Argentina, where citizens refuse to comply with government demands. As we shall see in detail, tax evasion, disbelief in democracy and the political elite, refusal to meet the terms of basic regulations and bills passed by congress, and, especially people's belief that they owe nothing to the state, and in many cases that the state is their enemy, are all features of an alarming divorce between government and citizen. This makes it increasingly difficult for the government to govern and for citizens to feel that they are part of a democracy.[20] The roots of this discontent are to be found in the framework of insecurity created by liberal reform in which the old rules of the game were rendered obsolete but the new ones are still not clear, except for a growing Darwinism and disbelief in social justice.

Mistrust in Neoliberal Argentina

To what extent did Argentina adopt neoliberalism? One could perhaps debate whether neoliberal economic policies were enforced with the same vigor during the two administrations of President Carlos Saúl Menem (1989–1999), and the following presidencies of Fernando de la Rúa (1999–2001) and Eduardo Duhalde (2001–2003). One could also debate whether the neoliberal package was applied with the same scope in all sectors of the economy and public institutions, and whether the current administration of President Néstor Kirchner (2003–) is moving away from liberalism toward a more protectionist economic policy. But there can be no doubt that during the 1990s and early 2000s, the government, the IMF, and at times the World Bank, collaborated closely in transforming the country into a world-class example of neoliberalism. Indeed, for more than ten years the IMF was directly involved in planning, implementing, and supervising neoliberal policies in Argentina.[21] In contrast, it provided assistance but did not partner with the government in policy implementation in Mexico in 1995, or with Indonesia, South Korea, or Brazil from 1997 to 1999. Thus, the Argentine adoption of neoliberalism and the resulting crisis of the model can not only be interpreted as the failure of corrupt and inefficient governments but also as a test of IMF policy itself.

The problems that emerged did not simply stem from maladjustments to IMF requirements. Argentina, in fact, fully adjusted. Rather, recession and social crisis resulted from a close partnership and coordinated action of the IMF and the Argentine government. Under IMF directives, less than three years after the first steps toward liberalization were taken during the first Menem administration, Argentina became the economy hosting the highest foreign investment and the largest number of foreign-owned firms in the whole of Latin America. In addition, the pace of reform was the fastest in the region, even compared to Chile, let alone Uruguay or Brazil. The only other country to keep pace was Turkey. In addition, unlike any other case, the IMF controlled some of the day-to-day implementation of neoliberal policies. To the IMF standard package, however, the Argentine government contributed some innovations. For instance, it implemented a number of bold liberalizing measures in monetary and exchange policy that the IMF first opposed and later felt compelled to support. One such measure was the creation in the early 1990s of the *Plan de Convertibilidad* that pegged the peso to the dollar. The plan was motivated more by political than economic reasons. Yet when the fixed rate for the peso survived the so-called tequila crisis in Mexico in the mid-1990s, the IMF (and those who had opposed the plan within Argentina) started to believe that *convertibilidad* was going to work.

We can conclude that Argentina became a testing ground for IMF policies and for its possible partnership with national governments in implementing policy. It is only fair to point out that the IMF did not participate in a number of crucial issues and that it overlooked some problematic aspects of governance in Argentina. For instance, the IMF could not fully determine whether tax revenues were spent wisely or adequately evaluate whether tax evasion—and the inadequacy of tax collection in the provinces—would end up jeopardizing the whole neoliberal strategy. The IMF also could do little about the strong political clientelism that permeated the whole taxation system. Yet, deviations from the "ideal model" and imperfections aside, Argentina still stood as one of the classic cases of neoliberalism, and as an example of close partnership in policy implementation between a government and the IMF.

Did the country reap any economic benefit from neoliberalism? Some aspects of the policy were no doubt beneficial. Imported goods became openly available in the Argentine market, contact with the outside world increased, and some industries became more competitive. Moreover, the orthodox application of neoliberal strategy fostered economic growth for almost a decade after its implementation. During the period from 1989 to 1998, the country experienced significant growth in comparison with its former performance. Between 1993 and 1998, the economy grew 4.4 percent annually. This was the best that the economy had done since the early 1960s. By the end of 1998 when the privatization of a number of state-owned industries and services was completed, however, a very important source of state revenue disappeared: simply, the state could no longer profit from the selling of public companies. At that point, unable to reform the tax system or attract more foreign investment, and with withering resources, the government could no longer thwart a deep financial crisis. Among other things, this triggered a deep recession that continued unabashed until December 2002, when a slight recovery in the export sector was noticeable.

By 2002, the Argentine media were comparing the situation to the one facing President Herbert Hoover in the United States in 1929.[22] From October 2001 to May 2003, more than 5 million middle-class Argentines fell under the poverty line. Taking the country as a whole, 53 percent of the urban population today is poor, while the situation in rural areas is much worse. In a country of 36.2 million inhabitants, this means that approximately 19 million are poor. Seventy percent of children live at or below the poverty level. Moreover, about 22 percent of the population cannot provide for its basic needs.[23] By 2005, official unemployment was almost 20 percent, and an additional 21 percent of working people were underemployed or working part-time as of 2005. By mid-2006, little had changed. Thus economic recovery faces serious obstacles. The ephemeral success and failure of neoliberalism to create jobs and erase inequality can be seen in figure 2.1.

Poverty and Unemployment in Greater Buenos Aires, 1988–2002

Figure 2.1 indicates some of the reasons for the decline in popularity of the neoliberal package. While at the onset of the 1990s most governments struggled to look "modern" and tried to march to the global neoliberal tune, by 2005 political elites associated with the orthodox application of the neoliberal doctrine faced growing discredit.[24]

One thing seems clear of late. Soon after the initial euphoria of liberalization, democracies in the area weakened and governments seemed unable to retain popular support. Mistrust is a problem in Argentina. While since 1984 trust in public institutions has decreased, after the mid-1990s, trust has reached the lowest levels ever. For instance, in 1984, 59 percent of Argentines believed in the country's justice system; in 2002, only 10 percent did.[25]

Before globalization, or at least before the initiation of what literature has called the second wave of globalization, Argentines already feared the future and were weary of instability. During the 1970s, a decade during which Argentina enjoyed only three years of democracy, the main source of uncertainty was, understandably, political and institutional. During the 1980s, it was inflation and hyperinflation that reduced people's capacity to plan for the future and added to uncertainty. During the early 1990s, the country enjoyed a relative period of stability under democratic governments and a fairly good economic recovery. Shortly after, however, globalization added new sources of uncertainty and instability.

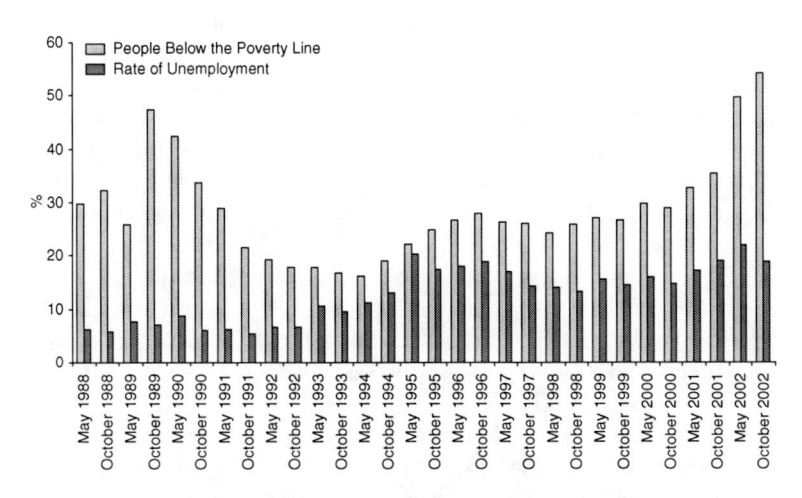

Figure 2.1 Unemployment and Poverty in Buenos Aires, 1988–2002

In other words, globalization could not resolve the old sources of uncertainty and added others instead; thus, since the second half of the 1990s, Argentines have experienced the highest levels of uncertainty in recent decades. This period has been characterized by institutional and political unpredictability, alarming and unprecedented unemployment rates in comparison with the past 20 years, widespread social insecurity, political chaos, increasing confrontation between citizens and government, and the perception that institutions are powerless to protect citizens from the negative effects of the market. Indeed, the most trusted institution in Argentina is the Catholic Church, which has enjoyed an average of about 50 percent of the population's trust since 1984. The negative effects of neoliberalism, once thought to be short-lived, now look permanent. At the same time, for the bulk of the population the long-term benefits remain elusive. One could argue that trust in public institutions was not really the main target of first- and second-generation neoliberal reforms: their major goal was to inspire trust in private capital. Yet this also is far from being accomplished. In the early 1990s itself, Argentines' trust in the private sector started to decline: from 24 percent in 1991 to 19 percent in 2001, to 9 percent in 2002 after the crisis of the financial system.[26] Mistrust did not abate in the ensuing years. As of 2003, only 9 percent of citizens trusted business.

The public's mistrust in politicians is stunning. In 2001, 87 percent of Argentines did not feel represented by any political party, and 93 percent did not trust political parties in general. When asked about the evils afflicting their country, 70 percent of Argentines thought that the major evil was politics.[27] By 2005, these opinions about politics and politicians had hardly changed. At least in the city of Buenos Aires, 76 percent of those interviewed did not feel represented by any party, 92 percent did not trust parties in general, and 74 percent believed that politics is the worst problem affecting the country. Among the youth, surveys find that growing uncertainty about the future continues to undermine the role of the political parties and the government. Only 47 percent of the youth in Buenos Aires (aged 18–29 years) still believe that the future holds some promise for them. Eighty percent of these same youth believed that the performance of political parties is bad or very bad, and 65 percent believed that parties have no contribution to make to the well-being of their country.[28] Of those interviewed in this survey, 69 percent believed that they would never feel close to any political party at all. In May 2006, a survey in the city of Buenos Aires found that 64 percent of residents do not feel that politicians can represent them and that 46 percent do not trust any person in public office.[29] One can conclude that these dismaying results are attributable not only to the incapacity of politicians and the performance of public institutions but also to something that is missing in neoliberalism and that has helped enlarge the gap between citizen and the state: *a guiding vision for the future.*

CONSTRUCTING AN UNCERTAIN FUTURE

The future is constructed in the present. The notion that societies forge their own collective vision of the future should come as no surprise. I suggest that this applies not only to authoritarian regimes but also to democracies.[30] A common project for the future contributes to collaboration; in democracies, there are obvious advantages when both ruling elites and grassroots organizations participate in the construction of a project for country and nation. The first Menem administration (1989–1995) was quite aware of this basic principle. It tried to articulate a sort of public discourse about the future to rally popular support for reform but, in the end, this project remained inarticulate and devoid of detail. It could be synthesized in just one line: "Argentina was on its way to find a place in the first world because of increasing foreign investment, privatization, and the parity with the dollar."[31]

During his second administration (1995–1999), however, Menem and his team seemed rather dubious as to the future of Argentina. It became apparent that the state had trouble delivering a discourse that could depict the future of the country for the short and long run. Public discourse remained grandiose but confusing in terms of what Argentines could expect from the near future.[32] Unlike prior expectations, the country did not seem at that time able to achieve the promised first world status. Worse still, the gains of the neoliberal reforms of the early 1990s seemed to run out fast, together with state revenues and public spending. Dissolution followed. The government created further confusion by insisting that the country needed to "catch up." Catch up with what and how? My suggestion is that, at least in the case of Argentina, neoliberalism as a doctrine seemed unable to offer policymakers the tools to articulate a promising public discourse about the future—except for its insistence on efficiency and free-market economics.

The following neoliberal presidency of Fernando de la Rúa (1999–2001) did even less in terms of spelling out a national project, a road to the future. Indeed, the president and his team remained suspiciously silent about their plans for the future of Argentina, including the role that the country should play in a complex and changing international community. Of great importance, plans for regional integration especially in the context of MERCOSUR during the de la Rúa administration seemed almost abandoned. In sum, beyond some economic forecasts and vague notions about the insertion of Latin America into a changing and more demanding global economy, neoliberal governments said almost nothing about the collective future awaiting this society as a result of reform.

What about MERCOSUR? Did it not represent a liberal promise for the future? It could certainly be argued that in the context of MERCOSUR the promise of a better future for Argentina and its partners was—and still is—implicit in the word "integration." Can we assume that integration, then, was the neoliberal vision? Perhaps. But the notion of integration remains insufficient as a picture of the near and long-term future. First, politicians keep giving mixed signs about integration. For most of them, integration is good as long as it does not threaten their control over taxes within their national territory and, especially, over custom duties. Second, government officials have remarked over and over that MERCOSUR is not the European Union, that is, it is not about the establishment of regional institutions of government and the creation of cultural bonds among members.[33] Third, although the last elections in Uruguay, Argentina, and Brazil were followed by further talk about strengthening MERCOSUR and opposing external influence in the Southern Cone, there has been no intention to create a public (or even governmental) consciousness regarding a shared future. To the common citizen, the notion of integration as a vision of the future stands, at best, vague and contradictory. The latest rift between Uruguay and Argentina regarding the installation of cellulose-processing plants on the Uruguay River that resulted in a diplomatic crisis separating two leftist governments and in the boycott of Argentine products in Uruguay is perhaps one of the most touchy crises between the two nations for more than 50 years. This has made the idea of a shared future even more fictional.

Was democracy enough in each of the countries involved in MERCOSUR to create some degree of certainty about the future? Not in the context of neoliberalism. While it is true that disenchantment with past military regimes and authoritarianism work in favor of democracy, widespread mistrust in institutions and politics do not. It is telling that while in Canada, the United States, or Switzerland two out of three people are satisfied with their political systems, by 1999 in Argentina (before, indeed, the 2001 financial crisis) 69 percent were not. In the city of Buenos Aires, 80 percent were unsatisfied.[34] After the 2001 financial crisis, 81 percent of Argentines nationwide were dissatisfied with their political system. So, even if 85 percent of the population still believes that democracy is preferable to any other kind of government, the dissatisfaction with the democracy under which they live is shocking.

Therefore, during the 1990s, but especially during the second half of that decade and the early years of the twenty-first century, growing pessimism about the personal future of citizens and about the collective future of the country overcame the optimism of the 1980s. The adoption of neoliberalism turned Argentines' newly found optimism into pessimism.[35] We find pessimistic attitudes toward the power of government, its capacity to lead, and the future of the country. Tellingly, what I have called elsewhere "neoliberal pessimism" has undermined a long-standing notion of Argentine culture: the notion of "progress."[36] Not surprisingly, in a country of immigrants such as Argentina, the concept of progress had deep and historical roots in the popular imagination. However, when in 2002 Argentines were asked whether they used the word progress in day-to-day conversations, and how often they used it in relation to their thoughts about the future, 62 percent of those interviewed answered that they seldom used the term, and only 51 percent said that they used it when talking about the future. When asked whether they thought that their parents or past generations used the word more frequently than they did, 85 percent thought that prior generations used the word much more.[37]

The Fracture between the Citizen and the State

Uncertainty about the future and the failure of the economic policies of neoliberalism provoked intense discontent that translated into collective action. From January to August 2002 alone, Argentina experienced an average of 20 protest demonstrations per day, with a total of 12,766 during that period.[38] Bearing a slight resemblance to scenes from the French Revolution, neighbors assembled and took action, erupting into provincial government headquarters while the legislature was in session. In many cases, protestors expelled the legislators and took over the decision-making process themselves. Some groups made decisions and sent them, signed and dated, to the central government. The so-called *piqueterismo*, a form of protest first adopted in 1997, became a regular and accepted form of channeling discontent and expressing popular demands. *Piqueteros* are those who block roads and the main arteries leading in and out of the urban centers, or simply block roads within the financial district or other crucial areas of the urban environment. The protestors are organized in several chapters and groups at the national and regional levels. While at the beginning the *piquetero* movement was divorced from political parties and government, almost immediately parties in the opposition started to penetrate the *piquetero* organization, especially the Peronist Party as part of its policy to undermine the government of President de la Rúa.

When President Kirchner took office in May 2003 and started to push a pseudo-populist agenda, many thought that *piquterismo* was over. Yet a number of *piquetero* organizations soon became a precious source of support for his administration (support that the presidency dutifully finances or sustains by granting political favors and prerogatives). Meanwhile, other *piquetero* organizations became supporters of the opposition to Kirchner within his own Peronist Party. In addition, similar grassroots organizations have evolved into social and political actors that remain independent from parties and government and acquired the status of active pressure groups. All of them have tried to gain mass support and most of them have organized assistant programs for the unemployed, such as shelters and food cooperatives. From January to December 2002, these groups, competing for social support and trying to demonstrate their power or acting as proxies for diverse political interests associated with government, staged a total of 3,490 *piquetes*. This, although very significant, was lower than their rate of activity during August 2001.[39] In the following years the number of demonstrations has remained steady at an average of 2,300 per year.[40]

As a result, Argentina today is one of the most highly mobilized societies in the world, and Buenos Aires perhaps the city home to most demonstrations on the continent. Such a high level of mobilization in urban areas, not only in Buenos Aires but also in some cities in the provinces, constitutes an important factor that adds to the growing divorce between the state and its citizens. In large sectors of the population there has been increasing and widespread discontent about the activities of *piqueterismo* and the constant disruption of the urban environment. Such unrestricted mobilization and the destruction of public facilities has also contributed to cement the notion that the government is either too inept or too corrupt to impose order. High and visible levels of mobilization and the failure of government to find a solution to this and other problems contribute to further uncertainty in a disrupted city.

Yet the roots of this divorce go deeper than these demonstrations and the incapacity of government to find a resolution to the *piquetero* problem. Both high levels of mobilization and the widening gap between the bulk of the population and the state represent one of the unexpected outcomes of neoliberal policies and globalization. Uncertainty about employment, the future of the country, and the personal prospects of the bulk of the population created this scenario in the first place. In short, liberal reform, with its emphasis on market wisdom, budget cuts, and the selling of state enterprises to foreign corporations, provoked increasing degrees of alienation between citizens and the state. It has also brought about an alarming weakening of political obligation and social trust.

Political Obligation and Citizen Duties

Argentines have good reasons to feel alienated from the state and to distrust the political elite. Until early 2003, the government spent $20 billion per year on a political class totaling 9,242 members. This excluded the executive but included senators, representatives, provincial governors, and vice governors. This made the Argentine political elite one of the most expensive on the continent. The national congress in recent years has been allocated an annual budget of about $336 million, which amounted to nearly 1 percent of the national budget.[41] After Kirchner came to office, the congressional budget suffered some reductions and cuts, but it is still spectacular. How is this money spent? It is telling that only 30 percent of the congress's budget is devoted to maintaining the Library of Congress, the congress bureaucracy (permanent and temporary) and services. The rest (70 percent) goes to salaries and other benefits, such as "special expenses"; these include travel, cell phone bills, per diem expenses, and other "costs of representation."

Before the December 2001 crisis, a widespread public feeling that the country was going astray or had no direction whatsoever was already eroding the government's legitimacy and weakening political obligation among citizens. The financial crisis at the end of that year added, of course, to uncertainty and the feeling that the country was heading in the wrong direction, whatever that direction was. The state was viewed more as an enemy than as a friend. In July 2001, a survey in the city of Buenos Aires found that most respondents believed that they did not owe anything to the state. Most of the respondents also refused to comply with their obligations toward government (see figures 2.2 and 2.3). After the resignation of President de la Rúa and the election of President Kirchner, which seemed to have provided a new hope for the country, many expected a change in this negative attitude toward government. Yet these attitudes persisted.

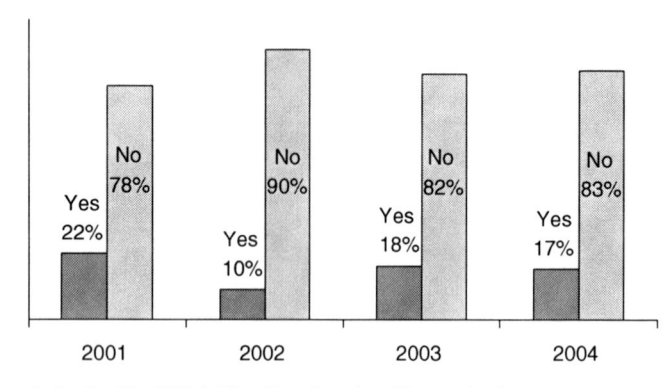

Figure 2.2 Do You Think That You Owe Anything to the State?

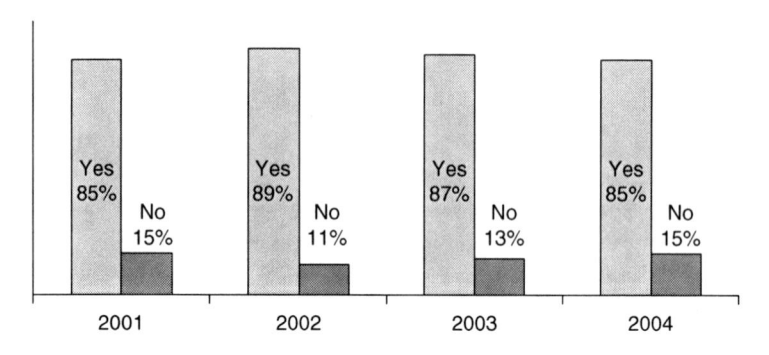

Figure 2.3 Are You Aware of Your Obligations Toward the State?

In 2002, 2003, and 2004, the same questions were repeated in identical surveys and the answers obtained were similar. When asked whether they felt that they owed anything to the state, an overwhelming majority of interviewees (90 percent in 2002, 82 percent in 2003, and 83 percent in 2004) said "no." When asked, however, if they were aware of their obligations toward the state, 89 percent in 2002 answered that they were. Almost similar figures apply to 2003 (87 percent) and 2004 (85 percent).[42]

In our 2002 survey, immediately after the December 2001 crisis, we obtained the highest percentages of negative responses to the question of whether respondents felt that they owe anything to the state; yet it became clear in subsequent surveys that the divorce between citizen and state preceded the crisis and continued strongly afterward. Therefore, we can conclude that the 2001 crisis and the fall of the de la Rúa government did affect public opinion. But we can also conclude that the public's antagonistic attitude toward the state and the erosion of political obligation that we detected preceded it (the very fall of the de la Rúa government speaks of prior discontent) and continued long after the financial crisis was over. This is shown in figures 2.2 and 2.3. We can also conclude that there is no indication that, at least in the city of Buenos Aires, citizens felt any different toward the state and their obligations toward government after President Kirchner took office in 2003.

In other words, this is a political system in which respondents feel highly antagonistic toward the state. It is also a system in which the public is aware of its obligations toward the state but chooses not to honor them. If the future of democracy and of the state depends upon the degree of legitimacy of government and the degree of respect that citizens may have regarding the fulfillment of basic civic duties, then democracy in Argentina may be at peril.

The Weakness of the State and an Uncertain Future

One important indicator of whether people believe the state is in control of national affairs lies in how they perceive the strength of foreign influences in domestic policy. In Argentina, people believe that foreign influences are stronger than the state in shaping the future of the country. People in the city of Buenos Aires perceive that the future of Argentina is decided elsewhere, outside the geographical and institutional borders of its territory. The belief that international organizations such as the World Bank or the IMF—rather than the state—are in control of economic and political decisions can be taken as a powerful indicator that the public views the state as weak and therefore unable to fulfill its social contract. This can be seen in figures 2.4, 2.5, 2.6, and 2.7.

It can be argued that these beliefs, at least in the city of Buenos Aires, by far the most important commercial, economic, political, and financial hub of the country, increase people's sense of uncertainty and the feeling that they are not in control of their own affairs. We detect this in other surveys as well. It also speaks of a sharp decline in the government's prestige and confirms the further weakening in political obligation toward the state.

As part of the same survey, we asked, "Who do you think makes the decisions that affect the present and future of your country?" The questionnaire offered the following choices: (1) other country; (2) other countries; (3) the national government; (4) international organizations (banks, etc.); and (5) citizens. In 2001, even before the crisis occurred in December, only 42 percent of respondents chose the national government as the organization responsible for the decisions

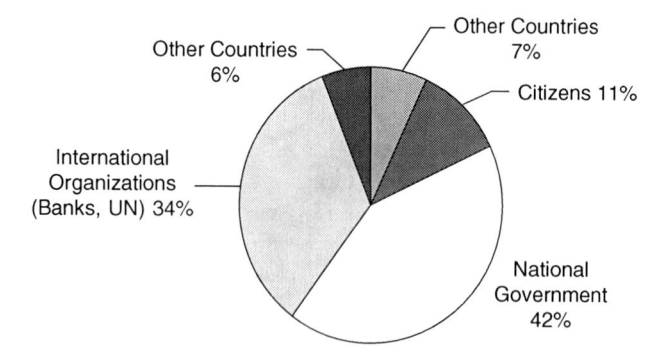

Figure 2.4 Survey 2001: Who Do You Think Makes the Decisions That Affect the Future of Your Country?

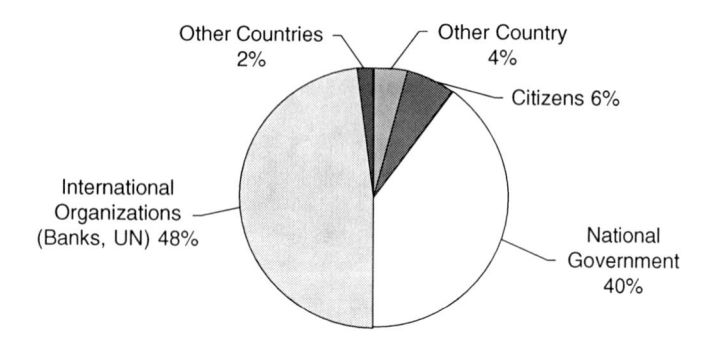

Figure 2.5 Survey 2002: Who Do You Think Makes the Decisions That Affect the Future of Your Country?

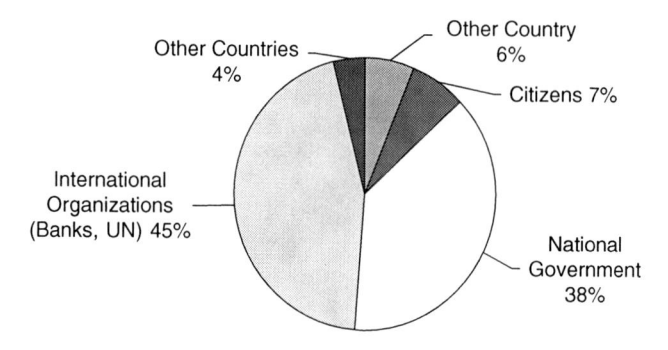

Figure 2.6 Survey 2003: Who Do You Think Makes the Decisions That Affect the Future of Your Country?

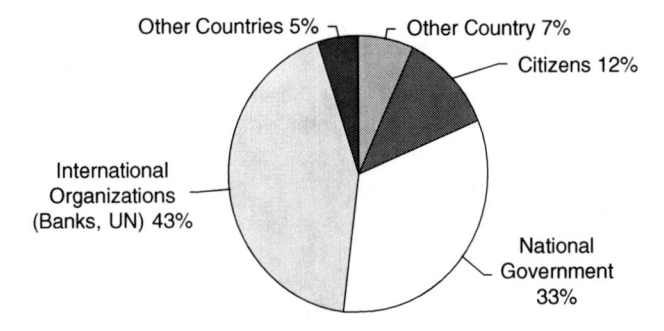

Figure 2.7 Survey 2004: Who Do You Think Makes the Decisions That Affect the Future of Your Country?

that shaped the country. Thirty-four percent thought that the major decisions affecting the country were made outside Argentina by international organizations such as the World Bank or IMF. And only 11 percent believed that citizens made decisions that mattered for the country at all. The percentage of those who thought that external influences were strongest increased in the following years.

As figures 2.4–2.7 show, only a few respondents from 2001 to 2004 believed that foreign countries (or a country) possess more power than the Argentine state in the making of public policy and economic planning. Yet when one lumps these responses together with those who believe that foreign institutions make the decisions that matter, the percentage of respondents who believe that the state wields little or no power regarding the most important decision affecting the future of Argentina reaches a stunning 50 percent or higher. Tellingly, while specific foreign countries are not targeted as the locus of decision making regarding national policies, international financial institutions are. Changes in the political elite of the country and even institutional reform in some public enterprises and bureaucracies did not seem to affect the opinion of those who thought that the real power lay outside the national territory and in the hands of strangers. For example, the results of these four identical surveys indicate that the advent of a new government under Néstor Kirchner and the reforms he instituted did not restore the public's faith in the state's ability to resolve the pressing issues affecting the nation, especially its future. Deep-rooted mistrust in government seems to be ubiquitous in the populace.

It makes sense to suggest that globalization and more specifically neoliberal reforms have affected the collective imagery, at least of the city and the province of Buenos Aires, by creating the idea that the country's future and that of its people were determined by external forces that the state cannot oppose, let alone control. And the intellectual and political influence of the city of Buenos Aires over the rest of the country is not mild. If government is powerless, citizens are even more so when forced to face powerful international influences. The country appears to have lost control over its own future. Again, we can conclude that this is a democracy in which citizens feel that their present and future are uncertain.

An interesting problem is that of finding the culprits. Whom did the inhabitants of Buenos Aires blame for social, political, and financial crisis? Whom do they blame for an unstable future? While the question of who makes the decisions that matter is one of who has the power, the question of who is to be blamed is a question of responsibility and accountability. In the same survey, we asked whether Argentina was a victim of international circumstances or whether it had "gotten what it deserved." To our surprise, given that the majority felt that the country was toothless when faced with international powerhouses, respondents believed that the responsibility for this state of affairs lay with the local elites and even with the people of Argentina. Indeed, a large majority thought that the country had gotten what it deserved. Therefore, government and citizens seem unable to successfully oppose international forces that determine the course of the future, but decisions made by local actors were perceived as responsible for this situation. Figure 2.8 compares the results for 2001, 2002, 2003, and 2004.

While at first glance the results shown in figure 2.8 seem at odds with the results obtained in the questions discussed above, they actually have much in common. Simply, they reflect people's beliefs that the state is to be blamed for the country's social and economic decline and for the empowerment of external influences. We can interpret that the country "got what it deserved" because the state was not able to deal with social issues in an adequate manner and because it had become weaker regarding international pressure. Thus, figure 2.8 suggests that respondents believe that the responsibility lies not only with the national government but also with those who elected it to office. One is tempted to speculate whether in the late 1960s and 1970s, at the peak of popular discontent in the midst of the cold war, and with the advent of authoritarian military regimes in the Southern Cone, people would have given similar responses to this survey. Overall, popular sentiment at the time blamed the United States and the clash between communism and capitalism for about everything that went wrong in Argentina or in the region in general. External

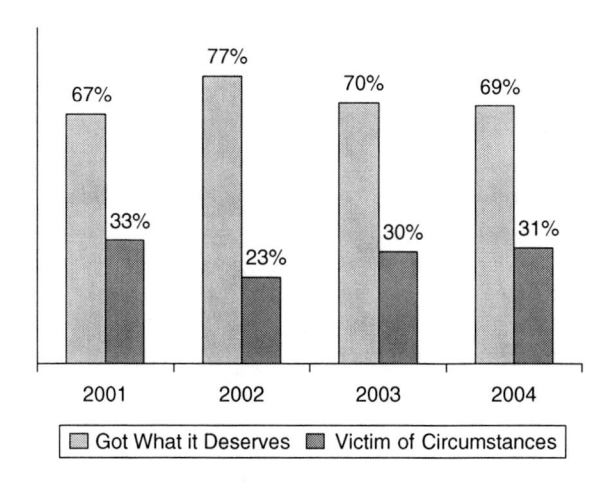

Figure 2.8 Do You Think This Country Got What it Deserves or Is a Victim of International Circumstances?

forces were indeed central to the popular imagery then, but the culprits, one could imagine, would have been of a different nature: countries, rather than international financial organizations. And maybe the public would not have blamed "dependent" ruling elites and the people who elected them to office as much as they do today.

It is worth noticing when looking at all the above figures, and especially at figure 2.8, that the surveys done in 2003 and 2004 were carried out at a time in which the Argentine economy was growing at 6 percent and 7 percent annually. By 2005 and 2006, at least at the macroeconomic level, one could no longer talk about a development crisis or a gloomy prospect for the Argentine economy. Yet at the micro level things still do not look good. Unemployment still remains high, and social problems have not been resolved; in fact, one can argue that they have worsened. Public health and other social services are still in decline, and most of those who fell below the poverty line have remained there with no foreseeable hope of recovery. The trickle-down effect of a healthier export economy has not reached the most impoverished sectors of the population and especially the "losers" of globalization. Uncertainty about the future surfaces in all aspects of social life and shapes decisions regarding education, family planning, emigration, and job searching.

A closely related question in the survey not only strengthened the finding that government is deeply discredited but also that the customary solutions to the problems of the country—the search for the right economic strategy or the advent of new political coalitions to power—no longer convince citizens. Respondents do not agree with these well-known strategies to resolve deep-rooted problems and open questions about the present and future of the country. They, indeed, want something different, or perhaps something reminiscent of ideologies associated with a shattered past. Asked what type of future they favor for their country—one based on collective action and united effort, one resulting from the right economic strategy (hopefully leading to material prosperity), or one resulting in political stability—most interviewees preferred the first choice (see figure 2.9). Most respondents wished to be a part of the decision-making process. They want to construct a future for the country on the basis of a collective and united effort rather than to delegate those decisions to the political elite. Under democracy, they want to be participants rather than bystanders.

Another interesting finding in the survey was that only a minority chose a future based exclusively on economic prosperity as the best alternative for the country. Where liberal reform emphasizes the wisdom of market forces and free trade as guarantors of a better future, at least in the city of Buenos Aires, most people emphasize collective endeavor and participation. Markets seem less reliable and more elusive than a collective and united effort; markets, by themselves, seem unable to foster collective responsibility, prosperity, and political peace. Tellingly, respondents believe that the very notion of political stability, traditionally seen as a condition for prosperity and key for a better future, remains insufficient as the ultimate goal for a better future.

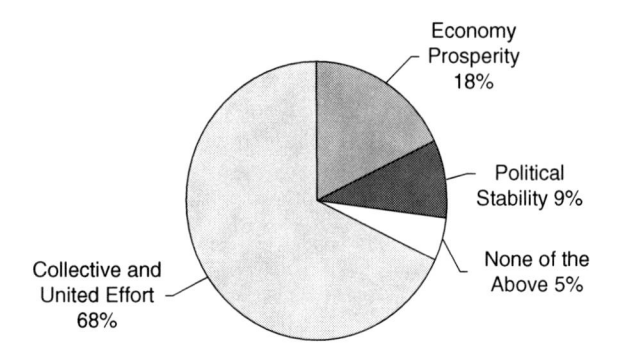

Figure 2.9 What Type of Future Do You Favor for This Country?

What Type of Future Do You Favor for Your Country? 2001–2004

One can suggest that disbelief in the wisdom of the free market and other forces associated with globalization is reflected in the respondents' incredulity regarding the wisdom of economists and planners who often take economic development as the major baseline upon which to build a better future. Argentina has certainly embraced this vision many times; the most important ministry in the country has traditionally been the Ministry of Economy. It is against this background that we should place the results of these questions about the most desirable future for the country. We can read a rejection to this strategy and the emphasis on economic strategy as the most desirable means to achieve a better future. In addition, we can infer that in the eyes of respondents, the future cannot simply be left in the hands of the state and its ministers. Rather, in the eyes of the public the best strategy to secure a healthier future is one in which the community actively participates in decision making.

When we break down the samples of these surveys by gender and levels of education, we see some interesting differences. For example, consistently in the four polls, more females than males thought that a strategy based on collective effort and economic prosperity (in equal dosages) was the best way to build a better future. Males, however, were a clear majority among those who thought that a strategy based on collective effort *alone* was the most effective to reach a better future. Females, for their part, were a bit more enthusiastic about a plan for the future exclusively based on the right economic strategy. When broken down by levels of education, those with a university education strongly supported a strategy based exclusively on collective effort to attain a better future, while respondents with less formal education did not.

Conclusions

We can conclude that starting in the mid-1990s, the neoliberal vision of a better society, with its emphasis on individual rationality, efficiency, free-market choice, and intense engagement in global market competition, faded away in Argentina. An unintended consequence of the enthusiastic adoption of first- and second-generation liberal reforms materialized in increasing uncertainty about social and political life and the near- and long-term future. Another unintended consequence of radical neoliberal reform was the emergence of a democracy with little trust in government, politicians, and public institutions. Still another was that Argentina inherited no concrete national project for the future of the country from ruling neoliberal elites, which further contributed to uncertainty and strengthened the divorce between citizens and the state. Under neoliberalism, both state and society in Argentina have suffered from increasing alienation. We can detect this alienation in the strong antagonistic and defiant attitude toward the state which has eroded legitimacy and political obligation.

In this democracy most people do not necessarily mistrust the idea of an electoral process to decide the allocation of power, but they do mistrust politicians and party politics, do not feel represented by any political organization, and think that they owe nothing to the state. This is a democracy in which government appears alien and distant despite its efforts to articulate a populist discourse and to reach to some popular sectors trying to rescue a well-known tradition of Peronism. And this is a democracy in which the public, not only in the city of Buenos Aires but also in the whole of the national territory, believes that democracy is better than authoritarian alternatives but also thinks that the political system does not work properly and is not to be trusted. The state is perceived as a weak actor and international forces as wielding most of the power.

Given this unabated mistrust toward the state and the market, at least in Buenos Aires, people seem to be demanding more control over their own prospects and country's future. Disheartening as it may sound for those who once believed in MERCOSUR as a hope for integration and as an empowerment of the international leverage of the countries involved, our research in Argentina shows that the public does not regard MERCOSUR as a possible future for the region and country. Regional integration does not seem central to the future of Argentina. Nor do Argentines believe that a run-of-the-mill democratic system based on regular elections and party contestation is going to deliver a better future. They do not even believe that finding the "right" economic strategy can gain a more promising future for the country. Rather, they want a future that is collectively built. This notion of the future is neither a new nor a revived rendition of Marxism, socialism, or anarchism. It is, however, an attempt to create mystique where neoliberalism was able to create none and to find meaning that can guide action using alternative strategies to produce stability and relieve uncertainty.

NOTES

Research for this chapter was possible thanks to two grants from the Inter American Foundation and the Universidad Abierta Interamericana in Buenos Aires under the auspices of its Center for Global Studies. For the opinion polls that provide an important part of the database used in this paper, I must thank

Raúl Aragon, Director of the Public Opinion Center of the Universidad Abierta Interamericana, and his wonderful team.

1. An important source of data for this paper was a series of four identical surveys done in the city of Buenos Aires using random samples from electoral lists (voting is compulsory in Argentina). Samples consisted of 1,000 cases each. Polls were run in 2001, 2002, 2003, and 2004. I have also drawn data from a similar opinion poll (sample size 1,000) carried out in the city of Buenos Aires in June 2005. The same poll was conducted by phone in the city of Montevideo in 2005, and I use some of those data only to compare and contrast. Surveys were conducted by the Center for Public Opinion of the Universidad Abierta Interamericana, Buenos Aires, and the Center for Global Studies of the same university.
2. For a detailed analysis of the role of the IMF in Argentina, see Michael Mussa, *Argentina y el FMI: Del Triunfo a la Tragedia* (Buenos Aires: Planeta, 2002).
3. These showed in a number of opinion polls conducted by Raúl Aragon, Sabrina Merlo, Gonzalo Screttini, Veronica Vidal, and Milagros Gaya in the cities of Buenos Aires and Montevideo. Interamerican University Call Center, September 2002 and July 2003. These were phone surveys based on samples of 1,000 cases in each city.
4. In the aftermath of September 11, Latin America has made little changes in its conception of national security and military policy. See Jorge Battaglino, "El Cono Sur y La Concepcion de Seguridad Regional Luego de Septiembre 11," paper presented at the conference Security and Defence in 21st Century Latin America, the National School of Defence, Buenos Aires, Argentina, July 15, 2005.
5. For an analysis of this particular aspect of U.S. foreign policy, see Joseph Nye, *The Paradox of American Power: Why the World Only Superpower Can Go It Alone* (New York: Oxford University Press, 2002).
6. See John Lewis Gaddis, *Surprise, Security, and the American Experience* (Cambridge: Harvard University Press, 2004), 15–19.
7. On the debate of whether the United States is becoming a new empire, see Zbigniew Brzezinski, *The Choice: Global Domination or Global Leadership* (New York: Basic Books, 2004); Michael Hardt and Antonio Negri, *Empire* (Cambridge, MA: Harvard University Press, 2001); Benjamin Barber, *Fear's Empire: Wars, Terrorism, and Democracy* (New York: Norton, 2003); Emmanuel Todd, *After the Empire* (New York: Columbia University Press, 2004); Chalmers Johnson, *The Sorrows of Empire* (New York: Metropolitan Books, 2004); Niall Ferguson, *Colossus: The Price of American Empire* (New York: Penguin Press, 2004); and Michael Mann, *Incoherent Empire* (New York: Verso, 2003).
8. For details, see Fernando López-Alves, "Cold War Paradoxes: Latin America and the US," paper presented at the conference Latin America at the CrossRoad in the 21st Century, Instituto Universitario CLAEH in Montevideo, Uruguay, July 2005.

9. See Walter Laqueur, "Save Public Diplomacy: Broadcasting America's Message Matters," *Foreign Affairs*, 73 (September/October 1994): 19–24.
10. The average percentage of those who failed to see the connection between U.S. foreign policy and democracy in the three cities was 72%. This fact is based on phone surveys conducted in March 2005 by the Centro de Estudios Globales of the Universidad Abierta Interamericana (Buenos Aires). Each poll had a sample size of 1,000.
11. Ibid. Most (97%) of the 12% of respondents who mentioned the connection with democracy thought that the United States favors a particular type of democracy that creates some kind of dependency upon the single remaining superpower.
12. As is well known, Chinese growth is staggering. China is now the world's third largest trading economy, following the United States and Germany. It is the sixth largest economy in the world and within a relatively short period of time will overtake the United Kingdom and France to rank fourth. In 2003, China alone accounted for one-fifth of global trade expansion. It is this extraordinary economic growth and its increasing need for energy sources that has led Beijing to focus on Latin America.
13. China has been aggressively forging ties with most of Africa's 54 countries. Energy resources have been of paramount concern but agreements also include political and military ties with more than a dozen African nations. Chinese firms are searching for oil and gas and in 2004 China spent almost $10 billion on African oil, accounting for nearly one-third of its total crude-oil import.
14. Luis Giglione, "El MERCOSUR y China: 2000–2004," paper presented at the conference China y America Latina en el Siglo 21, Universidad Abierta Interamericana, Buenos Aires, September 2004. It is worth mentioning that a Chinese delegation attended this conference during its 2004 visit to Argentina.
15. See Fernando López-Alves, "Chinese Expansion and the New Partnership with Latin America," paper presented at the conference China y America Latina en el Siglo 21, Buenos Aires, Argentina, September 2004. See also López-Alves, "Cold War Paradoxes."
16. China obtains needed minerals and other natural resources in addition to the recognition of Market Economic Status extended by Latin American governments (Argentina, Brazil, Chile, and Peru).
17. See Cynthia A. Watson, testimony to the Subcommittee on the Western Hemisphere of the House Committee on Foreign Affairs, April 6, 2005.
18. For a full discussion of Southern Cone countries as societies with no hope, see Fernando López-Alves, *Sociedades Sin Destino: America Latina Tiene Lo Que Se Merece?* (Buenos Aires and Madrid: Taurus, 2000).
19. Ibid., 4–6.
20. Regarding tax evasion in Argentina during the 1990s, see James E. Mahon, Jr., and Javier Corrales, "Pegged for Failure?: Argentina's Crisis," *Current History* (February 2002).

21. See Mussa, *Argentina y el FMI*, 12–14.
22. *El Clarin*, July 28, 2002, 5–6.
23. See *La Nacion*, August 22, 2002, 1.
24. Carlos Vilas, "Pobreza, Desigualdad y Susentabilidad Democratica: El Ciclo Corto de la Crisis Argentina," unpublished manuscript, Secretaria de Seguridad y Acción Social, July 2003.
25. See Marita Carballo, *Valores Culturales al Cambio del Milenio* (Buenos Aires: Nueva Mayoria, 2005).
26. Ibid.
27. World Values Survey–TNS Gallup Argentina, 1984–2002.
28. Survey by Ipsos Mora y Araujo for the Odiseo Foundation. The sample included 1,200 persons between the ages of 18 and 29. See also the newspaper *La Nacion*, July 24, 2005, 11–12.
29. Center for Public Opinion, Universidad Abierta Interamericana, based on 1,000 phone interviews. It was conducted on May 20, 2006.
30. See Lewis Siegel Baum and Andrei Sokolov, *Stalinism as a Way of Life: A Narrative in Documents* (New Haven, CT: Yale University Press, 2001); and Jeffrey Brooks, *Thank You Comrade Stalin! Soviet Public Culture from Revolution to Cold War* (Princeton: Princeton University Press, 2001).
31. See Marcelo Camusso, "El Discurso Publico en la Argentina del Neoliberalismo," paper presented at the Universidad Catolica Argentina, Buenos Aires, April 2003, 14.
32. Ibid., 16–17.
33. At a conference on globalization, for instance, former Uruguayan president Luis Alberto Lacalle (1990–1995), one of the crafters of MERCOSUR and still active in MERCOSUR politics today, expressed that the purpose of MERCOSUR was never to create real political and social integration. Its main objective remains "exclusively the creation of mechanisms that would facilitate and encourage trade among members." The conference was held at the Hotel La Capilla, Punta del Este, Uruguay, May 17, 2002.
34. Carballo, *Valores Culturales al Cambio del Milenio*, 79–81.
35. For a very interesting discussion on the concept of "pessimism" and its history in European philosophical thought, see Joshua Foa Dienstag, "Nietzsche's Dionysian Pessimism," *American Political Science Review*, 95 (December 2001): 923–937. For a discussion on pessimism in Argentina and Uruguay during the 1990s and its political consequences, see Fernando López-Alves, "Neo-Liberal Pessimism in Argentina: 1990–2002," paper presented at the Center of International Studies, Princeton University, May 2002. See also the same paper in its Spanish version in *Foro Abierto*, 1 (3) (December 2003), Buenos Aires.
36. López-Alves, "Neo-Liberal Pessimism in Argentina," 7.
37. Survey by the Public Opinion Center of the Universidad Abierta Interamericana, Buenos Aires, 2002. In 2004, the same survey obtained roughly the same results.
38. See *La Nacion*, August 22, 2002, 8–9.

39. *El Clarin*, June 23, 2002, 1.
40. Interview with Raúl Aragon, Director, Center for Public Opinion, Universidad Abierta Interamericana, July 2005.
41. The House of Deputies absorbed $195 million of that budget, with the rest going to the Senate and the Executive. See *La Nación*, February 26, 2002, 12–13. See also Guillermo Lanfrancon, *Yo Pago, Tu Pagas, Ellos Gastan* (Buenos Aires: Editorial Planeta, 2001).
42. Surveys conducted in 2001, 2002, 2003, and 2004 by the Public Opinion Center of the Universidad Abierta Interamericana, Buenos Aires, based on samples of 1,000 each.

3

ISOMORPHIC NEOLIBERALISM AND THE CREATION OF INEVITABILITY

Miguel Ángel Centeno

Winners tend to assume that their victory was inevitable. The appeal of postfacto functionalism is considerable, and it is understandable why those looking back may consider that history was on *their* side. Such an attitude seems to pervade among sympathizers of market economics throughout the globe but particularly in Latin America and eastern Europe. That markets should and would win the ideological battle is often seen as the most natural of processes. While not engaging in polemics regarding the desirability of such outcomes, I will address the extent to which neoliberal ideals have established both an ideological and a de facto policy monopoly. More importantly, I will ask how we account for the apparent victory of neoliberalism at the start of the twenty-first century. Among other things, and contrary to expectations, this victory has created a growing context of uncertainty in Latin America. Intellectual victories can be read as monopolies of thought and action that provide some paradigmatic stability. Yet the experience of neoliberalism in Latin America encourages the opposite reading: the overwhelming acceptance of the doctrine has changed the rules of the game to a point that the new ones are confusing and the old ones seem not to matter. To explain the outcome of this uncertainty discussed at some length in other chapters in this volume, one needs to explore the major question of how and why neoliberalism established its monopoly.

I will not address the process of, or prospects for, transition. The literature on what one author has called "transitology" is already massive.[1] Rather, I will discuss what I believe has been a largely neglected question: why did market ideology win so overwhelmingly in such a short period of time? Most of us can easily recall a time not so long ago when the term crisis was easily associated with capitalism.

Amidst the American triumphalism of the new millennium, we seem to have forgotten the common perspective of the world in 1979: a powerful Soviet Union increasingly allied with a commodity-rich developing world, both willing and able to challenge the West. Twenty years later, the United States and its economic principles are hegemonic. I begin with the observation that this practical homogeneity of economic and political views is in itself worthy of analysis.

My proposed answer will have three parts. In the first, I will attempt to define exactly what the neoliberal paradigm is and how it influences public policy. I will then suggest that part of its triumph may be understood through what DiMaggio and Powell (1982) have called "institutional isomorphism." Third, I suggest that the paradigm was spread through a series of connections between individuals and institutions (abetted by asymmetric distributions of power). Thus, the triumph of liberalism is not necessarily the victory of a "better idea" but the triumph of an imperial vision (Hall 1988). Finally and most important, I link this victory to the coercive property of finance capital and its ability to demand new forms of behavior and new policy paradigms from practically every country after 1975. The combination of (1) a ready policy solution; (2) a group ready to carry it out; and (3) the political leverage with which to force this solution accounts for the great second victory of liberalism.

I should note that this analysis is not necessarily concerned with the economic and social performance associated with the market. Few today would question the superiority of market economics in promoting growth (despite the events of the past years). Moreover, the positive relationship between improved performance in measures of aggregate living standards and both liberal economic systems *and* integration into the global economy is fairly well documented.[2] Thus, I do not wish to *necessarily* argue that there is a "better way." The actual benefits of liberalism, however, do not wholly explain its success. The victory of a policy paradigm or an ideological perspective cannot simply be assumed but must be explained politically, and this is what this chapter is attempting to do.

A second clarification concerns the unit of analysis. This chapter provides a "satellite's-eye-view" and necessarily neglects the domestic and even regional dynamics that may be involved. By doing so, I do not claim that global structures can account for all developments. But, I do take seriously the notion that with greater interdependence, the structures of a global system do have an independent causal role to play in determining policy choices and outcomes. Much of previous work on a global comparative scale has utilized long-standing categories from international relations (e.g., income, geography, or language). Much less has been done on how different countries' *relational position* in the process of integration itself is the key differentiation between them. An obvious exception is of course the world system tradition and dependency theory. However, both of these rely on relatively simple one or two dimensional models of global structure. More formal network analysis would allow for a more complex and interactive analysis.[3] Only this form of formally structural approach would allow us to begin to understand both the processes of global integration and different societies' and countries' position therein. While this chapter does not make use of such formal models,[4] I hope that it will stimulate research in this direction.

Explaining the Victory of the Market

The Neoliberal Paradigm

Let us begin by defining what we mean by neoliberalism. Obviously, there is a wide variance within the neoliberal model. Moreover, while some regimes have emphasized one aspect, others have concentrated on others. Nonetheless, there is enough commonality in the policy trends of the past few years that we may describe an "ideal type" neoliberal policy outlook.

The standard version of what neoliberalism looks like borrows from the so-called Washington Consensus a series of now familiar policy objectives:

- fiscal balance;
- trade openness; and
- monetary control

The overall objective is to control inflation over and above all other considerations. Inflation must be defeated even if the price is dramatic declines in production and increases in unemployment.

I would like to suggest that neoliberalism is much more than a set of policy prescriptions. Most importantly, it involves shift in (1) the kinds of logics used in policymaking; and (2) the intended audience of this policymaking.

Under neoliberalism the main thrust of political decision making is no longer guided by political reasoning—that is, the satisfaction of some domestic constituent demand (this does not necessarily imply democratic processes—authoritarian regimes have their clients as well). Rather, decisions are made largely on the need to encourage the implantation of macroeconomic goals. Obviously, compromises are made, but the starting point for much decision making is "will this be good for the economy as measured by x, y, z?" This shift is critical in a variety of ways, but most importantly, it requires that decision makers create autonomous spaces for themselves that will allow them not to respond to social or sectoral requests for relief. Much more so than in "political" regimes, decision makers need to trust their wisdom rather than their representation.

The conjunction of this economic emphasis with the construction of a global financial marketplace means that the key interests and opinions that must be satisfied are not necessarily inside the domestic economy. All countries now have to deal with the international response to their policies, but for those somewhere in the limbo between the Organisation for Economic Co-operation and Development (OECD) and the United Nations Development Programme (UNDP) basket cases, the international markets are all critical. The global opening means that domestic money is less institutionally loyal and may flee (i.e., act like it is itself an international investor), and the shift from direct investment to the stock and bond market means that international players can desert a sinking ship with surprising ease and rapidity.

The implication of these two trends is that signaling behavior has become ever more critical for policymaking. In fact, neoliberalism may often be described not so much as a set of concrete policies, but a well-recognized dramaturgical sequence that serves to assure that the right policies *will* be followed, the right instincts obeyed, and the right interests represented.[5]

Overall, neoliberalism signifies a shift in the kinds of rationales and expected responses that are given weight in policymaking toward more economically instrumental policies favored by international audiences. An interesting point here is that these policies favored by international audiences are not always clear to local actors. The local rules of the game that establish social and economic preferences in relation to the punishment or rewards imposed by the local market appear distorted in the eyes of local actors. Their preferences and market behavior no longer apply under this new logic, a logic that seems characterized by unpredictability and unjust punishment and reward. While no doubt there is such a logic here, it does not necessarily look clear or even "logical" to actors in specific countries.

The Global Reach of Neoliberalism

How pervasive is neoliberalism? To what extent can we speak of a global trend toward the kind of attitudes and policies described above? In part because of the haziness of any definition of neoliberalism, in part because of the difficulty in obtaining reliable and relevant data, it is impossible to define some "neoliberal" index that would provide a precise quantification of the trend in policymaking over the past 20 years. We can, however, address some general developments.

First, how much has the state exited from parts of social life? The data are somewhat contradictory on this score. On the one hand, we have various cases of massive privatization of parastatals. There is no question that Latin American states and those from the former Soviet bloc play a much less direct role in the economy of their respective countries. Yet the aggregate evidence does not indicate a massive pullback of the state. I have used two possible measures to determine the extent to which neoliberal policies have led to a decline in the central role played by the state. State expenses have not necessarily declined in absolute- and inflation-adjusted terms and deficits remain a perennial problem for Latin American governments (figures 3.1 and 3.2).

The evidence is hazier when it comes to government intervention in the social economy. While neoliberal regimes are stereotypically denounced for cutting welfare spending, it is critical to disaggregate such policies. In Latin America, for example, some countries associated with neoliberal policies such as Mexico and Argentina actually saw increases in health and welfare expenditures—both in absolute terms and as a percentage of (gross domestic product) GDP and of government

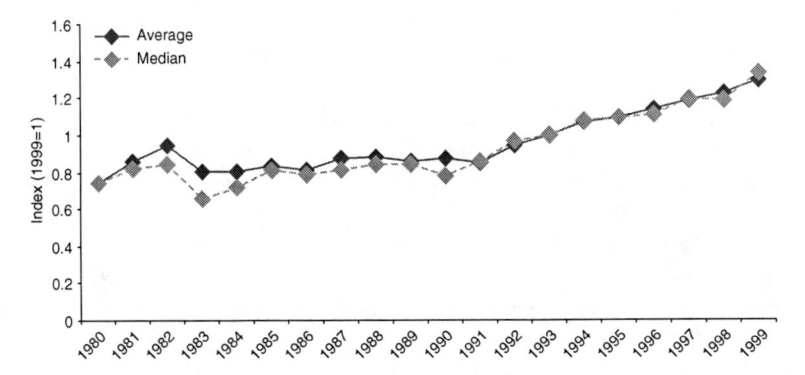

Figure 3.1 Government Expenditures
Note: Based on Mexico and ten South American countries.
Source: USAID 2000.

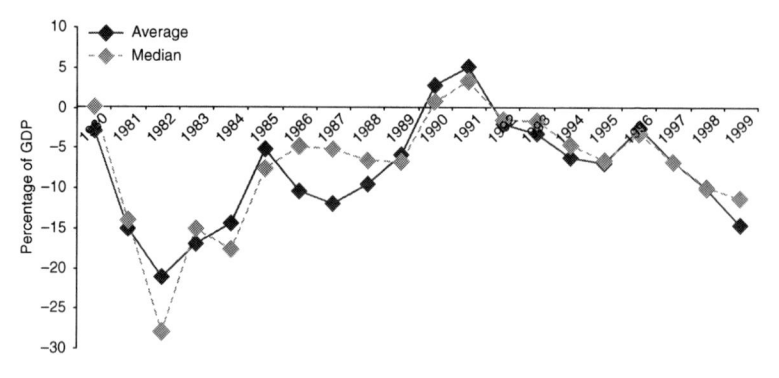

Figure 3.2 Latin American Government Deficits
Note: Based on Mexico and ten South American countries.
Source: USAID 2000.

spending. Recent studies have indicated, however, that social security provisions and pensions may have been much more adversely affected. Certainly in the case of eastern Europe, the past decade has been less than kind to those on fixed incomes. Significantly for some sectors, the government's role as an employer has declined (figures 3.3 and 3.4).

While reliable comparative longitudinal data are also largely unavailable, all observers have noted a significant increase in inequality as "market forces" have been allowed much freer play in a variety of regions. The logic of the market has been allowed to increase the social distance between the haves and have-nots, despite the dislocation this may create. In several countries, the trend toward greater inequality has been deepened by a rapid increase in urban unemployment and particularly the decline in the ability of many to sustain middle-class status (figures 3.5–3.7). Especially in the past ten years, there has also been a dramatic increase in urban poverty.

There is also an almost global trend in the overrepresentation of (1) economists; and (2) those with training in the OECD and particularly in the United States, among leading policy elites. In some cases (e.g., Mexico and Chile), this could be described as almost hegemonic control by a new kind of politician. Even in those cases where the official holders of power have not attended such institutions, the significant influence by international institutions may be said to make any differences in personnel practically irrelevant. One indication of the predominance of a particular form of economic policymaking is the drastic reduction in inflation that may be observed throughout the world since the mid-1980s, but particularly in Latin America (figure 3.8).

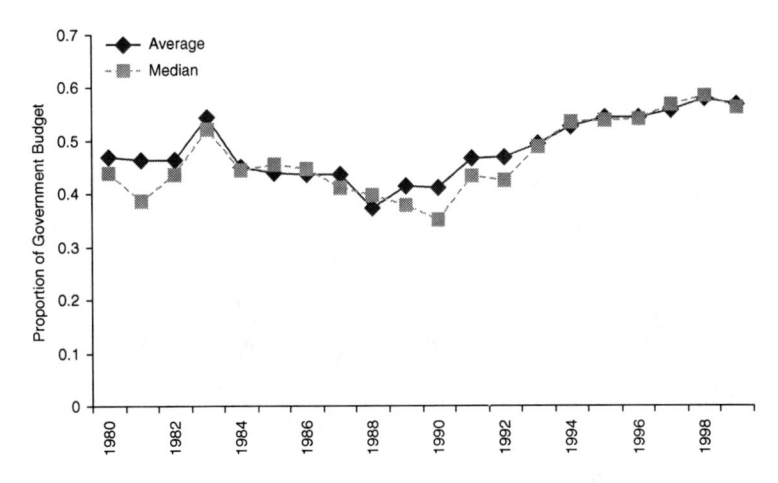

Figure 3.3 Social Expenditures
Note: Based on Health, Education, Welfare, and Social Security from Mexico and nine South American countries.
Source: USAID 2000.

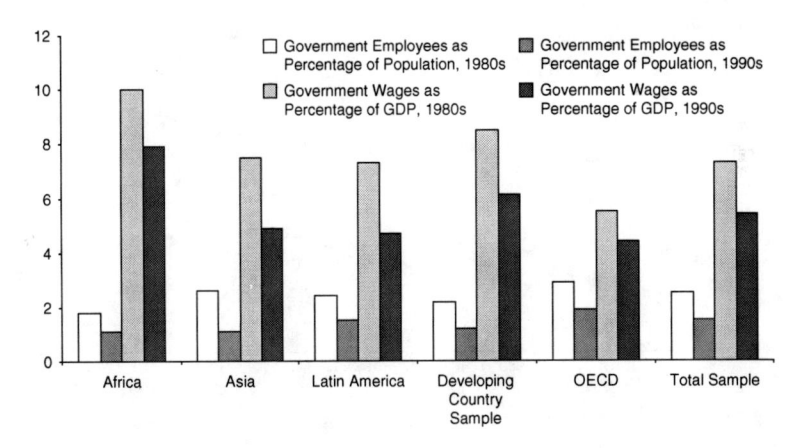

Figure 3.4 Government Employment
Source: Schiavo-Campo 1997.

The most obvious and best documented trend toward the neoliberal model has been the vast increase in the willingness of countries to open their economies to the international market. Practically every significant economy (but particularly among the middle-income countries most affected by neoliberalism) has reduced all possible

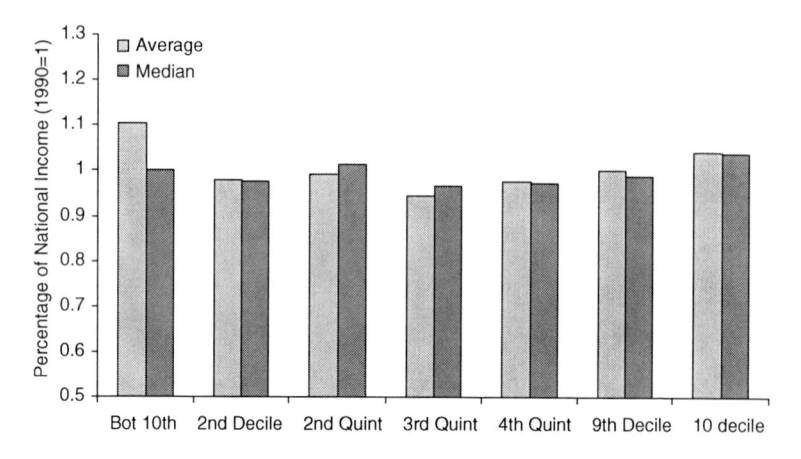

Figure 3.5 Growth of Inequality in Latin America
Note: Based on Mexico and ten South American republics.
Source: ECLAC 2000.

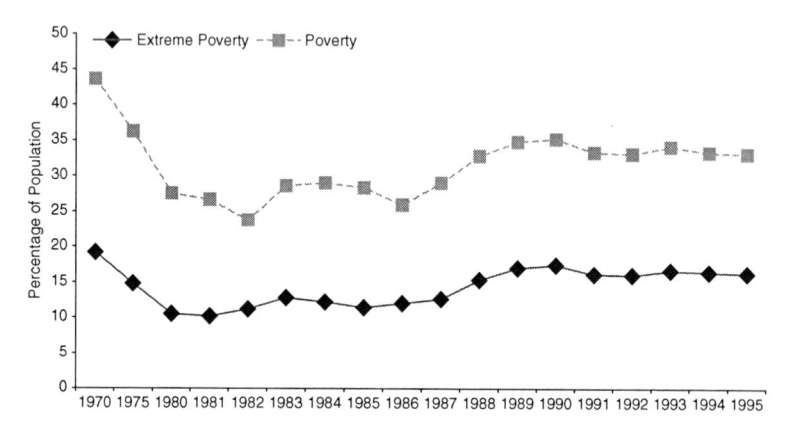

Figure 3.6 Poverty in Latin America
Source: Londono and Szekely 1997.

forms of market protection. The evidence for this may be best gleaned from the dramatic rise in the amounts of imports absorbed by ten representative cases as in figure 3.9.

Not coincidentally, this has been accompanied by two correlated trends: (1) a steep decline in the terms of trade associated with traditional products produced by developing countries; and (2) a marked shift in the distribution of income toward both the OECD and the newly emerging Asian economies (figures 3.10–3.11).

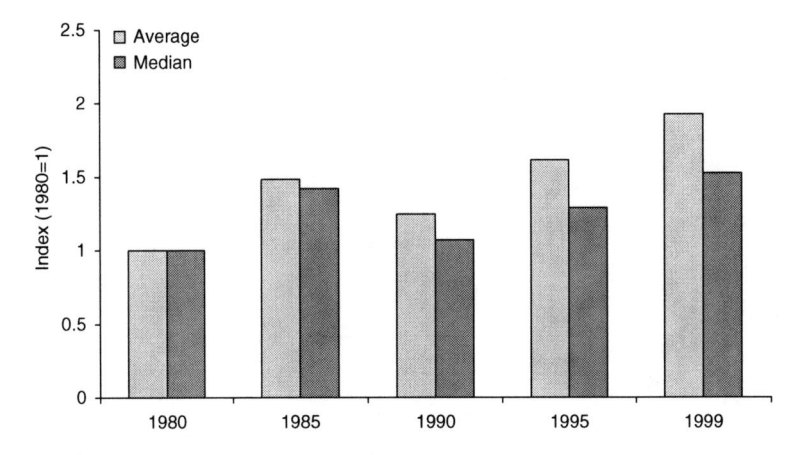

Figure 3.7 Urban Unemployment in Latin America
Note: Based on Mexico and ten South American countries.
Source: ECLAC 2000.

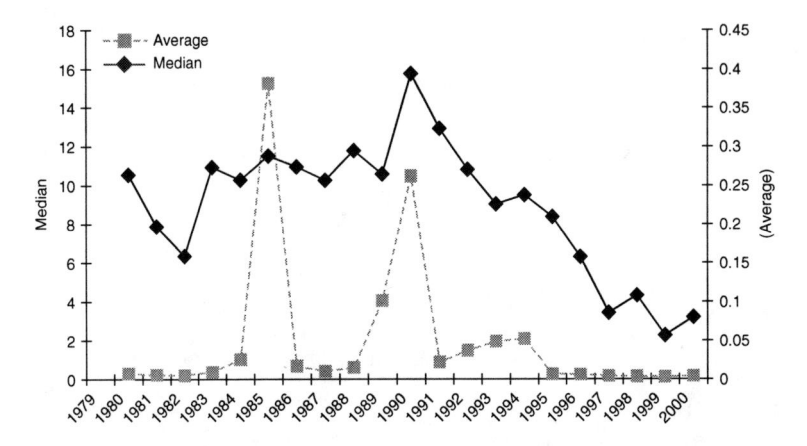

Figure 3.8 Latin American Inflation
Note: Based on Mexico and ten South American countries.
Source: USAID 2000.

How do we explain such an apparent global movement toward the same sets of policies? The trend is particularly puzzling, as almost all of these policies have had significant social and political costs. That is, the most obvious answer of politicians seeking votes does not necessarily fit the attributes of the model. (This is not to deny that some of the policymakers responsible for the shift have been able to obtain significant popular support, e.g., Carlos Salinas de Gortari prior to

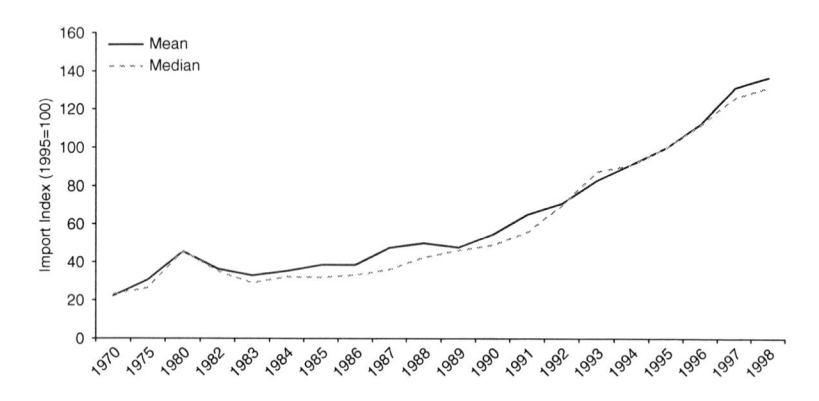

Figure 3.9 Openness to Trade
Source: Handbook of International Economic Indicators 2000.

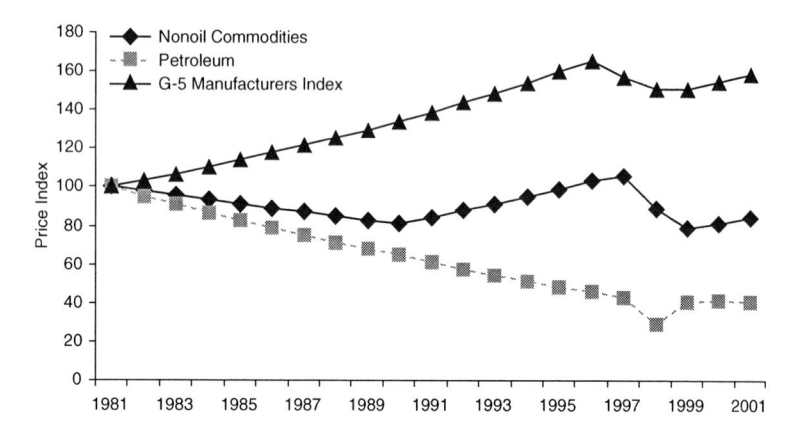

Figure 3.10 Terms of Trade
Source: IBRD, Global Economic Prospects 2000.

1994 in Mexico, Alberto Fujimori during most of the 1990s in Peru, and Carlos Saúl Menem prior to 1997 in Argentina).

In short, we have something of a behavioral mystery. Why have a wide variety of countries been willing to pay the high costs of "international discipline" when the immediate benefits thereof were so often both illusive and amorphous and while the costs (especially domestic) were so concrete and immediate? Why then do so many countries follow policies with no immediate or obvious payoff?

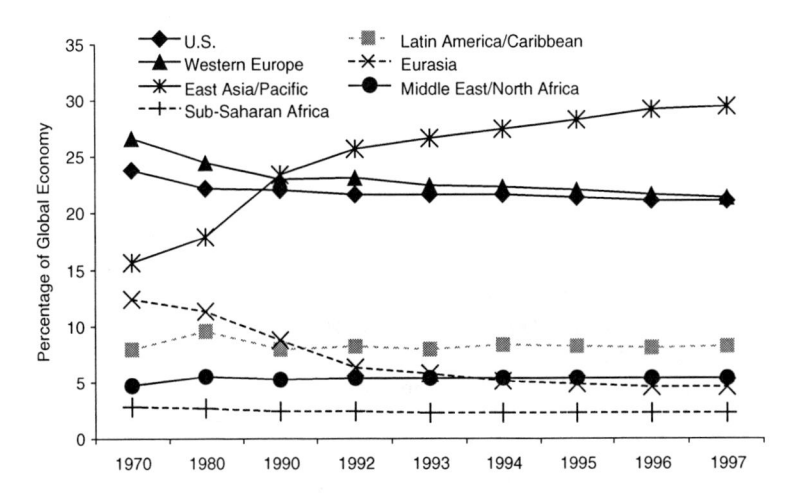

Figure 3.11 Share of Global Wealth
Source: USAID 2000.

Explaining the Rise of Neoliberalism

The answer preferred by many cheerleaders of neoliberalism and globalization in general (e.g., Thomas Friedman) is that the world has come to its senses and now recognizes the wisdom of the markets. Many of these go further in indicating that not only were countries smarter for having chosen the market but that "there was[is] no alternative." Nations hoping to avoid the pain associated with neoliberalism will find themselves shut out of opportunities and will fall further behind. The total collapse of the socialist alternative as practiced in the Soviet bloc, the apparent anomie of social democracy's third way in the OECD, and the undeniable capacity of market mechanisms to generate new forms of growth have led to the adoption of a functionalist teleological read on contemporary history. This was the best way to go, so this is the way we went.

A single chapter in a book is inadequate for a full discussion as to the costs and benefits of such policies. Moreover, such exercises in universal judgments neglect the critical differences in both a priori states, policies, selected speeds and form of implantation, and sheer contingency. Again, there is certainly no doubt as to the productive advantage of the market or the very good reasons for the collapse of alternatives. What may be debated, however, is the validity of claiming that because the markets did bear fruit, everyone decided to plant them. Rather, we might look to the work of Powell and DiMaggio and associated views of John Meyer and other neoinstitutionalists for a more complex and satisfactory answer.

This perspective has been used to explain organizational behavior. Simply put, neoinstitutionalists challenge the assumption that institutions (or individuals) are perfectly rational information-processing machines with clear maximizing goals. Rather, these actors are attempting to make their way through the fog of information and signals that their environment offers them. These signals are sometimes associated with policies or decisions that will lead to improvements in relevant performance (but we must recognize that such relevancy is also situationally contingent). At many other times, however, signals from the environment have nothing to do with how an organization or an individual performs but rather with how it/he/she is *perceived as performing*. Neoinstitutionalism emphasizes that it does not matter whether we know what we are doing as long as it looks like we do. Obviously, one cannot fool all of the people all of the time, but depending on the situation, we can fool quite a few of them for just long enough.

From this perspective, then, the rise of neoliberalism should not be understood as a necessarily purposeful turn toward "better" policies, but rather a discursive adoption of new policy language and interests. Countries have become more neoliberal because they are supposed to—if not, they run the danger of not being taken seriously or, much more relevant, being cut off from the flow of international resources.

Critics have accused neoinstitutionalists of positing a process of "institutional infection" without providing a mechanism by which these standards are passed or imposed. A neointuitionalist narrative must account for two things: transfer of models and enforcement of models. A discussion of the rise of neoliberalism provides a good example of how these mechanisms may have functioned.

If, as some have suggested, policy paradigms can be analyzed as forms of social epidemiology, then we need to identify the carriers of neoliberalism. As noted above there has been the rise of a particular type of policy elite. The Mexican technocrats whom I have analyzed in previous works are perhaps the prototypical example, but other countries have had their equivalents. These men (with very few women) could "infect" their states from the inside by pushing for a new way of making policy decisions and a new economic paradigm. The fact that almost all of these newly powerful individuals did push for at least some set of neoliberal policies goes far in explaining the global convergence that we have observed. These individuals had powerful institutional allies. First, within their own countries they often came from ministries with a great deal of bureaucratic influence. Second, they were supported by a network of private banks, international monetary institutions, and even the sovereign governments of the most powerful countries. These institutions provided the domestic policymakers with support at critical junctures. Moreover, and perhaps most important, they often exercised an implicit veto over the rise of alternative elites or policy models.

I would like to emphasize what may be called a global cultural shift partly driven and perhaps best understood through diffusion models. The available data point toward an increasing centrality of the OECD countries in terms of cultural production and reproduction, but particularly to a hegemonic role played by the United States. While this part of the project is still ongoing, some representative trends already indicate the nature of the change. Figures 3.12–3.14 depict some important and, I believe, representative changes in the possible mechanism of cultural diffusion. The first depicts the balance of trade in audiovisual materials between the United States and Europe. The second figure shows the distribution of phone calls within and between Latin America. The third depicts trends in tourism flows in that continent. Each indicates the increasing centrality of the United States in the "global web."

But more important than a shift in the cultural centrality or autonomy of a region is the flow of financial resources and its

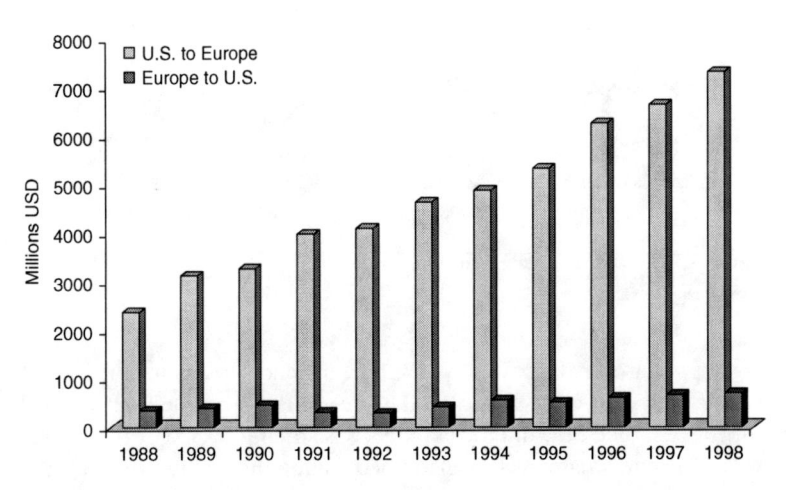

Figure 3.12 U.S. and European Audiovisual Trade (Includes Theatrical Films, Videos, and TV Programs)

Source: Cannes Market, *Focus* 2000.

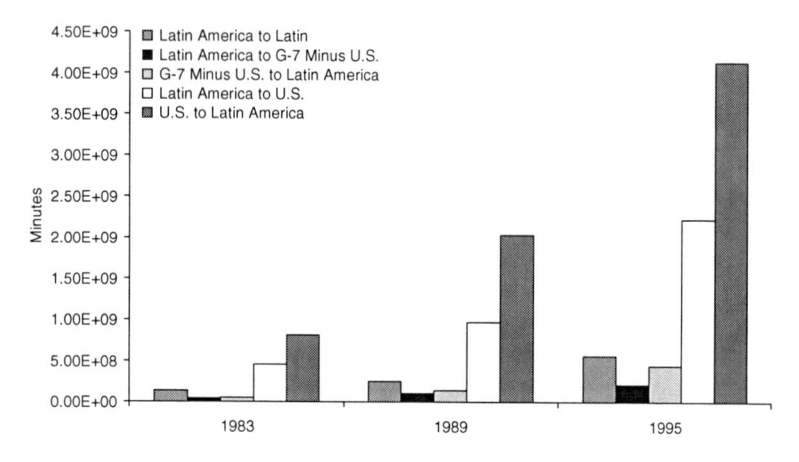

Figure 3.13 Latin American Telephone
Source: International Networks Archive (www.princeton.edu/~ina) 2005.

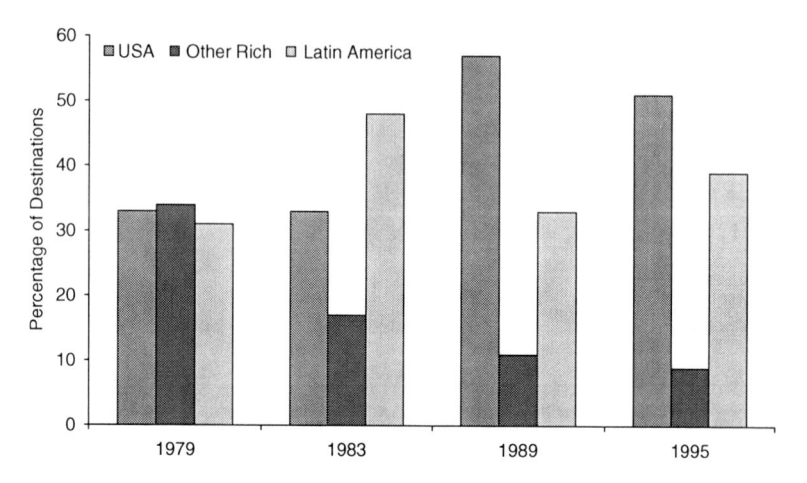

Figure 3.14 Latin American Tourism
Source: Mapping Globalization Project, Princeton University 2005.

development over the past 20 years. If in the end, the neoliberal policies owe at least part of their rise to the preferences of some international institutions, then how did the latter exercise their power? For the answer we can turn to what may be called "neo-Hilferdingism": simply put, the power of financial capital to impose its discipline on these countries.

In order to understand this, it may be worthwhile to return momentarily to the definition of neoliberalism. The set of policies under this rubric shared more than an apparent devotion to the market. They also venerated monetary and fiscal stability. If any attribute was considered paramount by neoliberalism, then it was the ability of countries to pay their bills—especially their international obligations. Thus, from the most cynical view (to which I do not necessarily subscribe) neoliberalism may be understood as a payment program to make sure that obligations to major financial institutions are met.

Why are these so critical? Why are countries so willing to impose a discipline on their societies for the sake of the financial well-being of the world? The story has two parts.

Beginning in 1973, massive amounts of global lending allowed almost all the countries later to have neoliberal policies to borrow beyond their wildest dreams. From Mexico to Poland and from Hungary to Indonesia, governments went on a borrowing binge (figure 3.15). As has often been noted, these loans were rarely used to generate increased capacity to pay them back, but were often consumed in nonproductive ways. Much as in the case of a drug addict, countries thus found themselves beholden to those who had initially sought them out as consumers. For a wide set of social, political, and economic reasons countries needed foreign exchange. Given limited export capacity, financial institutions were their only source of "ready money." Yet, such moneys were unavailable unless these same countries could maintain their viability as international debtors. In part this involved paying back some of the debt. But as these amounts became truly astronomical, the actual payment became less important than providing the banks and relevant institutions with a reasonable case that such payment would occur at an unspecified future time.[6] This required countries to adopt a series of behaviors and polices associated with responsible international actors. As long as they were judged responsible—that is, as long as they were seen as moving toward a neoliberal paradise, they would be rewarded with more loans. Interestingly, the very imposition of these policies often made exit from such a bargain increasingly difficult. As countries opened their markets to satisfy the conditions of their continued access to international cash, they saw previous domestic suppliers of a variety of goods and services disappear. As they were replaced by imports, the need for steady sources of cash with which to pay for these naturally increased. Neoliberalism not only justified itself but also appeared to make its adoption irreversible.

Beginning in the 1990s, access to debt was augmented by the development of new sources of cash through portfolio investments.

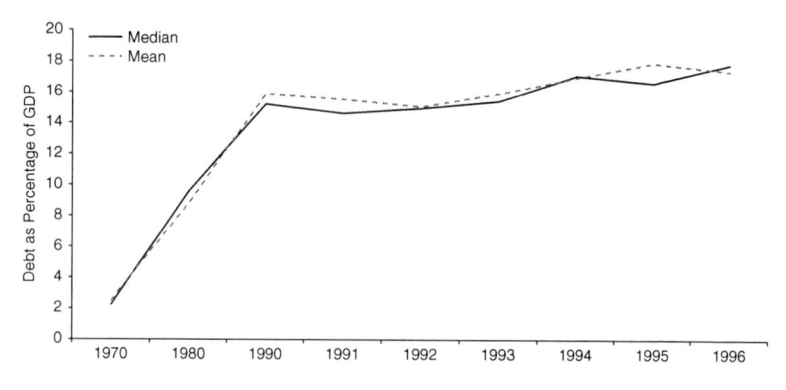

Figure 3.15 Debt Growth

Note: Countries—Brazil, Mexico, India, Turkey, Philippines, Poland, Malaysia, Algeria, Egypt, Nigeria, Pakistan, Peru, Colombia, Chile, Hungary, and Czech Republic.
Source: *Handbook of International Statistics* 2000.

The dramatic rise in the number of stock exchanges in "emerging markets" often had little to do with the equity requirements of local capital. Rather, many of these markets served as auction houses for a plethora of financial papers issued by both the sovereign governments and the largest corporations. In the early 1990s, investments in these new instruments became Wall Street's newest rage. National economies came to be increasingly dependent on international flows of capital (figure 3.16). Note that this dependence took two (correlated) forms: (1) a direct flow from external sources; and (2) retention of domestic capital from flowing to better returns elsewhere (figure 3.17).

Perhaps more important than the sheer amount of investment was the shift in its composition. Where previously, foreign investors had to remain committed to their bet in the form of factories or other infrastructure, the increasing popularity of portfolio investments made exit a matter of literally minutes, if not seconds (figure 3.18).

These two instruments—debt and investment—provided the positive and negative incentives for the kind of neoliberal convergence we noted above. Enough anecdotal examples exist of the power of such signaling as to confirm at least the potential role played by the mechanism described. We may begin with the counterexample of Alan García's disastrous first term as president of Peru. His refusal to play by the game led to a massive capital drain and the practical collapse of Peru's economy. In the same country, Fujimori's populist rhetoric soon turned decisively neoliberal

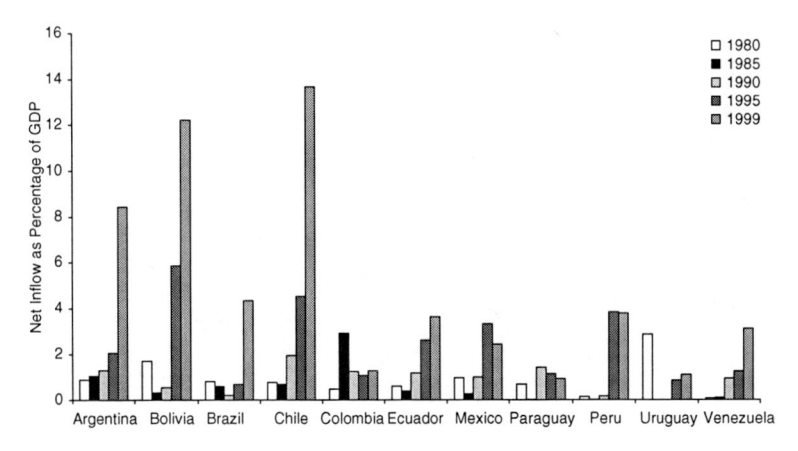

Figure 3.16 FDI in Latin America
Source: USAID 2000.

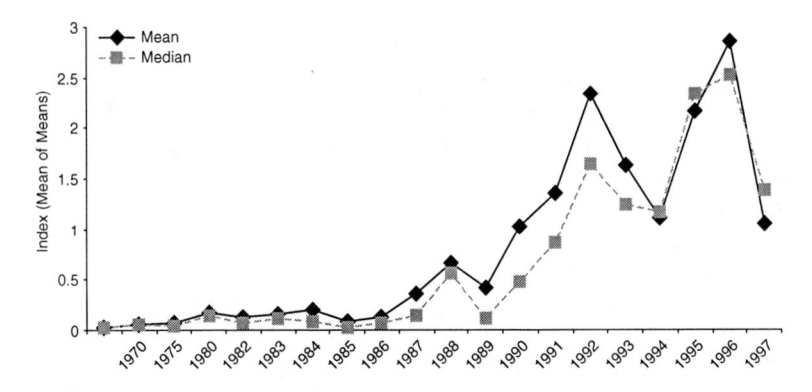

Figure 3.17 Total FDI
Note: Countries—Argentina, Brazil, Chile, China, Colombia, Czech Republic, Mexico, Poland, Russia, and Turkey.
Source: World Bank Tables 2000.

following an extended visit to the United States after his election. All accounts of this indicate that the new president had the facts of international life quite explicitly explained to him. For the Chinese, pursuit of some aspects of neoliberalism has allowed that state much freer rein in a variety of other areas. In perhaps the most interesting case, signaling of neoliberal intentions allowed a small elite in the former Soviet Union to essentially pillage their own country as well as $100 billion in international aid.

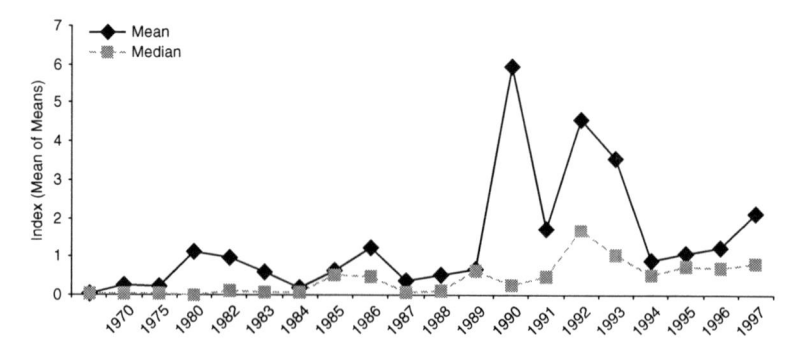

Figure 3.18 Types of Investment: Portfolio/Direct
Note: International Monetary Fund 2000.

Conclusions

Obviously, the role of many factors—cultural, political, and epistemological—is not to be dismissed. What I have done here is to give one side of the story that seeks to combine aspects of cultural and organizational explanations with the type of resources needed to give them force.[7] I think we need to perhaps view much of the past 20 years *not* as a radical departure from historic international relations and to ask ourselves whether the rules of power have really changed. This is of course debatable. What seems certain, however, is that neoliberalism has deeply changed the prior rules of the social and economic game. However, other chapters in this book offer evidence that while neoliberalism did bring about important changes at the local level, the rules of engagement in the new system are still changing and remain confusing. Uncertainty is the result.

I would like to point out that this outcome stands completely opposed to some of the key motivations that led to its adoption in the first place. Those who advocated neoliberalism knew that a competitive market would bring uncertainty, but this was a positive feature of the reforms. In a competitive market, uncertainty would be temporary; it was equated with increasing productivity, future well-being, and progress. Yet as argued elsewhere in this volume, uncertainty did not vanish easily and resulted in the progressive detachment of citizens from government, growing disenchantment with neoliberalism, and increasing probing into what, at some point, seemed inevitable about its adoption. No doubt today more than ever the inevitability of neoliberalism is questionable. In this chapter I have shown that some things may be inevitable but not for the reasons we might attribute to them.

Notes

1. See Kaufman and Haggard (1992, 1994).
2. But Latin America remains an interesting exception to some of the measures. See Hoffman and Centeno (2003).
3. The theoretical model closest to this enterprise is the work of Breiger (1981) on international interdependence.
4. For examples, see Louch, Hargittai, and Centeno (1999); and Hargittai and Centeno (2001).
5. Here I am borrowing from Ben Schneider's work on the adoption of these policies in Brazil.
6. The standards were often not very high. For example, how anyone could believe after 1975 that Mobutu Sese Seko would ever pay back any of Zaire's massive debt is somewhat puzzling.
7. Some correlations between trends in trade openness, debt, and foreign investment are greater than 0.75!

References

Breiger, Ronald L. 1981. *The Social Class Structure of Occupational Mobility.* Albany: State University of New York, Department of Sociology.

DiMaggio, Paul, and Walter W. Powell. 1982. *The Iron Cage Revisited: Conformity and Diversity in Organizational Fields.* New Haven, CT: Institution for Social and Policy Studies, Yale University.

Hall, Peter, ed. 1989. *The Political Power of Economic Ideas: Keynesianism Across Nations.* Princeton, NJ: Princeton University Press.

Hargittai, Eszter, and Miguel Ángel Centeno, eds. 2001. *Mapping Globalization.* Thousand Oaks, CA: Sage Publications.

Hoffman, Kelly, and Miguel Ángel Centeno. 2003. "The Lopsided Continent: Inequality in Latin America." *Annual Review of Sociology* 29: 363–391.

Kaufman, Robert, and Stephan Haggard. 1992. *The Politics of Economic Adjustment: International Constraints, Distributive Conflicts, and the State.* Princeton: Princeton University Press.

———. 1994. "The Challenges of Consolidation." *Journal of Democracy* 5 (4): 5.

Louch, Hugh, Eszter Hargittai, and Miguel Ángel Centeno. 1999. "Phone Calls and Fax Machines: The Limits to Globalization." *Washington Quarterly* 22 (2): 83–100.

4

CAN THE BACKLASH AGAINST GLOBALIZATION BE CONTAINED?

Benjamin J. Cohen

At the dawn of the twenty-first century, it has become a cliché to say that we live in an era of globalization—a time of rapidly accelerating economic interdependence among nations. Overall, the trend toward globalization seems beneficial. Growth of output has been promoted as economies everywhere open up to the opportunities of international trade and investment. Millions of people around the world have experienced substantial increases in living standards. The material benefits, in the aggregate, are obvious.

But this does not mean that the trend toward globalization is unchallenged. Around the world threats of backlash are intensifying, generated by the uncertainty associated with massive economic change. The unknown is naturally unsettling. Unhappiness focuses on what has come to be known as the Washington Consensus—a newly triumphant neoliberal economics emphasizing the virtues of privatization, deregulation, and liberalization wherever possible, which has been widely promoted by the U.S. government together with the Washington-based International Monetary Fund (IMF) and World Bank. What about the costs of neoliberalism, ask a growing number of critics. What about the potential losers from economic change, the growing inequality of incomes, the possible environmental decay or cultural degradation? To many, globalization seems not benevolent but malign—not a friend to be welcomed but an enemy to be resisted. Therein lies the central challenge for international economic policy today. Can the backlash be contained? Can today's open, multilateral system be defended against the forces of protectionism and economic nationalism?

The aim of this chapter is to consider what might be done to cope with globalization's challenge to economic policy. The costs of globalization cannot be denied. Plainly there are losers as well as winners as national economies become increasingly subject to the discipline of integrated markets. The anxieties provoked by the uncertainties of economic change are hardly misplaced. But neither can the material benefits of globalization be denied. Uncontained backlash would put world prosperity at risk, in effect throwing out the baby with the bathwater. The challenge for policymakers is to preserve the gains of a system that has worked so obviously to the advantage of millions, while at the same time responding constructively to the system's many legitimate critics. Needless to say, the task will not be an easy one.

Some would argue—somewhat optimistically—that no special initiatives are needed. The threat of backlash, it is alleged, is really more smoke than fire. Globalization is here to stay, whatever the uncertainties it generates; thus its benefits must be here to stay too. So why worry? Such optimism, however, is misplaced. The premise of this chapter is that the threat of backlash is real and could indeed be highly damaging to standards of living around the world unless countered by effective policy reform. New responses to globalization's uncertainties are needed in the spheres of both trade and finance.

Is Globalization Irreversible?

In economic discourse, the term globalization is used as a shorthand expression for the increasing integration of national economies around the world—a process of commercial and financial interpenetration driven by the forces of market competition and technological innovation as well as by governmental policies of deregulation and liberalization. In trade, globalization can be seen in the growing openness of markets for goods and services: greater and greater dependence on foreign commerce as a source of domestic prosperity. In finance, it is manifest in a rising level of capital mobility: ever-higher volumes of private lending and investment across national frontiers. Both open trade and capital mobility exercise significant discipline on the policy behavior of governments.

Admittedly, we are still far from anything that might be described as a fully globalized world economy. Numerous national markets, particularly in developing areas, remain well insulated from outside influence; and even in more developed regions, the industrial centers of North America, Europe, and Japan—the so-called Triad countries—as well as in the emerging markets of East Asia and

Latin America, significant divergences persist. Cross-border integration is limited not only by formal restrictions imposed by governments (tariffs and other trade or capital controls) but also by all kinds of informal barriers as well, including exchange-rate uncertainties, informational asymmetries, and linguistic and cultural differences. As economist Dani Rodrik, a leading expert on globalization, has written, "international markets for goods, services, and capital are not nearly as 'thick' as they would be under complete integration" (Rodrik 2000, 179). Still, the direction of change is unmistakable. Even if not yet completely integrated, markets clearly are growing ever "thicker" in terms of both the range of transactions encompassed and the number of people affected.

For some, the trend is also inexorable, akin to letting the genie out of the bottle. Once unleashed, it is suggested, the forces of competition are too powerful to be reversed. Governments cannot resist the tides of international trade and finance. Rather, the best they can do is adapt to the new world economy that is emerging, competing for the material benefits of globalization by accommodating themselves as much as possible to the preferences of market agents. In trade, this means opening the economy to foreign competition through both commercial exchange and direct investment. In finance, it means creating an environment of "sound" monetary and fiscal policies that will sustain the confidence of lenders and portfolio managers. That is what political scientist Philip Cerny intends by the notion of the "competition state." "The very concept of the national interest," he contends, "is expanding to embrace the transnational dimension in new ways: the so-called competition state is obliged by the imperatives of global competition to expand transnationalization" (Cerny 1994, 225). The competition state, from this perspective, is simply an acceptance of reality—an acknowledgment of globalization's disciplinary force. The genie cannot be put back in the bottle.

But is that in fact reality? History suggests otherwise, despite the evident power of market forces. The present era, after all, is not the first time that a seemingly inexorable process of transnational integration has taken hold. A century ago the world economy also seemed to be well on its way toward something approximating globalization. Indeed, by some measures national markets were even more closely tied together prior to World War I than they are now. Investment funds moved freely between countries, tariffs were comparatively low, and nontariff barriers and capital controls had still not even been invented. Yet when circumstances warranted, governments felt little inhibition in sacrificing the benefits of trade and finance for the sake of other policy objectives. During the interwar period and beyond, the seemingly irresistible momentum of economic integration was decisively reversed, before the start of what some are now calling the second age of globalization. If the genie could be put back into the bottle once, it does not seem implausible to assume that it might happen again, as economic historians have frequently noted (James 1999).

The reason lies in the logic of politics—specifically, in the logic of national sovereignty, which remains the core organizing principle of world politics. However challenged they may feel by the forces of global competition, states remain, in the most fundamental sense, masters of their own destiny—still capable, when motivated, of exercising their legal authority to limit the openness and vulnerability of their economies. Globalization's disciplinary force may be powerful, but it is not omnipotent. As political scientist Louis Pauly has written, "states can still defy markets" if they wish (Pauly 1995, 373). Governments are not condemned simply to accommodate the preferences of multinational corporations. The competition state is not the only choice. Other policy options exist, including overt limitations on trade or capital flows. Globalization will never be irreversible so long as sovereignty continues to reside at the national level.

The argument for the presumed irreversibility of globalization rests implicitly on an assumption that governments value the material benefits of economic integration above all else. Typical is Rodrik's sanguine remark that "short of global wars or natural disasters of major proportions, it is hard to envisage that a substantial part of the world's population will want to give up the goodies that an increasingly integrated (hence efficient) world market can deliver" (Rodrik 2000, 184). In fact it is not so hard to envisage at all, since the "goodies" are not the only things that matter to much of the world's population. Numerous other core goals and values also figure prominently in the calculations of rational policymakers. Economic nationalism, therefore, could easily come to take precedence over international integration. Time and again, governments have demonstrated their willingness to limit market openness, sacrificing the benefits of economic integration when deemed necessary for the sake of national security, cultural preservation, or environmental protection. Globalization's discipline has frequently been defied.

Most important, policymakers could feel driven to limit openness abroad by popular discontent at home. Worried about an uncertain future, workers and companies may lobby for protection against lost income or jobs. Public-interest groups may protest risks to the environment or a traditional way of life. A prime example is provided by France where, in early 1999, an obscure farmer named José Bové bulldozed a McDonald's restaurant to protest the perceived invasion of foreign (particularly U.S.) corporations—and became a national hero. The event unleashed a torrent of antiglobalization sentiment across the country to which politicians felt compelled to respond. Never particularly loath to criticize the United States, which French leaders have taken to calling the world's "hyperpower" (*hyperpuissance*), France now has happily accepted the mantle of leadership in the opposition to globalization. "France feels that nothing short of its identity is at stake," writes one observer. "The debate has been recast as 'Anglo-Saxon globalization' versus the preservation of France's national and cultural values" (Meunier 2000, 105). In turn, French opposition to "Anglo-Saxon globalization" has resonated across the world, in Latin America no less than elsewhere. Echoes are even evident in such advanced industrial economies as Canada and Japan, which are also known to be sensitive to the cultural consequences of what they see as the McDonaldization of the world.[1]

Another example came later in 1999 in the notorious Battle of Seattle, where a coalition of nongovernmental organizations successfully disrupted a meeting of the World Trade Organization (WTO) intended to launch a new round of trade liberalization. Inauguration of the round had to be postponed by two years until a subsequent WTO meeting in Doha, Qatar, in 2001. Grievances at Seattle ranged from targeted complaints about labor conditions and pollution to more inchoate concerns about social justice and alleged capitalist exploitation. Similar demonstrations also erupted in April 2000 in Washington at a joint meeting of the IMF and World Bank, where again many grievances were aired. Among the aims of the self-styled Mobilization for Global Justice was international debt relief. The enemy, in the words of the *New York Times*, was a system seen as "hooking lower-income nations on cheap debt and then insisting that they adopt free markets, unlimited investment, privatization and restrained government spending, or risk a cutoff in new aid."[2] Such is the stuff of the backlash against globalization. "Globalism is the new 'ism' that everyone loves to hate," said the former director general of the WTO.[3] Antiglobalization demonstrations have now become a regular feature at intergovernmental meetings.

Admittedly, fears for the future can be overdone. Ever since the end of the cold war, specialists have bewailed the risk of renewed protectionism around the world. With the waning of the Soviet threat, we have repeatedly been told, the major industrial powers could fall to squabbling among themselves, no longer willing to restrain their mercantilist impulses for the sake of the Western alliance. That dour theme was developed most eloquently by political scientist Robert Gilpin in his jeremiad *The Challenge of Global Capitalism* (Gilpin 2000), which worried that the clock could soon be turned back to the interwar period when economic rivalries similarly raged unchecked. Faith in the irreversibility of globalization, Gilpin wrote, "may turn out to be valid, but it is important to recall that world has passed this way before" (Gilpin 2000, 12).

In fact, however, much has changed in the last half century to lessen the risk of systemic disintegration or breakdown. Most important are the many international regime structures that have been constructed to help promote intergovernmental cooperation and collective economic management, in most instances formally institutionalized in multilateral organizations like the IMF, World Bank, and WTO or in regularized procedures such as those of the Group of Seven (G-7). In any event globalization continues to move forward, seemingly inexorably, despite its diverse critics. "So far," as one informed observer comments, "the manifestations of a backlash are more likely to be found in speeches than in legislative or executive actions" (Naím 2000, 12). U.S. commentator Bruce Stokes speaks of the protectionist myth. "Free trade is not in retreat," he insists. "Crying wolf about false chimeras of protectionism impugns credibility" (Stokes 1999–2000, 89).

Nonetheless, there are valid grounds for concern. That the clock has not yet been turned back is no guarantee that popular protests will not be more successful in the future, as more McDonald's restaurants get bulldozed and more Seattles hit the TV screens. Globalization may be powerful, but neither history nor the logic of politics gives comfort to the view that a liberal world economy is truly irreversible. Even Stokes acknowledges that "if these problems are not dealt with, protectionism could return with a vengeance in the first years of the new millennium, with devastating consequences" (Stokes 1999–2000, 101–102). The threat of backlash cannot be ignored. Effective responses are called for in the spheres of both trade and finance.

International Trade

The threat is surely evident in the trade sphere, where protectionist impulses are never very far from the surface. Over the past decades, the scale of import liberalization around the world has been impressive—but so too has been the scale of resistance to further opening of domestic markets. Not all the growing pressures for protectionism can be dismissed as mere self-interested parochialism or a misguided reaction to uncertainty. Broader issues are implicated, involving inter alia legitimate questions of income distribution, cultural diversity, the global environment, and national sovereignty. Finding effective responses to the diverse concerns of trade's many critics while at the same time preserving the benefits of closer international integration will not be easy.

Past Achievements, Present Problems

Trade liberalization has been high on the world diplomatic agenda in recent years, with many noteworthy results. At the global level, governments acted decisively to push completion in late 1993 of the Uruguay Round, after some eight years of often torturous negotiations. Easily the broadest and most comprehensive trade agreement in history, incorporating no fewer than 29 separate accords in a document running to over 22,000 pages, the Uruguay Round represented a new high in the globalization of the world economy. In the industrialized Triad economies, numerous import quotas were liberalized or eliminated, while tariffs on most manufactured goods were reduced to not much more than nuisance levels. On a broader scale, traditional rules previously embodied in the General Agreement on Tariffs and Trade (GATT) were extended to whole new economic sectors such as agriculture, services, intellectual property rights, and foreign investment. And perhaps most importantly of all, the old GATT was folded into the newly created WTO, an agency endowed with much wider powers to govern the multilateral trading system. Subsequent negotiations produced further openings in several key sectors, including information technology products in 1996 and financial services and telecommunications in 1997.

Liberalization was also promoted at the regional level, especially in the Western Hemisphere. In the late 1980s, in a historical rapprochement, Argentina and Brazil led the way in creating the Common Market of the South (MERCOSUR). Membership also included Paraguay and Uruguay along with, in later years, associate agreements with Bolivia and Chile. MERCOSUR was soon followed by the North American Free Trade Agreement (NAFTA) in 1993, creating a major new free-trade zone between the United States and neighbors Canada and Mexico. And in late 1994, at a Summit of the Americas in Miami, 34 Western Hemisphere governments agreed to negotiate a

Free Trade Area of the Americas (FTAA), aiming for a full and open market within ten years to stretch from Alaska to Tierra del Fuego. Regional liberalization was also promoted elsewhere. In November 1994, the United States and 17 other countries of the Asia-Pacific region, under the auspices of the recently established Asia-Pacific Economic Cooperation (APEC), declared their intention to achieve full mutual free trade within twenty five years. And for a brief moment there was even talk of a Transatlantic Free Trade Agreement (TAFTA), combining the United States and European Union, though the idea never gained much political momentum. Instead, at a 1995 summit meeting in Madrid, Washington and the European Union settled for a vaguer new Transatlantic Marketplace, rephrased in 1998 as a Transatlantic Economic Partnership, involving few commitments on either side.

Yet for all these achievements, many problems remain. Resistance to liberalization has grown too—all part of the broader backlash against globalization's discipline. The result is a long agenda of unfinished business for the world's trade negotiators.

At the global level, there were great hopes for a new Millennium Round to begin shortly after the start of the new century—only to be postponed by the Battle of Seattle, before being reborn as the Doha Round. Numerous issues had been left unresolved by the Uruguay Round. Some were included in a so-called built-in agenda for the new WTO. These were items formally mandated for further sectoral bargaining, involving most prominently agriculture and services. In agriculture, the main achievement of the Uruguay Round was agreement to convert existing nontariff barriers, like import quotas, into more transparent—and hence more negotiable—tariffs. Protection levels, however, remain high, limiting market access in most countries. In services, the main achievement was a new General Agreement on Trade in Services (GATS) providing a basic legal framework for future liberalization. The pioneering accords on information technology products, financial services, and telecommunications that followed in 1996–1997, impressive as they were, only began the task of converting principle into practice.

Other issues, which many call the New Trade Agenda, remain to be taken up. These include such highly charged matters as labor standards, environmental protection, and cultural policy—all sensitive regulatory questions reaching deep into domestic political and social affairs. Should trade agreements incorporate such issues as workers' rights, fair labor practices, and prohibition of child or prison labor? Should governments be permitted to use import barriers to promote environmental or cultural objectives? Global trade rules have traditionally limited the role of factors like these on the grounds that they could become an excuse for hidden protectionism—a subterfuge used arbitrarily by powerful constituencies to promote their own material objectives. But as the Battle for Seattle made clear, they are questions that cannot be ignored if the backlash against globalization is to be contained.

At the regional level, little visible progress has been made in turning the earlier visions of FTAA and APEC into reality. In part this is simply the result of traditional protectionism, as import-sensitive sectors have lined up to defend their particularist interests. In part as well, it is the result of new geopolitical rivalries that have sprung up since the end of the cold war. In the Western Hemisphere, Washington's regional aspirations have been resisted by Brazil, Latin America's leading economy, which has its own ambitions to expand MERCOSUR into a South America Free Trade Area (SAFTA) as a counterweight to NAFTA. In East Asia, the attractions of freer trade have been overshadowed by emerging great-power struggles involving the United States, China, and Japan. Progress seems stalled on all fronts.

Future Strategy

What can be done about these problems? Can further liberalization be promoted in the face of determined resistance from globalization's critics? Though difficult, the task is not impossible. What is needed is a strategy that explicitly addresses the uncertain costs of liberalization as well as the benefits—an approach that formally recognizes that trade-offs are required to reconcile trade promotion with other legitimate goals of policy. Market opening matters, but so too do such matters as income inequality, the environment, culture, and national sovereignty.

On the one hand, this means a refusal to retreat from the long agenda of business left unfinished at the outset of the twenty-first century. Governments should publicly commit themselves anew to persevering on past initiatives—global liberalization in areas of agriculture, services, and other New Trade Agenda items, along with regional efforts to complete APEC and FTAA. At the global level, once the Doha Round is completed, the traditional approach of huge multilateral rounds would best be abandoned, given the increased number and complexity of issues and the rapid growth of WTO membership. One source observes that "the low-hanging fruit in multilateral trade negotiations has already been picked. . . . The 'global-round' approach to trade talks ... [has] outlived its usefulness" (Cutter, Spero, and Tyson 2000, 91). More efficient would be the more narrowly targeted type of bargaining that produced the later accords on information technology products, financial services, and telecommunications. Regional talks should continue to emphasize the importance of enhanced market access.

On the other hand, policymakers must explicitly couple liberalization with the legitimate concerns of its opponents. No longer is it possible to separate trade negotiations from their consequences, as bargaining reaches ever deeper into traditionally domestic issues, generating ever-greater uncertainty. If the backlash against globalization's discipline is to be contained, critics must be persuaded that policymakers have not abandoned their social responsibilities. The trading system cannot become identified with limiting the broader authority of governments to promote the public weal. This does not mean giving mercantilists a free rein. But it does mean recognizing the legitimacy of other core social values. Three groups have been at the forefront of the assault on the trade regime: labor unions, social activists, and economic nationalists. Highest priority, therefore, should be given to the issues of most salience to each.

For labor unions, particularly in the older industrial economies, the main issues obviously are job security and income. Can unions be turned away from protectionism? The most direct approach would be one that formally ties liberalization to parallel aid measures for those in the Triad nations whose incomes and jobs are likely to be most threatened—blue-collar workers. In effect, this would mean making domestic adjustment assistance as an integral part of foreign-trade policy. Union hostility to open markets will not be eased without a major new emphasis on programs designed to compensate workers for their losses—enhanced unemployment insurance, moving allowances, retraining programs, and the like. Mobilizing political support for such interventionist measures in today's climate of triumphant neoliberalism will certainly not be easy. But turning labor away from protectionism without offering a safety net of some kind will be even more difficult.

For social activists the main issues are, above all, the New Trade Agenda questions of labor standards, environmental protection, and cultural policy. Concerns about pollution or cultural degradation can no longer be dismissed as irrelevant to international trade negotiations. The likes of José Bové have made such issues relevant. The challenge is to design rules that explicitly balance the oft-competing goals of economic efficiency and social welfare in the broadest sense—guidelines that carefully define when governments may legally sacrifice gains of trade in order to limit the ancillary costs of open markets. Opportunistic use of such rules as a rationale for hidden protectionism is always a risk, of course. But that would seem a small price to pay if the alternative is ever-more violent street protests.

Finally, for economic nationalists, the main issue is the threat that WTO supposedly poses to the historical principle of state sovereignty. Most at issue is the WTO's mechanism for dispute resolution, which was greatly strengthened by the Uruguay Round as compared with the earlier GATT system. Critics argue that adverse rulings by WTO panels of experts, which are convened whenever a country is formally accused of a trading violation, can compel a nation to change its laws against its will. In fact, that is an exaggeration. It is true that governments may no longer single-handedly forestall an adverse ruling, as in the past. But it is also true that the WTO lacks enforcement powers of any kind, other than a right to authorize retaliatory sanctions against offending states. Nonetheless, there is ample room for improvements that might ease concerns of this sort. Even its supporters admit that the WTO's dispute settlement process is opaque and slow. Procedures could provide for much greater public access and participation to enhance transparency and accountability. That too seems a small price to pay to preserve the benefits of a liberal trading system.

INTERNATIONAL FINANCE

Threat of backlash is equally evident in the sphere of finance, where market integration has proceeded even more rapidly than in the trade sphere. As the global mobility of capital has risen, so too has the frequency and amplitude of financial crises, generating mounting discontent and denunciation. Here as well broad issues are implicated—most importantly, the question of what globalization of finance means for the ability of sovereign states to manage their own economic affairs. Who knows when the next crisis will hit or what its consequences will be? And here too, finding effective responses to critics while preserving the benefits of closer integration will not be easy.

Phoenix Risen

Of all the many changes of the world economy in recent decades, few have been nearly so dramatic as the resurrection of global finance. A half century ago, after the ravages of the Great Depression and World War II, financial markets everywhere—with the notable exception of the United States—were generally weak, insular, and strictly controlled, reduced from their previously central role in international economic relations to offer little more than a negligible amount of trade financing. Starting in the late 1950s, however, private lending and investment once again began to gather momentum, generating a phenomenal growth of cross-border capital flows and an increasingly close integration of national financial markets. Like a phoenix risen from the ashes, global finance took flight and soared to new heights of power and influence in the affairs of nations.

Like trade liberalization, financial liberalization has ranked high on the world diplomatic agenda in recent years, again with many noteworthy results. In this sphere the United States helped lead the way in the mid-1970s by removing the various capital controls it had introduced in the 1960s, followed by other Triad countries in the 1980s. In the 1990s came the turn of the emerging economies of Latin America and East Asia, which were all urged to phase out existing controls as quickly as possible. Open financial markets, governments were told, were essential to attaining healthy, self-sustaining growth. Like trade based on comparative advantage, capital mobility could lead to a more productive employment of investment resources; it also offered increased opportunities for effective risk management and potentially higher returns for savers. Free capital mobility, therefore, no less than free trade, should be enshrined as a universal norm. The high point came in early 1997 when, at the urging of the United States, the IMF began to prepare a new amendment to the organization's charter to make promotion of financial liberalization a specific IMF objective and responsibility.[4]

But then came the Asian financial crisis of 1997–1998, with reverberations that were still being felt at century's end. Crises in global capital markets were nothing new, of course. During the 1980s there was Latin America's prolonged debt problem, triggered by Mexico's near default on its foreign bank loans in 1982. In 1992–1993 there was the collapse of the European Union's so-called Exchange Rate Mechanism—a pegged-rate precursor to today's Euro—under the pressure of massive currency speculation. And in late 1994 there was yet another near default in Mexico, which quickly spread to a number of other countries, most prominently Argentina, in what came to be known as the "tequila effect." Later dubbed by Michel Camdessus, then managing director of the IMF, "the first financial crisis of the twenty-first century," Mexico's new emergency was distinguished by the fact that unlike during the 1980s, the debts involved were not bank loans but securities—in particular, government bonds—which could be sold quickly by foreign investors. This greatly accelerated the pace of events and complicated the task of negotiating a satisfactory solution. Default was avoided only with the help of a line of credit of some $20 billion from the U.S. Treasury, which eventually succeeded in reversing the tide of capital flight.

None of these prior episodes, however, had prepared policymakers for the ferocity of the storm that hit East Asia, beginning with an attack on Thailand's currency, the baht, in mid-1997. Though a rescue package of some $25 billion was quickly assembled for Bangkok, the crisis soon proved contagious—"bahtulism," some called it—spreading first to regional neighbors such as Malaysia, Indonesia, and Korea; and then later as far afield as Brazil in 1999 and Argentina in 2000–2001. Governments across the developing world were forced to turn for assistance to the IMF, which prescribed tough policy conditions. Monetary and fiscal policies were tightened sharply in hopes of sustaining the confidence of foreign investors, even at the risk of prolonged recession and higher unemployment. Economic development stalled, and living standards tumbled.

Criticisms, not surprisingly, soon followed. Why, many asked, should sovereign states be forced to tailor their policies to the preferences of private interests? Why should freedom of capital movements be given absolute priority over other considerations of public welfare? In the words of economist Paul Krugman, it was all a cruel "confidence game":

> The need to win market confidence can actually prevent a country from following otherwise sensible policies and force it to follow policies that would normally seem perverse.... Policy ends up having very little to do with economics. It becomes an exercise in amateur psychology.... It sounds pretty crazy, and it is. (Krugman 1998)

Across the developing world, accordingly, resistance to financial liberalization has rapidly increased—also part of the broader backlash against globalization's uncertainties. The phoenix of global finance is now seen as more rapacious than benign. Many in East Asia took encouragement from the example of Malaysia which, in September 1998, reintroduced strict controls on capital outflows in order to provide room for more expansionary domestic policies. Temporary capital controls had long been dismissed as a relic of an earlier, more interventionist era. But now, as one source commented, they seemed to become "an idea whose time, in the minds of many Asian government officials, has come back" (Wade and Veneroso 1998, 23).

Authorities in Latin America too have begun to reconsider the virtues of capital mobility, as discomfort with the confidence game increases. Here too the core issue is clear: can the benefits of open markets be reconciled with the legitimate grievances of critics?

Taming the Phoenix?

Can the phoenix be tamed? Once again, what is needed is a strategy that explicitly addresses the uncertain costs of liberalization as well as the benefits. Since the Asian crisis, there has been much talk of reform of the "international financial architecture"—the rules and institutions governing monetary relations among states. The challenge of reform is to find some way to reconcile capital mobility with the demands of national sovereignty. In this sphere too, critics must be persuaded that policymakers are not being compelled to sacrifice social responsibilities on the altar of open markets. Improvements are called for in both crisis prevention and crisis management.

First, reforms are needed to reduce the probability of more Asian-style financial storms in the future. Consensus already exists on the need for strengthening domestic banking and capital markets, to avoid the kind of uncertainties and fragilities (e.g., currency mismatches and excessive short-term borrowing) that are known to have contributed to East Asia's difficulties. Indeed, many governments have already been persuaded to upgrade the supervision and regulation of their financial markets, emphasizing in particular better risk-management practices and disclosure requirements in order to enhance market discipline. But that is only a beginning, as I have suggested elsewhere (Cohen 2001). In addition, the case for temporary capital controls must be seriously reconsidered—particularly the case for flexible curbs on liquid inflows of the sort that Chile maintained, with considerable success, for many years to minimize the risk of massive outflows. Controls are indeed an idea whose time has—or should—come back. The IMF, for instance, has dramatically changed its tune since the Asian crisis, dropping active discussion of a new amendment on liberalization and talking instead of the possible efficacy of selective financial restraints.[5] Most desirable would be a new set of rules similar to those proposed for core New Trade Agenda issues—guidelines that, in parallel fashion, would carefully define when and how governments may legally sacrifice the benefits of capital mobility in order to limit the ancillary costs of open markets. Though this approach too runs the risk of abuse by opportunistic governments, it would again seem a small price to pay if the alternative is arbitrary market closure.

Reforms are also needed to cope more effectively with crises when they do occur, to reduce their severity and minimize the threat of contagion. At one level, this means creating more orderly market procedures for restructuring problem debts, perhaps along lines suggested by IMF deputy managing director Anne Krueger (2001)—an international workout mechanism modeled on the lines of a domestic bankruptcy court. At a second level, it means taking another look at the role of the IMF, which until now has acted mainly as guardian and enforcer of the Washington Consensus. Conservatives have criticized the IMF for creating a serious moral hazard: a risk that countries will deliberately take on higher levels of debt in the knowledge that the IMF is there to rescue them if they get into trouble. Their solution would be to limit the IMF's activities strictly to the provision of emergency liquidity—in effect, aiding just the most solvent borrowers—as a U.S. congressional commission recently recommended.[6] In fact, however, it is hard to see how such a narrow mandate could really reduce the spread of panic in financial markets, once a crisis begins. More to the point would be a streamlining of the IMF's lending programs, as advocated by former U.S. Treasury Secretary Lawrence Summers,[7] to enable it to move more quickly and effectively to stem market unruliness. Fund policy conditionality must also be reassessed, to put less single-minded emphasis on domestic austerity, particularly fiscal austerity, when governments are forced to play the confidence game with international investors.

Conclusion

The agenda for the world's governments is long. At the outset of the twenty-first century the backlash against globalization's discipline is intensifying, threatening prosperity. The irreversibility of globalization cannot be taken for granted. If the material benefits of open markets are to be preserved, the legitimate concerns of globalization's critics must be directly addressed. Anxieties born out of uncertainty are by no means irrational. In trade, this means doing more to compensate for the effects of open markets on income inequality, the environment, culture, and national sovereignty. In finance, it means doing more to limit the impact of capital mobility on the ability of states to manage their own economic affairs. Otherwise the clock could indeed be turned back, as many fear, to an earlier era of rampant protectionism and economic nationalism. In that event, we would all lose.

Notes

1. Canadian cultural concerns are well illustrated by its repeated efforts to limit the circulation of U.S. magazines like *People* or *Sports Illustrated*, which outsell Canada's own magazine industry. The governments's purpose, in the words of the prime minister, is to protect "part of our national identity" (as quoted in *The Economist*, February 6, 1999, 36). Japanese concerns are well illustrated by the country's determination to continue a long tradition of whale hunting despite U.S. opposition to the destruction of endangered species. Whale meat is considered a delicacy in Japanese cuisine. "Americans are a bunch of culinary imperialists," one Japanese restaurant owner has said. "Telling the Japanese not to hunt whales is like telling the British to stop having their afternoon tea" (as quoted in *The New York Times*, August 10, 2000, A8). How different is this from José Bové's denunciation of McDonalds as *la mal-bouffe* ("lousy food"). Echoed the respected newspaper *Le Monde*, "resistance to the hegemonic pretenses of hamburgers is, above all, a cultural imperative" (as quoted by Meunier 2000, 107).
2. Kahn 2000, 4.
3. Michael Moore, as quoted in *The New York Times*, January 29, 2000, B2.
4. Under the plan, two articles of the IMF charter were to be amended—Article 1, where "orderly liberalization of capital" would be added to the list of the Fund's formal purposes; and Article VIII, which would give the Fund the same jurisdiction over the capital account of its members as it already enjoys over the current account. The language would also *require* countries to commit themselves to capital liberalization as a goal. For more detail, see *IMF Survey*, May 12, 1997.
5. See, e.g., Ariyoshi et al. 2000.
6. This was the International Financial Institutions Advisory Commission (2000)—otherwise known as the Meltzer Commission after its chair, Allen Meltzer, a prominent academic economist. The Commission was comprised of some eleven private-sector specialists appointed by the Congress. Its report was issued in March 2000.
7. See, e.g., *The New York Times*, December 15, 1999, C4.

References

Ariyoshi, Akira, Karl Habermeier, Bernard Laurens, Inci Otker-Robe, Jorge Iván Canales-Kriljenko, and Andrei Kirilenko. 2000. *Country Experiences with the Use and Liberalization of Capital Controls*. Occasional Paper, Washington DC: International Monetary Fund.

Cerny, Philip G. 1994. "The Infrastructure of the Infrastructure? Toward 'Embedded Financial Orthodoxy' in the International Political Economy." In *Transcending the State-Global Divide: A Neostructuralist Agenda in International Relations*, edited by Ronan P. Palan and Barry Gills (Boulder, CO: Lynne Reinner), chapter 12.

Cohen, Benjamin J. 2001. "Taming the Phoenix: Monetary Governance after the Crisis." In *The Asian Financial Crisis and the Structure of Global Finance*, edited by Gregory W. Noble and John Ravenhill (Cambridge: Cambridge University Press), 192–212.

Cutter, W. Bowman, Joan Spero, and Laura D'Andrea Tyson. 2000. "New World, New Deal: A Democratic Approach to Globalization." *Foreign Affairs* 79 (2) (March/April): 80–98.

Gilpin, Robert. 2000. *The Challenge of Global Capitalism: The World Economy in the 21st Century* (Princeton, NJ: Princeton University Press).

IMF Survey, May 12, 1997.

International Financial Institutions Advisory Commission. 2000. *Report to the U.S. Congress* (Washington, DC).

James, Harold. 1999. "Is Liberalization Reversible?" *Finance and Development* 36, part 4 (December): 11–14.

Joseph Kahn. 2000. "Seattle Protesters are Back, With a New Target." *The New York Times*, April 9, 2000, 4.

Krugman, Paul. 1998. "The Confidence Game." *The New Republic* (October 5): 23–25.

Krueger, Anne. 2001. "International Financial Architecture for 2002: A New Approach to Sovereign Debt Restructuring." Address prepared for the National Economists' Club Annual Member Dinner, American Enterprise Institute, Washington, DC, November 26.

Meunier, Sophie. 2000. "The French Exception." *Foreign Affairs* 79 (4) (July/August): 104–116.

Naím, Moisés. 2000. "Editor's Note." *Foreign Policy* 118 (Spring): 11–12.

Pauly, Louis W. 1995. "Capital Mobility, State Autonomy and Political Legitimacy." *Journal of International Affairs* 48 (2) (Winter): 369–388.

Rodrik, Dani. 2000. "How Far Will International Economic Integration Go?" *Journal of Economic Perspectives* 14 (1) (Winter): 177–186.

Stokes, Bruce. 1999–2000. "The Protectionist Myth." *Foreign Policy* 117 (Winter): 88–102.

The Economist, February 6, 1999.

The New York Times, January 29, 2000.

The New York Times, August 10, 2000, A8.

Wade, Robert, and Frank Veneroso. 1998. "The Gathering Support for Capital Controls." *Challenge* 41 (6) (November/December): 14–26.

Part 2

Uncertain Relations between the State and Civil Society

The two chapters in this section examine some of the important ways in which globalization has altered relations between the state and civil society in contemporary Latin America. This is a vast subject, of course, and the authors focus on how the forces of globalization have affected the formation of public policy and the interplay between government officials, business elites, interest groups, and nongovernmental organizations. While the discussions are directed specifically toward two policy areas, mass media and environment, the authors suggest that the ideas are applicable to a far wider range of policy issues. Both chapters stress that globalization has led to important changes in state-society relations, and both suggest that the changes have often increased the level of uncertainty among stakeholders in the policy process—rather than leading to greater predictability as was promised by the proponents of neoliberal economic reforms.

In the first selection, Diane Johnson directs the reader's attention to recent changes in state policies regarding media ownership. This is a critical issue, since an independent and diverse mass media has long been considered one of the pillars of liberal democracy. Although in some ways the South American states have followed the global trends in media ownership, they seem to be retaining their own flavor. Meanwhile, the rules of the game have changed—but without being replaced by clear new rules in many cases. Likewise, Jonathan Rosenberg argues that economic globalization has had complex and uncertain effects on developing states, altering long-standing relations with the global North. New policy requirements attached to loans and grants to the global South demonstrate these changes and the resultant uncertainties.

5

Globalization and Public Policy in the Americas: Are We Heading Toward Convergence?

Diane E. Johnson

Introduction

In the late 1990s, Jeffrey Stark argued that "an indispensable area of research is the systematic study of how individual Latin American democracies respond and adapt to globalization" (1998, 88). In this chapter, I contend that one of the clearest expressions of the state's response to globalization is in its formation of public policy.[1]

It is hard to imagine a policy area that would not be affected by the sweeping global developments of the last quarter century, from trade to immigration to education to health to the environment. A popular assumption is that globalization will lead to a greater uniformity of policy across regions, and that these policies will increasingly resemble those of the advanced industrialized countries. Here, I ask whether we are witnessing a convergence of policy in Latin America in the critical area of communication. I approach the question by looking specifically at policy regarding media ownership, with a focus on the major South American countries and Mexico. This is a particularly important issue because the mass media play such an important role in liberal democracies. They have become the major conduit through which the state transmits information to, and receives information from, its citizens. Control of the media is thus critical, and I argue that globalization is helping to reshape the rules about ownership. In the past few years in the United States, for example, the Federal Communications

Commission (FCC) voted to further relax long-standing regulations regarding the number of media outlets that one corporation can own, and the size of the media audience that one corporation can reach. This has raised concerns that an increasingly concentrated group of media outlets will broach a smaller range of issues and that the diversity of voices will diminish.

The notion that globalization has influenced the rules regarding media ownership reinforces the importance of exogenous factors in the formation of public policy. I am not suggesting that international forces have replaced or even outpaced domestic factors, as I make clear later in the chapter. But surely we need to consider both. Moreover, for analytical clarity it is essential to define which particular aspects of globalization are involved. In the case of media ownership, I argue that we should focus on three: the rise of foreign investment and the multinational corporations that act as the agents of this investment, privatization, and deregulation. The evidence in this chapter shows the importance of these three global trends and that one of the most profound—albeit often unintended—effects of economic globalization has been the growing concentration of ownership in ever-fewer hands. This is particularly visible with Televisa in Mexico and Globo in Brazil, giant media monopolies with large transnational operations that enjoy, as Fox puts it, "practically monopolistic control of their enormous domestic markets" (1996, 160). The Venezuelan media are based on a similar model, with two large family-owned companies dominating the market. At this time, the media in countries such as Argentina, Peru, and Colombia remain more fragmented but are moving toward greater private control, monopolization, and political influence. As a whole, excluding Cuba, the region appears to be heading toward a greater concentration of ownership and the development of multimedia conglomerates, with relatively little effective media regulation (Fox 1996).

Although the trends in media ownership appear to be converging, however, it is clear that countries are forging individualized responses to the pressures of globalization. In sum, the rules of the game are shifting everywhere but not always in precisely the same direction, at the same speed, or with identical results. Globalization has both directly and indirectly affected the shape of media ownership, sometimes dismantling existing rules without replacing them with a coherent substitute. In this climate of uncertainty, the outcome for policy has to a significant degree depended on the response of the stakeholders in the process. Thus it is still far from certain whether this trend will lead to policy uniformity across the Americas.

Three Dimensions of Media Ownership

Media ownership has been a widely debated topic in recent years, particularly with the growing concentration of ownership in North America and western Europe (e.g., Alger 1998; Bagdikian 2000; Compaine and Gomery 2000; Humphreys 1996; MacLeod 1996; McChesney 1998, 1999; and McQuail and Siune 1998). A much smaller body of literature examines this in a Latin American context, approaching the question either directly (Cajías 1999; Fox 1996) or indirectly through an examination of global changes and the media (Fox 1997; Fox and Waisbord 2002; Mastrini and Bolaño 1999; and Sinclair 1996). We can distinguish among three overlapping but analytically distinct dimensions of media ownership: public versus private, domestic versus foreign, and concentrated versus diffuse. Important changes in each of these areas in recent decades have led some to predict a global convergence in policy.

With respect to the first dimension, for instance, the two basic models have been the commercial model of privately owned media best exemplified by the United States, and the public-service model traditionally exemplified by countries in western Europe.[2] Between 1983 and 1993, however, we saw a transformation in European communication policy. Some of the most important changes were in television, where governments paved the way for private ownership in both terrestrial (open-air) television and new cable and satellite television. Within a decade, public-service broadcasters had to begin sharing the stage with new advertising- or subscription-funded commercial services (Gunther and Mughan 2000; Humphreys 1996, chapter 6). This brought ownership in Europe closer to the commercially owned model found in the United States.

The second dimension is whether media ownership is predominantly domestic or foreign. One characteristic of the recent wave of globalization has been increasing foreign investment in media enterprises. Although foreign investment was a significant aspect of the last big wave of globalization between the late nineteenth century and World War I, its ramifications for media ownership were limited. Until the past decade or two, most countries legally prohibited foreign ownership of the media (especially broadcast media). In their quest for increased foreign investment, however, a number of countries in recent years have opened up the media to foreign investment or have loosened existing restrictions. India, for example, has decided to permit full ownership of the broadcast media by a foreign entity, although it maintains restrictions on ownership of the print media.

In another example, Russia's Mass Media Law of 1992 states that foreigners may not establish a mass media operation, but they are not restricted from outright ownership.

Many other countries, such as Australia, Singapore, South Africa, and most European countries, limit the percentage of foreign ownership that they allow. This is often a controversial issue. A heated debate in the United Kingdom in 2002 occurred when the Tony Blair administration proposed a draft communications bill that would have ended the ban on foreign ownership in the broadcasting media by countries outside the European Union; the administration then revised its proposal to allow investment only from those whose own countries allow European ownership of their media. This would prevent ownership by those in the United States, Canada and Brazil, for instance, since those countries still forbid foreign ownership of the broadcast media based on the belief that this is too sensitive an industry to make it open to foreign control.[3]

The third dimension measures ownership on a scale from concentrated to diffuse. Concentration can be either "horizontal" or "vertical." Horizontal concentration typically happens in one of two ways. The first is ownership of numerous individual outlets within the same medium; say, the creation of a large newspaper chain or television monopoly. The expansion of newspaper chains actually began in the late nineteenth century, when corporations began buying family-owned newspapers, in some cases building media empires (Fang 1997, 55), but this has grown tremendously since the mid-twentieth century in many areas of the world. The concentration of radio and television ownership under the state has long existed in most European countries and other democracies as well as in authoritarian countries, although the restrictions on content varied enormously. In most instances, this had to do with the scarcity of airwaves, although there was also an impulse regarding the social responsibility of the media to present various issues to the public in countries like England, Canada, and most of continental Europe. This contrasted with the commercial model found in the United States. The contemporary controversy, however, pertains to the growing concentration of media—both print and broadcast—under private, profit-oriented ownership.

A second type of horizontal concentration is cross-ownership, which includes the ownership of more than one type of medium—usually a newspaper and either a television or a radio station. Today, this would extend to cable and satellite television interests. At some point, when one or a few companies in either of these categories (or both) accrue enough media properties, people begin to talk about "concentration."

The development of vast multimedia corporations has received scholarly and popular attention in the last couple of decades, particularly in light of the growth of corporations such as AOL–Time Warner, Bertelsmann, the News Corporation, and Viacom. The central concern in a democratic society is that the concentration of ownership will limit the range of viewpoints found in the media and gives a particular group or groups disproportionate influence both in what the public reads and hears and in government policy decisions regarding the media. Along with the global trends toward privatization of the media and decreasing restrictions on foreign investment, the deregulatory impulse seems to be leading toward the relaxation of once common restrictions against multiple licenses or cross-ownership in many countries (see, e.g., MacLeod 1996).

As opposed to horizontal concentration, which refers to ownership across one medium or among mediums, vertical concentration occurs when the same firms gain ownership of both content and the means to distribute it. This would include, for instance, a company that owns a factory that produces printing presses or newsprint, as well as publishes a newspaper (or newspapers). It would also include a media corporation that owns a telephone company if the media are distributed through the Internet and users require telephony for Internet access.

The Theoretical Link between Media Ownership and Globalization

In thinking about the effects of globalization on communication policy, specifically as it relates to the mass media, we can draw on two disparate bodies of theory. The first addresses the role of the media in liberal democracies. Although this work traditionally has focused on the impact of domestic forces, it is possible to draw out some international implications. The second set of theories focuses on the economic and cultural impacts of globalization. For the most part, these globalization theories do not explicitly address public policy, but they do provide some clues about the state's capacity to formulate policy in light of global market and cultural forces.

The prevailing view in U.S. media studies about the role of the media in a liberal democracy is the liberal-pluralist perspective. According to the logic of the market on which the liberal view is based, the media will be privately owned and ownership will be diffuse. A rise in foreign investment in the media and multinational media corporations will lead to proportionately more foreign ownership. Pluralists expect the profit motivation and the ability to publish in a free market to increase competition among the media and increase the range of views that is presented, particularly during a period characterized by the emergence of new media technologies (Wheeler 1998, 6–7).[4] Thus, we might expect the state to respond to pressures to open up the market by relaxing existing restrictions on media ownership. The liberal-pluralist view was reinforced by modernization theory in the 1960s, which assumes the importance of a modern communications system in making the transition from tradition to modernity (e.g., Lerner 1963; Pool 1963). Although it does not refer specifically to "globalization," modernization theory suggests that the spread of ideas and information from North to South will lead to an increasingly uniform type of media-state relationship, based on the liberal-pluralist ideal favored in the North. This in turn suggests a global homogenization of media policy.

My research mainly confirms the pluralists' predictions regarding the increasingly private and international nature of media ownership. I also find some evidence that policy regarding ownership is converging across the Americas. Importantly, however, the pluralists cannot explain why ownership is becoming less rather than more diffuse. In a competitive environment, especially with the advent of "new media" such as cable and satellite television and the Internet, liberal reformers anticipated the entrance of new players in the market. This would be good for the economy and for democracy. Indeed the number of media outlets has risen, but this ownership has become more concentrated. Moreover, this has occurred in an atmosphere of global deregulation. As I will argue, uncertainty among policymakers trying to adapt to the pressures of globalization is one explanation for the failure of the market to behave as expected.

The major alternative to liberal-pluralist theory, especially in Latin America, is the media imperialism or media dependency approach (see, e.g., Beltrán and Fox 1980; Schiller 1969, 1976, 1998). This perspective posits that media systems represent unequal core-periphery relations by promoting foreign ideas and interests beneficial to multinational corporations (MNCs) and their allies, the reactionary domestic classes (vis-à-vis technology, expertise, programming, etc.). In short, it predicts a privately owned and commercially driven media characterized by a small number of owners dependent on foreign values and interests, rather than an independent national media functioning freely in a competitive arena (Curran and Park 2000, 5). It also expects new media to be developed and monopolized by the dominant economic interests, which can capture the market and bear the costs of new technology far more easily than new entrants. Thus media imperialism theory can easily explain the growing concentration of media ownership. Its major weakness is that it cannot explain the continuing importance of domestic politics in media-state relations or why the state remains a "central actor in the evolution of media systems" (Waisbord 2000, 53).

The second relevant strand of theory is globalization theory. Although there are many variants, we can place them in two main groups. The first group consists of theories of economic globalization borrowed from international relations, which focus on the state's autonomy vis-à-vis the market, including liberal theory, dependency theory, and realist theory. The liberal school contends that the market shapes both domestic and international policies and that states will increasingly lose the autonomy to act independently of global market concerns. Thus, economic globalization will constrain the state's ability to regulate the media. The dependency school contends that the United States and western European economies constitute the core of global capitalism, and the economies of Asia, Africa, and Latin America constitute the periphery of the system; while there is some state autonomy in the core, there is virtually none in the periphery.[5] Finally, the realist school contends that the distribution of power among states largely determines international relations, so powerful states such as the United States will retain considerable autonomy from other states despite the increasing globalization of the economy, while weaker states will have less autonomy from other states.

Although these theories of economic globalization have important distinctions, each suggests that many (or most) contemporary democracies will have little ability to resist market forces in forming policy.[6] This is potentially crucial to communication policy as it inhibits the state's ability to control the type of media that exist within its own borders. This also suggests a significant level of predictability or certainty, to the extent that states will need to conform under the pressures of globalization. Pressures to open to greater foreign investment, for example, would theoretically inhibit the state's choices when it comes to regulating media ownership. Hence, theories of economic globalization generally lead us to expect the erosion of state sovereignty. The admittedly limited evidence, however, suggests otherwise. Empirical studies do indicate a global trend toward media liberalization and market control (see, e.g., Curran and Park 2000). However, globalization theory understates the continuing importance of the state in shaping media systems, regardless of political or economic regime type (Curran and Park 2000). And as we have seen elsewhere in this volume, while the rules of the game have changed, the new rules are often amorphous and not at all clear.

The second group consists of theories of cultural globalization. Again, these vary significantly, but they share two central ideas. First, globalization is becoming increasingly decentralized (see, e.g., Giddens 1999). It is not, in other words, controlled by any group of nations or any group of MNCs. This is a departure from the traditional view of globalization as the "modernization" (or "exploitation," depending on one's view) of developing societies by the developed world. Second, globalization is extending the basis of communication and cultural exchange in positive ways (see, e.g., McLuhan 1964; Ang 1990; Robins et al. 1997). This includes the opportunity to form cultural communities and to gain access to information that national governments have long sought to suppress. A frequent example is the Zapatista revolt in southern Mexico that began in early 1994. In this case, rebels used the Internet to disseminate their story to the international community, circumventing the mainstream Mexican media that had long served as the mouthpiece of the state. In short, the United States and other economically powerful countries in the North are *less* likely to impose policy on the South, and we would not expect to see a convergence in communication policy. This is contradicted by evidence in this chapter and elsewhere, however (see, e.g., Curran and Park 2000).

In sum, both economic and cultural globalization theories fail to explain the persistent role of the nation-state in media matters. According to economic theories, the state is losing its ability to shape its own destiny in light of the growth of multinational corporations and international institutions. According to cultural theories, the nation is becoming an imagined community that does not reflect the reality of the contemporary world. Neither of these claims is borne out by evidence. States have retained significant influence in media systems in at least three ways. First, they license broadcast media, and national channels remain dominant. Second, they make laws and regulations regarding media operation. Third, they influence the media through informal means such as the provision of loans or the withholding of information. Thus states are finding effective ways to resist some of the theoretical effects of globalization on public policy.

At the same time, as we shall see, some evidence supports the idea of a convergence in policy regarding media ownership. I believe that the most fruitful approach to addressing this seeming paradox between a trend toward convergence and the continued importance of the state is a historical institutionalist or path-dependency approach. This says that specific patterns of timing and sequence matter, and that these patterns are extremely resistant to reversal (see, e.g., Pierson 2000; Thelen 1999). Thus while international factors play a crucial role in shaping media ownership, institutional inertia can filter the effects of globalization. This suggests that changes in media ownership will be gradual or uneven rather than immediate or consistent. It also suggests that the players who most benefit from existing arrangements will either resist the effects of globalization or try to adapt in order to preserve their advantage, while those who benefit least may be more receptive to change in the hopes of improving their position. All of this has contributed to a significant level of uncertainty on the part of both policymakers and those who are affected by the policies.

Finally, there is the issue of reciprocal causation. In theory, the media-state system's response to the forces of globalization could (1) accelerate and foster more globalization; (2) resist or retard globalization; or (3) have no bearing on globalization. In the first case, we would see both positive and negative feedback, making the response into an independent variable of its own in a second-stage chain of causation. Figure 5.1 represents this simple argument graphically.

The Global Trend Toward Deregulation

A key development during the current wave of globalization has been the trend toward deregulation, which merits special attention here because it has had such an important impact on policy regarding media ownership. Countries that are highly regulated cannot experience high levels of globalization, because globalization assumes the freedom to accommodate a rapid increase in the flow across borders of goods, capital, technology, people, and ideas and information. Indeed, a major reason that historians and others refer to the interwar period as one in which globalization declined is because it was characterized by the erection of trade and tariff barriers. Conversely, a lack of regulation—or deregulation following a period of regulation—does not guarantee globalization. Hence deregulation (or a lack of regulation) is a necessary but not sufficient condition for globalization. Moreover, it is theoretically likely that the process of deregulation as a correlate of globalization will lead to changes in the media-state system, which will then lead to greater deregulation (see figure 5.1). In United States, Canada, and most of western Europe, the evidence suggests that this does indeed occur. In the area of communication policy, the trend is perhaps most clearly shown in the area of media ownership.

We would thus expect to see a decrease in the state's formal legal and regulatory control over the media during periods of globalization. As Gunther and Mughan (2000, 14) put it, "media deregulation [in established democracies] has been part of a broader neoliberal

```
┌─────────────────────────────────┐
│  Globalization processes in the │
│      international system       │
└─────────────────────────────────┘
                │
                ▼
┌─────────────────────────────────┐
│    Globalization processes      │
│       within the state          │
└─────────────────────────────────┘
                │
                ▼
┌─────────────────────────────────┐
│        Response of the          │
│     media-state system to       │
│     globalization processes     │
└─────────────────────────────────┘
```

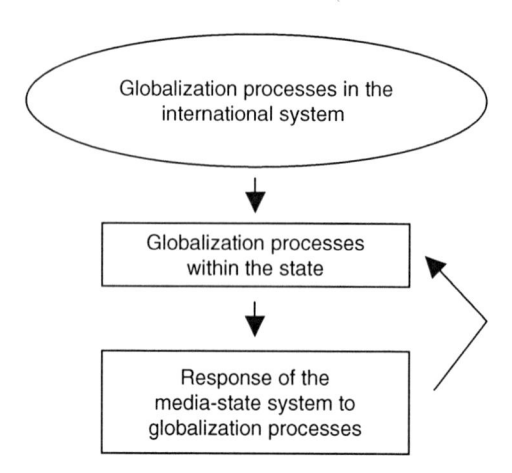

Figure 5.1 The Media-State System and Globalization

reaction against intervention in social and economic life." In fact, however, in one sense the state role shifts from being a producer to a regulator as a result of privatization (Galiani and Petrecolla 2000, 92). Somewhat paradoxically, then, the state is unlikely to cease regulating but likely to adopt a new role vis-à-vis industry and thus perhaps to practice a different type of regulation. This is important for a number of reasons. The restructuring of the economy during deregulation, particularly as a result of privatization, raises questions about the state's role in the various economic sectors (Galiani and Petrecolla 2000; Zuleta Puceiro 1999), including the media. Moreover, Waisbord (1998) argues that if deregulation occurs, so will further conglomerization and concentration of ownership.

Corresponding with the wave of globalization that began in the 1970s and 1980s, we can indeed detect a global trend toward deregulation of the media, as the state's role in broadcasting shrunk for different reasons and with different consequences. Gunther and Mughan (2000, 13–15) classify this deregulation into two basic types. The first is the liberalization of political control, mainly in formerly authoritarian systems such as Chile and the Soviet Union. The second is the opening of airwaves to private commercial broadcasters with few or no public-service obligations. We have seen the latter development in countries such as Germany, Britain, and the Netherlands, which early adopted a public-service model of broadcasting. The Latin American region has shared this trend toward deregulation of the media, particularly with regards to the privatization of television stations.

In reference to Latin America, Fox and Waisbord explain,

> During the 1990s, media policies shrunk the participation of state and public interests and helped consolidate market principles. Such policies were part of a wider change in the region's political zeitgeist. . . . As in other industrial sectors, privatization, liberalization, and deregulation were responsible for dismantling the old media order and strengthening market forces. (2002, 9)

Hence, despite the onset of globalization and the general trend toward deregulation, the state has continued to regulate the media in terms of operation and content. In fact, the most recent period of globalization has actually led to an increase in some areas of media regulation. Moreover, there have been some important qualitative changes in the laws and regulations during the past two decades. Some of these are best explained by the change in political regime from authoritarianism to democracy in many countries. Others are best explained by globalization, specifically the forces of economic liberalization. Perhaps more than any other type of medium, this has affected the television industry.

Historical Development of Media Ownership in Latin America

Although we can detect some broad historical similarities among government policies regarding media ownership, there are also important differences. The variation is due in part to the vacillation between laissez-faire and authoritarian control that has long characterized Latin American politics. In the next section of the chapter, I ask whether these policies are now converging. In the final section, I offer a case study of Argentina, where media ownership has changed significantly as a result of globalization. Ultimately, I argue that we are likely to see similar trends in ownership policy across the Americas but that similarities will vary in degree and in the manner and timing that they occur. At least in the short term, this has resulted in a certain level of unpredictability for the stakeholders in the media, in civil society, and in government bureaucracy.

The first question is whether the media developed under private or public ownership. The print media in Latin America have traditionally been under private ownership, similar to those in western Europe and the United States. Broadcasting media were somewhat different. Like the United States and unlike western Europe, Latin America never developed a strong commitment to public-service broadcasting. Although we typically classify the media in Latin America as "mixed" public–private systems, they have been mainly private and commercial along U.S. lines.

Radio emerged in the 1920s under private ownership in most Latin American countries, including Argentina, Brazil, Mexico, Paraguay, Uruguay, and Venezuela. In most instances, the state followed this with the creation of a national public radio station, but these public stations did not provide much competition for the privately owned channels in terms of audience or advertising revenues. In Peru, the first radio station in 1924 was state-owned (and commercial), but due to the expense, the government subsequently opted for a model of private ownership. The two exceptional cases are Chile and Colombia. The former did not develop any important national radio industry prior to 1950 (Fox 1997, 118). When radio did emerge in Chile, it followed the mainly private and commercial model found elsewhere. Colombia was more interesting. It developed a unique hybrid system in which the state owned the broadcasting frequencies and infrastructure and bid out the time to private programming companies that then sold advertising time (Calero Aparicio 2002). The state guaranteed the programming companies relatively harmonious competition for advertisers as well as a significant audience and supported national programming production.

We see a little more variation in the emergence of television ownership. The first TV station in Argentina in 1951 was financed by the state under President Juan Perón (1946–1955). The state retained a monopoly on TV ownership until Perón's ouster in the mid-1950s. The succeeding government maintained the original station as a public channel but began selling commercial licenses to private interests in 1958. In Brazil, Mexico, Paraguay, and Uruguay, television was born commercial and developed mainly under private ownership. Governments in these countries granted licenses to newspaper owners and owners of commercial radio, starting with Mexico in the late 1940s, and followed by Brazil and Uruguay in the 1950s, and Paraguay in the mid-1960s. As in Argentina, the first television station in Peru was state-owned, but as it had done with radio, the Peruvian government shortly turned instead to a private, commercial model.

Again, Chile and Colombia were exceptional. When television emerged in Chile in the late 1950s—nearly a decade after Argentina—the government decided to limit station ownership to the state and the universities. The first three stations were established at three major universities in 1959; a decade later, the government set up a national channel called TVN to compete with them. Colombia adopted the same hybrid model that it had used for radio.

The second dimension of interest is the degree of foreign ownership of Latin American media. The vast majority of print media in the region have always been in domestic hands; foreign influence was limited mainly to the broadcast media. While this influence was important, it was not as critical as domestic factors (Fox 1996, 1997). In most cases, governments erected some kind of barrier to foreign ownership of the media—especially television. When foreign ownership did occur, it was usually controversial. Argentina, for example, early established that only Argentine citizens could own broadcast media. In the 1950s, U.S. television networks invested in Argentine television indirectly through their respective production companies, but this was not outright ownership; moreover, the U.S. companies withdrew in the 1960s.

Mexico, Brazil, and Venezuela also sought to limit foreign ownership of the media. The 1940 Law of Communication in Mexico barred foreigners from owning broadcast licenses. Likewise, the Brazilian legislature passed a Telecommunication Law in 1962 that prohibited private media from signing contracts with foreign capital; however, the military regime of 1964–1985 looked the other way when the U.S.-based Time Life Company invested in the young TV Globo. A new Telecommunication Code in 1967 fixed the problem by allowing foreign investment in communication industries. A somewhat similar situation occurred in Venezuela, where a 1941 law limited foreign ownership in commercial broadcasting stations to a maximum of 20 percent. This was violated in the late 1950s and early 1960s, when the U.S. network ABC acquired 43 percent of the newly formed Venevisión. But in the early 1970s, President Carlos Andrés Pérez took the opposite course of his Brazilian counterparts by prohibiting new foreign investment in the media and requiring any foreign firm to divest itself of 80 percent of its stock within three years (Fox 1997, 69, 72).

Although Chileans established no legal prohibition against foreign ownership in the absence (until 1970) of a comprehensive media law, the fact that the universities and state controlled all TV channels reduced the importance of foreign investment while simultaneously checking the development of a strong domestic media industry (Fox 1997, 117). In Colombia, the hybrid ownership system also dissuaded foreign investors; a rare exception was ABC's investment in the country's second TV channel after 1965 (Fox 1997, 93). Finally, in Peru, foreign investors acquired a stake in two of the first four private TV stations licensed in the late 1950s. The military regime of 1968–1980 sought to free the media from what it perceived to be extensive foreign influence, passing a new General Law of Telecommunications that prohibited foreign investment in a TV station.

The final dimension is the degree to which media ownership in Latin America was historically concentrated. In general, the ownership of the print media in Latin America was diffuse, while the ownership of broadcast media was frequently monopolistic. Fox (1996, 1997) attributes the latter in part to the weakness of political parties and of elected democratic governments through much of the region during the last quarter of the twentieth century. She argues that authoritarian governments in the 1960s and 1970s gave commercial autonomy to the media in exchange for "political docility," and in the absence of state oversight and regulation, the private media industries grew strong. Two of the best examples of media monopolies in the region, and indeed the world, are Globo in Brazil and Televisa in Mexico.

Brazil is a case in which cross-ownership of, and concentration in, the broadcast media developed particularly early and especially intensely. By the late 1930s, the media group Diarios e Emmissoras—owned by Assis Chateaubraind—already owned 5 radio stations, 12 newspapers, and a magazine. Within a decade, the group's ownership increased to include 36 radio stations, 31 newspapers, and several magazines, in addition to 18 TV channels, a news agency, and a public relations firm (Fox 1997, 55, 57). By the early 1940s, two other multimedia groups joined Diarios e Emmissoras, including Radio Globo. Although concentration occurred a little later in Mexico, it was also extensive. The most significant multimedia company to emerge was Televisa in 1972, which created a virtual monopoly of private broadcasting in Mexico.[7]

Cross-ownership was in some ways less pronounced elsewhere. In most countries, only a small number of TV licenses were issued, typically going to existing media companies. In this sense, the broadcast media were both concentrated and monopolistic. But the multimedia empires that developed in Brazil and Mexico were unrivaled, especially prior to the 1980s. Moreover, virtually every country was characterized by a greater or lesser degree of horizontal concentration, rather than the vertical concentration that has occurred in recent decades. In Chile, the universities, rather than media conglomerates, owned the TV stations. Nor was the fragmented hybrid system in Colombia conducive to the creation of big media companies; in fact, Colombia was somewhat unique in its avoidance of media monopolization (Calero Aparicio 2002, 91). Thus among the broadcast media, concentration of ownership in Latin America is hardly new. But as we shall see, the nature of the phenomenon has altered somewhat, and the process has accelerated as a result of globalization in the past two decades.

Recent Changes in Media Ownership

Policies regarding media ownership have evolved significantly during the past couple of decades, a period characterized by the renewed forces of economic globalization. Amaral (2002, 39) writes that "beginning in the 1980s, the combined effects of deregulation and privatization together with the proliferation of new technologies accelerated the globalization of communications." We can detect some clear trends in Latin America in the area of media ownership policy, along the three dimensions now familiar to the reader. The forces of globalization, namely those linked with economic liberalization such as privatization and deregulation, have played a critical role in that change. However, there is still considerable variation among nations in one or more areas of ownership policy, as well as in the enforcement of the policy. Moreover, the changes have often created a sense of confusion among the concerned parties.

One clear change in recent decades has been the trend toward more private ownership of the media. An important consequence of globalization in Latin America during the late 1980s and 1990s was the privatization of most state-owned industries, required by international lending agencies such as the International Monetary Fund and World Bank. This included the state-owned media. In countries such as Argentina, Brazil, Peru, and Uruguay, where military dictatorships from the 1960s through the 1980s assumed direct or indirect control over the media, ownership returned to private hands. All of the large media groups in these countries today are again privately owned, and although each state maintains some public radio and TV channels, the preponderance of broadcasting is private and commercial.

In Mexico, the government has privatized most of the broadcasting industry. In 1991, after two decades of state ownership, the government sold the Imevision educational network comprised of 40 stations. One of the few remaining state-owned broadcasting enterprises is TV Channel 11 located in Mexico City. In the late 1980s and 1990s, the Chilean government privatized most of the state media and opened up television to private enterprise.[8] In Colombia, the old hybrid model has given way to private ownership, following a 1995 law that made the private sector responsible for a channel's entire operations, rather than a "tenant of rented time slots" (Calero Aparicio 2002, 96). Privatization occurred in the Venezuelan broadcasting industry mainly under Carlos Andrés Pérez's second administration from 1989 to 1993.[9] In Paraguay, which has no public TV stations, the state retains the National Radio Network and two radio stations, but they have a small reach and audience. Moreover, some Latin American governments such as Venezuela in the late 1980s, and Paraguay and Peru in the early 1990s, have dramatically increased the number of broadcasting licenses for private owners in recent years, in part as a result of the introduction of FM radio frequencies, UHF television frequencies, and cable and satellite TV (Peirano 2002; Orué Pozzo 2002; Mayobre 2002).

A second important development is the internationalization of media ownership in Latin America. Extreme cases such as Argentina and Colombia have virtually no restrictions against foreign ownership of the media. Most countries allow foreign investment but place some restrictions on it. This is the case in Chile, which limits foreign ownership of TV stations to 49 percent. By the mid-1990s, three of the important Chilean television stations had significant foreign ownership: Mexico's Televisa owned 49 percent of Megavisión (Channel 9), Venezuela's Venevisión owned 49 percent of Chilevision (Channel 22), and the Canadian company CanWest had stock in La Red (Channel 4) (Fox 1996). Tironi and Sunkel (2000) assert that internationalization has been a particularly important tendency in the media's evolution in Chile. The policy toward cable ownership is open to foreign investment, and companies based in the United States, Argentina, Canada, and Mexico have invested heavily in the Chilean cable industry.[10]

As in Chile, Brazilian law prohibits outright ownership of the broadcast media by foreign companies (World Association of Newspapers 2002), but foreign investment has had the effect of strengthening existing national media monopolies (Amaral 2002, 44). A new Cable TV Law in Brazil also allows foreign investment up to 49 percent (Amaral 2002, 43). Similarly in Mexico, foreign investment in the media is now permitted, although as in Brazil, this has little chance of posing a serious challenge to existing media monopolies (Fox 1997, 50). Extensive foreign investment has also affected the Peruvian media, which have more lax restrictions than some other countries. In 1992 for instance, the Mexican giant Televisa acquired 76 percent of Peru's second-ranked TV network, Compañía Peruana de Radiodifusión (Sinclair 2002). On the other hand, foreign investment has been less influential in media ownership in Uruguay (Faraone 2002) and Venezuela (Mayobre 2002).

The third trend observable in Latin America in recent decades has been the growing concentration of media ownership. As I pointed out in the previous section, concentration is not new among the broadcasting industries and thus is not entirely attributable to globalization. However, globalization has altered or exacerbated some aspects of concentration. The first is the growing trend toward cross-ownership in light of relaxed regulation. The second is the accumulation of "new media," namely cable and satellite television, by the most important traditional media companies.

We see the most extreme examples of both horizontal and vertical cross-ownership in Mexico and Brazil. In Mexico, Televisa remains dominant—although in the past decade it has faced a growing challenge from a second multimedia company, TV Azteca, which bought Channel 13 from the state in the early 1990s. TV Azteca is a 50-member consortium headed by Ricardo Salinas Pleigo, who also owns a large chain of electrical parts stories and other retail chains in Mexico and Central America (Sinclair 2002, 129). A similar development has transpired in Brazil, where the megamedia Globo today faces a challenge from the multimedia company Abril. While Globo continues to dominate domestic broadcast television, it has strong competition from Abril in subscription (pay-TV) services (Fox 1997, 61). Grupo Abril grew from a strong base in the print media: Editora Abril founded in 1950 is the largest publishing operation in Latin America (Sinclair 2002, 133).

In Venezuela, the two commercial television networks Radio Caracas Televisión and Venevisión dominate audiences and advertising (Fox 1996). Similar to the situation in Brazil and Mexico, concentration is both horizontal and vertical in Venezuela. Radio Caracas Televisión and Venevisión have significant holdings in TV stations, radio stations, and newspapers, as well as media distribution companies. In addition, Venevisión has invested widely in nonmedia holdings including department stores, supermarket chains, and soft drink manufacturing.

Laws against cross-ownership in Argentina have been eliminated or relaxed since the late 1980s. By far the most important multimedia company is Grupo Clarín, whose flagship is *Clarín*, with the highest circulation among Spanish-language newspapers. Unlike in Brazil, Mexico, and Venezuela, however, concentration in Argentine media ownership at this time is mainly horizontal, rather than vertical. Likewise in Colombia, media ownership has become increasingly concentrated in the hands of a few multimedia owned by large economic conglomerates (Fox 1996). The most important is the group that owns the daily newspaper *El Tiempo*, along with other newspapers and publishing houses, and a cable company. Chile is unusual because for the most part we do not see the patterns of cross-ownership prevalent elsewhere in the region; however, cross-ownership does exist in cable TV (mainly with phone-cable multimedia groups) (Fox 1997, 128).

Another area in which the concentration of ownership is apparent is in the growth of new media. Cable television has grown tremendously in Latin America since the 1980s, particularly in Argentina, Mexico, Venezuela, Brazil, and Chile (Fox 1996). In almost every case, control of cable is concentrated in the hands of a few players, generally the same companies that dominate the traditional media. This has occurred for one of two reasons: either the government has failed to produce a comprehensive law dealing with the new media, or the government has produced a law that permits concentration. Argentina is an example of the former. Cable ownership is concentrated in the hands of two groups: (1) Grupo Clarín and (2) Hicks, Muse, Tate & Furst; moreover, Clarín is the largest and most important multimedia company in the country.

Brazil is an example of a country that passed a Cable TV Law in the mid-1990s with few restrictions on horizontal or vertical concentration. By the time the law was passed, the two most important multimedia— Globo and Abril—had already established virtual control of the industry. In Mexico, again we see cable TV dominated by the country's two most important multimedia groups, Televisa (Cablevisión) and TV Azteca (Multivisión) (Sinclair 2002). In Chile, one of the most important cable interests is Intercom, which is controlled by the same company that owns the largest daily newspaper, *El Mercurio*. In Uruguay, the dominant media companies that own the three commercial stations in Montevideo (including one that also owns the country's most influential newspaper) dominate the cable TV industry (Faraone 2002, 174). Likewise in Venezuela, cable TV is largely controlled by just two networks, Omnivisión and Cablevisión.

A Case Study: Argentina

Argentina is a particularly good example of a country in which policy regarding media ownership has altered in light of globalization. The three crucial changes in media ownership in the past decade and a half have been the (re)privatization of the broadcast media, a series of bilateral investment treaties that for the first time officially permitted foreign ownership of the media, and a new law that allowed cross-ownership of the media (i.e., of different types of media). These have paved the way for a growing concentration of media ownership in Argentina, which we have seen elsewhere. Yet the Argentine case also nicely demonstrates the kind of institutional inertia and the continued importance of the state in shaping communication policy to which I previously referred. Thus the results of globalization have not always been predictable.

Since the late 1980s, media ownership in Argentina has gone from mostly public to mostly private,[11] from almost entirely domestic to significantly foreign, and from relatively diffuse to relatively concentrated. Globalization has played a critical role in these changes. The most important aspects of globalization in this case are deregulation and privatization, and the explosive rise in foreign investment and media-related MNCs. Other explanations, such as regime change or economic crisis, are not particularly illuminating. While Argentina did indeed make a transition from authoritarian to democratic government in 1983, changes in media ownership did not occur until a half dozen years later. Moreover, until the most recent wave of globalization, democratic governments in western Europe and elsewhere were not characterized by media ownership that is private (referring again to the broadcast media), foreign, or concentrated. Thus, democratization is not a satisfying explanation.

Nor is the effect of economic crisis. Although Argentina indeed experienced a short economic crisis in 1989 and a longer one from 1998 to relatively recently, many of the changes in media ownership—notably the key decision to allow foreign investment—occurred during the "boom" times of the mid-1990s, when Argentina was experiencing annual levels of economic growth of 4–7 percent. Likewise, similar moves toward privatization of the broadcast media and the elimination of cross-ownership restrictions have occurred in states in western Europe and elsewhere in the absence of economic crisis. Moreover, although the change in Argentina is partially attributable to the political goals of certain government officials and to the economic interests of the big media owners in Argentina, this cannot explain the parallel trends in media ownership policy elsewhere in the region.

The reprivatization of the broadcast media took place under the administration of Carlos Menem (1989–1999). Although radio had been mainly under private ownership since its inception in the early 1920s, and television was mainly under private ownership starting in the late 1950s, various regimes periodically placed the media under direct or indirect state control. This was the case from 1974 to 1989, first during the civilian regime of Juan Perón (1973–1976),[12] then under the military regime (1976–1983), and continuing during the civilian regime of Raúl Alfonsín (1983–1989). Shortly after his inauguration in 1989, Menem decreed the Law of State Reform, which among other things called for the immediate divestiture of state-held radio and television stations. Today, the majority of radio stations and open-air television stations are privately owned, along with cable and satellite networks.

The second change was to allow foreign ownership of the media. During the 1990s, the national government made aggressive efforts to encourage foreign investment, but the Broadcasting Law of 1980 (22.285) prohibited foreign investment in the broadcast media and limited the granting of operating licenses for television and radio to Argentine nationals or Argentine-owned companies. Although most media experts agree that the 1980 law is outdated, infighting among the various stakeholders has prevented the passage of a new comprehensive communication law. Rather than wait for the Argentine congress to act, the Menem administration annulled the ban on foreign ownership indirectly. In 1991, Menem signed a bilateral investment agreement with the United States that became effective in 1994. Among other things, this allowed U.S. companies to invest in Argentine media. The treaty was not discussed or approved by the Argentine congress, but according to the reforms made to the constitution in 1994, the treaty takes precedence over national law (Galperín 2002, 31). This action then opened the media to foreign investment by all countries that sign commercial and investment treaties with Argentina (Candurra 2002).[13] As a result, Argentina is now one of Latin America's most internationalized TV markets, and one of "the most liberal TV business environments in the world" (Galperín 2002, 31, 22). Argentina may in fact be the paradigmatic case, given its openness toward foreign ownership in an industry that many Western countries exempt from external investment. In fact, as one prominent Argentine journalist suggests, in this case Argentina seems to have "out-liberalized" the liberalizers (Escribano 2002).

The third change was to allow greater cross-ownership of the media. The Broadcast Law of 1980 prohibits the ownership of multiple licenses for one type of medium in one zone, although its enforcement has been somewhat inconsistent. The law also bans print media companies from holding broadcasting licenses. Along with mandating the privatization of state-run media, however, the Law of State Reform passed one month after Menem came to office ended the prohibition of cross-ownership of the media. This led immediately to the creation of large multimedia corporations. There are currently some two dozen multimedia groups in the federal capital. By far the largest and most important is Grupo Clarín, which owns the country's largest daily newspaper (*Clarín*), the largest radio station and leader in news audience (Radio Mitre), the most important cable channel (Multicanal), the television channel with the second largest news audience and market share (Canal 13), and numerous smaller newspapers, magazines, and radio and television stations in Buenos Aires and elsewhere in the country. It also has part ownership of one of the major news agencies and an array of other diverse businesses from cellular phones to cinema to Internet. Currently, the other most important media conglomerations are the U.S.-based Hicks, Muse, Tate & Furst; the Spanish Telefónica; and the Mexican-based CIE.[14]

Journalist and media historian Pablo Sirven (2002) posits that congress permitted Menem to change the articles regarding ownership because it was a part of his larger economic program, which included tax-free zones and eliminated protections and tariff barriers. This reflected the trend toward neoliberal economic reform associated with contemporary economic globalization. Menem's decision to allow a greater concentration of ownership benefited some of his strongest supporters, who took advantage of the opportunity to increase their media holdings. His decision was also in part a result of intense lobbying by the biggest newspaper and publishing companies. This was not unique to Argentina, of course. Alger (1998) demonstrates that large media conglomerates in North America and western Europe have successfully pressured governments to rescind monopoly laws, which has led to a growing concentration of media ownership.

However, the concentration of media ownership in Argentina has been flavored by its own institutional arrangements and historical media-government relations. We can point to several examples. First, it has not been characterized by the growth of big newspaper chains as we have seen in the United States. Second, McChesney's (1999) observations about the vertical integration of the global market, "with the same firms gaining ownership of content and the means to distribute it," do not appear to be the case in Argentina. There is no equivalent of a General Electric owning the National Broadcasting Corporation (NBC), as we have seen in the United States. As Waisbord (1998, 83) notes, the logic of media concentration in Argentina is different than elsewhere in the developed and developing worlds. Rather than vertical integration, media groups in Argentina have primarily sought to expand horizontally into areas such as cable. The tremendous growth of cable has encouraged mergers with television companies and other media, and at this time, most of the country's cable systems are concentrated in the hands of Grupo Clarín (Multicanal) and Hicks, Muse, Tate & Furst (Cablevisión). Third, the trend toward foreign ownership that we see in Argentina appears to be much more common in the developing world than among the advanced industrial countries. Fourth, despite a common trend toward concentration in media ownership, the biggest media groups in Argentina "still pale in comparison" with communication giants in the United States, Europe, and Japan, and even with those in Mexico and Brazil (Waisbord 1998, 93).

Finally, Argentine communication policy during the recent wave of globalization has been notable for its lack of clarity. Media experts both inside and outside the government tend to agree that the existing laws and regulations are both incoherent and ineffective, and are enforced somewhat inconsistently.[15] Why has the country been unable to formulate a comprehensive policy to replace a series of media laws and regulations made obsolete by the development of new information technologies? I argue that the best explanation for this is institutional inertia, exacerbated by conflicting interests among the many actors in and out of the state who are responsible for formulating media laws and regulations. Thus despite the onset of a second wave of globalization in the 1970s and 1980s, many of the institutions originally formulated in the 1940s and subsequent decades have persisted.

Conclusion

In sum, most of Latin America has followed the global trend toward deregulation of media ownership, especially the easing of prohibitions against multiple licenses and cross-ownership. The changes in ownership have occurred in the direction anticipated by liberal-pluralist theory, with one important exception: while ownership has become more private and more foreign-held, it also has become more concentrated and less diffuse. The forces of globalization, especially deregulation, and the capital investment necessary to become a player in the so-called new media, have greatly increased the privileges of the large owners vis-à-vis the smaller owners, rather than allowing new entrants into the media and expanding the playing field. This runs counter to the expectations of liberal-pluralist theory and creates uncertainty, especially for the small owners or those hoping to break into the market. By lifting the ban on cross-ownership and foreign investment, a relatively few multimedia were allowed to form that during the 1990s came to enjoy ever greater influence in the formation of media policy. This is more consistent with the predictions of the media imperialism thesis than liberal pluralism. Moreover, the evidence suggests that a relatively large level of foreign investment has served more to empower existing national players than to introduce new internationally based influences on media policy. This runs against some expectations found in much of the globalization literature.

An important point in this chapter is the notion that the state can balance the loss of sovereign control through its regulation of the media. Thus despite the very real influence of international trends, domestic factors remain important in public policymaking. In this case, the market helps to shape—but does not determine—media policy. The case study of Argentina suggests that despite the general trend that points to a convergence of policy (at least in the area of media ownership) across the Americas, we should expect to see important variation in the means, the manner, the extent, and the timing of policy reform in each case. This indicates that while globalization has the potential to have an important effect on public policy formation, the results in terms of policy outcomes still remain somewhat uncertain.

Moreover, while it is likely that globalization is exerting similar pressures on policymakers throughout the world, we would expect to see regional variation. For example, Latin America is unique in the sense that the region is predominantly monolingual (Spanish) and has been subject to significant U.S. interventionism for more than a century. The relative linguistic homogeneity, in tandem with the dominance of a handful of media giants in the North, might make it more attractive for Latin American media corporations to cater to a regional media market and to try to find ways to resist the expansion of the global media market. And since "globalization" is often understood as shorthand for U.S. cultural dominance, we may see a greater backlash against the incursion of U.S.-based media corporations than in areas where the United States has historically been less involved—especially if left-leaning (and often anti-United States) candidates continue to win electoral victories in the region. This will require Latin American governments to seek a balance between their desire for foreign investment and international recognition and the desire to preserve and protect their own national, state, and local media.

Notes

1. As it is used in the popular and scholarly literature, globalization refers to a package of phenomena, including such things as increased trade flows, increased foreign investment, immigration, and technology transfers. My focus in this paper is on the contemporary wave of globalization starting in approximately 1970 (see O'Rourke and Williamson 1999).
2. The distinction here applies to the broadcast media; print media in both North America and western Europe have traditionally been privately owned and commercial.
3. The situation regarding foreign ownership is very much in flux at this point, so the literature quickly becomes outdated. A good but slightly old comprehensive source on media ownership is MacLeod (1996).

4. Moreover, pluralists would predict that because satellite and cable television have largely eliminated the need for states to regulate scarce airwaves, this should open up entry into, and competition in, the broadcast media.
5. A variant of this is that the ruling classes in the periphery are tied economically to international capital, hence they manage or intermediate for international capital within their own state using their control of state power. This results in states with little autonomy in relation to their own dominant economic interests *or* to the global (capitalist) political economy.
6. Even the realist or dependency schools that grant autonomy to the "core" countries withhold that capacity from those in the developing world. Staniland (1985) provides a helpful outline of the main "schools" of global political economy that are relevant to this discussion, which I adopt here. Although he does not directly address the implications for media policy, I have attempted to draw out some logical ties.
7. Televisa came about as a merger between Telesistema Mexicano and a competitor, in order to challenge the government's creation of a state-owned TV network in the early 1970s.
8. In 1992, the Aylwin-Navarette Reform Law sought to restructure the national TV channel, TVN. This resulted in tremendous growth in audience share, making it first in the ratings by 1999 (Fuenzalida 2002). But Chile is an exceptional case; this is the only public station in the region to show audience growth during the period.
9. Despite laws against the concentration of media ownership, important banking and media groups close to the president bought interests in radio, television, cable, and the print media. Under the subsequent administration, President Caldera nationalized banks with close ties to Pérez, temporarily bringing many radio and television stations under government control.
10. In the Chilean case, the major changes in media ownership, both in privatizing and internationalizing ownership, were initiated by the military dictatorship of Augusto Pinochet during a period of economic liberalization. In fact, most owners or managers of most media in Chile today are people with links to the former authoritarian regime (Tirana and Sunkel 2000, 189).
11. This refers to the broadcast media. Print media in Argentina and elsewhere in Latin America have traditionally remained in private hands, except during times of military dictatorship.
12. Perón became president for the second time after an 18-year exile. He died in 1974 and was succeeded by his vice president (and wife), Isabel Perón.
13. The web page of the Argentine consulate shows bilateral investment treaties with 17 countries in the 1990s (only two of which were signed with congressional approval). There are 12 others designated "signed only," and 10 designated "being negotiated." See www.consargtoro.org/invest.htm. These bilateral investment treaties are a relatively recent phenomenon.

14. One of the most spectacular examples of foreign investment in the Argentine media came in late 1999, when Goldman Sachs acquired 18% of Grupo Clarín for $500 million. The remaining 82% remains in Argentine hands. Investment has been particularly prevalent in cable television.
15. For example, there have been instances of media ownership that have been clearly illegal. The usual example concerns the Spanish company Telefónica's full ownership of television Channel 11 and partial ownership of Channel 9, both in the federal capital. Although foreign ownership of the media is now permitted, prohibitions remain against ownership of more than one of a single type of medium in a single zone. The Federal Broadcasting Commission (Comité Federal de Radiofusión or COMFER) did eventually rule in late 1999 that Telefónica must sell one or the other of its properties by the end of 2002, which it did. Other examples included the continued operation of approximately 5,000 unlicensed (illegal) radio stations in the country, and inconsistent of fines for programming violations.

References

Alger, Dean. 1998. *Megamedia: How Giant Corporations Dominate Mass Media, Distort Competition, and Endanger Democracy.* Lanham, MD: Rowman and Littlefield Publishers.

Amaral, Roberto. 2002. "Mass Media in Brazil: Modernization to Prevent Change." In *Latin Politics, Global Media*, edited by Elizabeth Fox and Silvio Waisbord. Austin: University of Texas Press.

Ang, Ien. 1990. "Culture and Communication: Towards an Ethnographic Critique of Media Consumption in the Transnational Media System." *European Journal of Communication* 5 (2/3): 239–260.

Bagdikian, Ben H. 2000. *The Media Monopoly.* 6th ed. Boston: Beacon Press.

Beltrán, Luis Ramiro, and Elizabeth Fox. 1980. *Comunicación Dominada: Los Estados Unidos en los Medios de América Latina.* Mexico City: ILET/Nueva Imagen.

Cajías de la Vega, Lupe, and Guadalupe López. 1999. *Concentración de medios de comunicación en América Latina: ¿Amenaza o fortaleza?* La Paz: Friedrich Ebert Stiftung.

Calero Aparicio, Fernando. 2002. "The Colombian Media: Modes and Perspectives in Television." In *Latin Politics, Global Media*, edited by Elizabeth Fox and Silvio Waisbord. Austin: University of Texas Press.

Candurra, Luis Antonio. 2002. Interview by author. Tape recording. Buenos Aires, March 1.

Compaine, Benjamin M., and Douglas Gomery, eds. 2000. *Who Owns the Media? Competition and Concentration in the Mass Media Industry.* 3rd ed. London and Mahwah, NJ: Lawrence Erlbaum Associates Publishers.

Curran, James, and Myung-Jin Park. 2000. "Beyond Globalization Theory." In *De-Westernizing Media Studies*, edited by James Curran and Myung-Jin Park. London and New York: Routledge.

Escribano, José Claudio. 2002. Personal interview. Buenos Aires, March 14.
Fang, Irving. 1997. *A History of Mass Communication: Six Information Revolutions*. Boston: Focal Press.
Faraone, Roque. 2002. "Television and the New Uruguayan State." In *Latin Politics, Global Media*, edited by Elizabeth Fox and Silvio Waisbord. Austin: University of Texas Press.
Fox, Elizabeth. 1988. "Media Policies in Latin America: An Overview." In *Media and Politics in Latin America: The Struggle for Democracy*, edited by Elizabeth Fox. London: Sage.
———. 1996. "Latin America." In *Media Ownership and Control in the Age of Convergence*, edited by Vicki MacLeod. London: International Institute of Communications.
———. 1997. *Latin American Broadcasting: From Tango to Telenovela*. Luton, UK: University of Luton Press.
Fox, Elizabeth, and Silvio Waisbord, eds. 2002. *Latin Politics, Global Media*. Austin: University of Texas Press.
Fuenzalida, Valerio. 2002. "The Reform of National Television in Chile." In *Latin Politics, Global Media*, edited by Elizabeth Fox and Silvio Waisbord. Austin: University of Texas Press.
Galiani, Sebastián, and Diego Petrecolla. 2000. "The Argentine Privatization Process and Its Aftermath: Some Preliminary Conclusions." In *The Impact of Privatization in the Americas*, edited by Melissa H. Birch and Jerry Haar. Miami: North-South Center Press, University of Miami.
Galperín, Hernán. 2002. "Transforming Television in Argentina: Market Development and Policy Reform in the 1990s." In *Latin Politics, Global Media*, edited by Elizabeth Fox and Silvio Waisbord. Austin: University of Texas Press.
Giddens, Anthony. 1999. "Comment: The 1999 Reith Lecture. New World without End." *Observer*, April 11.
Gunther, Richard, and Anthony Mughan. 2000. "The Media in Democratic and Nondemocratic Regimes: A Multilevel Perspective." In *Democracy and the Media: A Comparative Perspective*, edited by Richard Gunther and Anthony Mughan. Cambridge: Cambridge University Press.
Humphreys, Peter J. 1996. *Mass Media and Media Policy in Western Europe*. Manchester and New York: Manchester University Press.
Lerner, D. 1963. "Toward a Communication Theory of Modernization." In *Communications and Political Development*, edited by Lucian Pye. Princeton: Princeton University Press.
MacLeod, Vicki, ed. 1996. *Media Ownership and Control in the Age of Convergence*. London: International Institute of Communications.
Mastrini, Guillermo, and César Bolaño, eds. 1999. *Globalización y monopolios en la comunicación en América latina*. Buenos Aires: Editorial Biblos.
Mayobre, José Antonio. 2002. "Venezuela and the Media: The New Paradigm." In *Latin Politics, Global Media*, edited by Elizabeth Fox and Silvio Waisbord. Austin: University of Texas Press.

McChesney, Robert Waterman. 1998. "Media Convergence and Globalisation." In *Electronic Empires: Global Media and Local Resistance*, edited by Daya Kishan Thussu. London: Arnold.
———. 1999. *Rich Media, Poor Democracy: Communication Politics in Dubious Times*. Urbana: University of Illinois Press.
McLuhan, Marshall. 1964. *Understanding Media*. London: Routledge.
McQuail, Denis, and Karen Siune, eds. 1998. Media Policy: Convergence, Concentration and Commerce. London: Sage.
O'Rourke, Kevin H., and Jeffrey G. Williamson. 1999. *Globalization and History: The Evolution of a Nineteenth-Century Atlantic Economy*. Cambridge, MA: MIT Press.
Orué Pozzo, Aníbal. 2002. "The Transitional Labyrinth in an Emerging Democracy: Broadcasting Policies in Paraguay." In *Latin Politics, Global Media*, edited by Elizabeth Fox and Silvio Waisbord. Austin: University of Texas Press.
Mayobre, José Antonio. 2002. "Venezuela and the Media: The New Paradigm." In *Latin Politics, Global Media*, edited by Elizabeth Fox and Silvio Waisbord. Austin: University of Texas Press.
McChesney, Robert Waterman. 1998. "Media Convergence and Globalisation." In *Electronic Empires: Global Media and Local Resistance*, edited by Daya Kishan Thussu. London: Arnold.
———. 1999. *Rich Media, Poor Democracy: Communication Politics in Dubious Times*. Urbana: University of Illinois Press.
Peirano, Luis. 2002. "Peruvian Media in the 1990s: From Deregulation to Reorganization." In *Latin Politics, Global Media*, edited by Elizabeth Fox and Silvio Waisbord. Austin: University of Texas Press.
Pierson, Paul. 2000. "Increasing Returns, Path Dependence, and the Study of Politics." *American Political Science Review* 94 (2): 251–67.
Pool, Ithiel de Sola. 1963. "The Mass Media and Politics in the Development Process." In *Communications and Political Development*, edited by Lucian Pye. Princeton: Princeton University Press.
Robins, Kevin, James Cornford, and Asu Aksoy. 1997. "Overview: From Cultural Rights to Cultural Responsibilities." In *Programming for People*, edited by Kevin Robins. Newcastle: Centre for Urban and Regional Development Studies, University of Newcastle and European Broadcasting Union.
Rockwell, Rick. 2002. "Mexico: The Fox Factor." In *Latin Politics, Global Media*, edited by Elizabeth Fox and Silvio Waisbord. Austin: University of Texas Press.
Sinclair, John. 1996. "Mexico, Brazil and the Latin World." In *New Patterns in Global Television: Peripheral Vision*, edited by John Sinclair, Elizabeth Jacka, and Stuart Cunningham. Oxford: Oxford University Press.
———. 2002. "Mexico and Brazil: The Aging Dynasties." In *Latin Politics, Global Media*, edited by Elizabeth Fox and Silvio Waisbord. Austin: University of Texas Press.
Schiller, Herbert I. 1969. *Mass Communication and American Empire*. New York: Kelly.

Schiller, Herbert I. 1976. *Communication and Cultural Domination*. White Plains, NY: International Arts and Sciences Press.

———. 1998. "Striving for Communication Dominance." In *Electronic Empires*, edited by Daya Kishan Thussu. London: Arnold.

Sirven, Pablo. 2002. Interview with author. Tape recording. Buenos Aires, April 5.

Skocpol, Theda. 1992. *Protecting Soldiers and Mothers: The Political Origins of Social Policy in the United States*. Cambridge: Belknap Press of Harvard.

Stark, Jeffrey. 1998. "Globalization and Democracy in Latin America." In *Fault Lines of Democracy in Post-Transition Latin America*, edited by Felipe Agüero and Jeffrey Stark. Miami: University of Miami, North-South Center Press.

Thelen, Kathleen. 1999. "Historical Institutionalism and Comparative Politics." *Annual Review of Political Science* 2: 369–404.

Tironi, Eugenio, and Guillermo Sunkel. 2000. "The Modernization of Communications: The Media in the Transition to Democracy in Chile." In *Democracy and the Media: A Comparative Perspective*, edited by Richard Gunther and Anthony Mughan and translated by Richard Gunther. Cambridge: Cambridge University Press.

Waisbord, Silvio. 1998. "The Market Deluge: Privatization and Concentration in the Argentine Media Industries." In *Global Media Economics: Commercialization, Concentration and Integration of World Media Markets*, edited by Alan B. Albarran and Sylvia M. Chan-Olmstead. Ames, IA: Iowa State University Press.

———. 2000. "Media in South America: Between the Rock of the State and the Hard Place of the Market." In *De-Westernizing Media Studies*, edited by James Curran and Myung-Jin Park. London and New York: Routledge.

Wheeler, Mark. 1998. *Politics and the Mass Media*. Cambridge, MA and Oxford: Blackwell.

World Association of Newspapers. 2002. *World Press Trends 2002*. Paris: World Association of Newspapers.

Zuleta Puceiro, Enrique. 1999. "State Reform and Deregulatory Strategies in Argentina." In *Competition Policy, Deregulation, and Modernization in Latin America*, edited by Moisés Naím and Joseph S. Tulchin. Boulder, CO: Lynne Rienner Publishers.

6

Development Assistance, the Environment, and Stakeholder Participation: Toward a New Conditionality?

Jonathan Rosenberg

Introduction

Economic globalization has had complex and uncertain effects on developing states. For the most part, since World War II, aid flows from the global North to global South have reinforced asymmetries of power, dependent relationships, and the foreign policy objectives of developed states. But with globalization, the nature of these relationships has changed in content and character, and possibly in their effects as well. The changing nature of conditionalities (i.e., the policy requirements attached to loans and grants) stands as an illustration of these changes and the resultant uncertainties.

Three sources of uncertainty, each one a function of the changing political economy of the late twentieth and early twenty-first centuries, shape the developments described in this chapter. First is the general trend from public to private capital flows as means of funding development in the global South. Second is the systemic change brought about by the end of the cold war. And third, is a heightened awareness of and concern for the environmental effects of development.

In the recent history of global development, conditionality conjures up some heated and painful controversies. Typically, conditionality is associated with neoliberal discipline imposed by the International Monetary Fund and World Bank on highly indebted developing states. The stringent conditions attached to loans emphasized short-term growth objectives, deemphasized social and distributive criteria, and usually proved antithetical to environmental sustainability and substantive participation by grassroots actors. But debt-related social, economic, and political turmoil in the 1970s and 1980s, and growing awareness of the environmental effects of conventional, growth-oriented development assistance have yielded two important results. One is the inclusion of sustainability as a consideration in development planning and funding. The other is the association of sustainability with the use of participatory methods.

On a practical level, concern for the environmental effects of economic development, and the linkage between sustainable development and participatory practices, has led to new international agreements and protocols, and new policies for international lenders and donors. International organizations and the governments of developed countries now provide support explicitly for sustainable development, and they routinely require recipient governments to use methods of implementation that identify and include relevant stakeholders.

The reasons for these changes have been analyzed elsewhere, but two points bear mention. First, grassroots activism was instrumental in getting development assistance agencies to consider the environmental sustainability of the projects they support and helped associate sustainability with participatory practices. Second, these bottom-up pressures—emanating from environmental movements in both developed and underdeveloped countries—played a major role in changing the development assistance policies of developed countries and major international organizations (Reed 1997; Rajagopal 2000).

The effects and sincerity of the new policies have been extensively argued and critiqued (see, e.g., Hunter 1996; Rich 1994; and Kiely 1998). But little has been done to compare the methods used by development assistance agencies to elicit stakeholder participation or to assess the effectiveness of particular methods. Therefore, I ask two basic questions: (1) Have new directions in development assistance led to effective stakeholder participation? (2) Can we generalize about the effectiveness of the methods employed by development assistance agencies and recipient countries?

To answer these questions, I posit the existence of a "new conditionality" and look at three externally funded attempts to implement participatory methods in three small island democratic states in the Eastern Caribbean—Grenada, Dominica, and St. Lucia. Each case resulted in a distinct type of participatory arrangement and displays different approaches to delivering development assistance.

I assess success and failure in promoting substantive stakeholder participation by tracking the interaction of three factors: the conditions related to participation placed on external support and the ways in which they are implemented by development assistance agencies; the methods of stakeholder inclusion in the project; and the structural autonomy from national government and the development assistance agency of the resulting participatory arrangements.

HISTORICAL BACKGROUND AND RECENT TRENDS

Historically, the Caribbean has been a nexus of global development, reflecting the recognizable trends and patterns of global change as well as the resultant uncertainties. European imperial adventures immediately and irrevocably affected the Caribbean islands, culturally, socially, politically, economically, and ecologically. Due to their centrality to the imperial project, Caribbean islands were quickly transformed. The taking of timber for transatlantic and transcaribbean shipping; the clearing of land to plant crops imported from other colonial possessions; the introduction of new systems of land tenure and political authority; the destruction of indigenous populations and cultures; the importation of African slaves; and the forging of a global, imperial economy based in Europe and tied to the Americas, Africa, and Asia are all of a piece. Caribbean natural resources became a source of wealth for European colonial empires, and Caribbean geography linked the islands inextricably to international trade and strategic interactions, apparently, for all time. Imperialism caused often chaotic disruptions in Caribbean life and created constant uncertainty over who would control the islands. During the eighteenth century the three states discussed in this chapter—Grenada, Dominica, and St. Lucia—changed hands frequently as the British, French, and Dutch battled for regional supremacy (Singh 2002, 19–20).

After independence—achieved during the cold war—local political struggles were still imbued with a global dimension. In the early 1980s, for example, while Grenada's People's Revolutionary Government attempted to establish democratic socialism and maintain friendly relations with Fidel Castro's Cuba, Prime Minister Eugenia Charles of Dominica positioned herself as a staunch supporter of Reagan administration foreign policy goals, including the reversal of the Grenadian Revolution by military means (Ferguson 1990, 113–118). Until the late 1980s aid flows and economic opportunities in the region were heavily influenced by the cold war interests of donor countries and the multilateral aid and lending institutions. Following the debt crisis of the 1980s and the accession to power of neoliberal regimes in the United States and United Kingdom, the so-called Washington Consensus linked promotion of market economies to the political goals of democratization and support for friendly regimes. Therefore, even as official development assistance was deemphasized in favor of foreign direct and portfolio investments as the main sources of development capital, official development assistance exacted a heavy price from the recipient.

The neoliberal orientation of official development assistance left little room for the active pursuit of environmental values through funded projects. Such "quality of life" considerations were treated as residual to the more immediate need for market-based economic growth. Nevertheless, pressure was mounting, both on and within development assistance agencies, to take the environment into account. Change came slowly. Agenda 21, a product of the 1992 UN Conference on Environment and Development in Rio de Janeiro, marked a turning point in the official doctrine of international development aid by linking development with environmental sustainability and environmental sustainability with stakeholder participation (see Bryner 1999; Rajagopal 2000). After making a nod to sovereignty in the use of resources, Agenda 21 urges developed countries to support environmentally sustainable development globally, and all states to consider the global environmental effects of their development practices.

In a formal sense, international lending and aid agencies have responded. By the mid-1990s, World Bank operational directives included guidelines for environmental assessment and suggestions on how local stakeholder participation could advance environmental sustainability (World Bank 1996, 1998). Other development assistance agencies made similar attempts to operationalize Agenda 21 by making environmental sustainability a prerequisite for development aid and prescribing participation by the affected populations in the assessment, implementation, and/or evaluation of projects. These included, to varying degrees, the Global Environment Facility (GEF), the Organization of American States (OAS), the United States Agency for International Development (USAID) and the British Department for International Development (DFID) (OAS 1998; GEF 1996; Department for International Development 1999).

Although official doctrine has clearly evolved, considerable skepticism remains. What if this new doctrine is a new conditionality as onerous and disruptive as neoliberal conditionality? Could participatory conditions lead recipient governments to take measures that would negatively affect economic growth and empower new groups whose long-term contribution to sustainable development is questionable? How do states and agencies contend with the uncertainty created by a changing natural environment and their own attempts to consider environmental sustainability in resource development and management practices?

Among the recipients of development assistance—including officials of development assistance agencies, government officials, and organizations and grassroots actors—we find a mixture of attitudes toward this new conditionality. Some interviewed for this study see the funding agencies' newfound commitment to stakeholder participation as yet another example of insensitivity to local conditions that creates delays and political complications in much needed programs.[1] Others, arguing the intrinsic value of participatory methods, admit that by making participation a condition of support, funding agencies may help push the cause of sustainability further and faster than would otherwise be the case.[2]

Is the New Conditionality Different?

I will argue that the new conditionality *can* be different from the old, but that positive results are not guaranteed simply by changes in the policies of development assistance agencies, no matter how sincere. I find strong evidence that the small island states of the Caribbean are responding to the connections Agenda 21 makes between economic development, environmental protection, and the responsibilities of wealthy nations and international organizations to aid poor countries pursuing these goals. Although support is not pervasive, there are individuals within governments, regional organizations, NGOs, and the private sector who pay considerable attention to the need for economically, socially, and environmentally sustainable development.

But the local politics can be contentious. Agenda 21 calls for increased participation of traditionally underrepresented groups and encourages "international and national governments, businesses, and NGOs to integrate environmental and economic objectives" (Bryner 1999, 167–168). Here we find disagreement over the suitability of participatory methods for the current political climate of the Eastern Caribbean, and widely varying approaches to implementing participatory methods. When faced with the demands of foreign lenders and donors, the governments of the region see themselves as having great need and little bargaining power. Of necessity, small island states often take their cues from the growing number of international agreements on sustainable development and the funding agencies that support them. In part, this is inevitable given their dependence on aid and lending. But the effects of that dependence may not be as negative as they once were. In fact, within a generally mixed record, we find some positive trends in government-to-government aid and lending. And more generally, as Miller argues, global concerns and the common pool nature of environmental resources may be undermining the international power relationships assumed by traditional realist and structuralist analyses, providing "Third World countries with a potential basis for leverage" (1998, 175).

Therefore, the new conditionality can be different from older forms in important ways. First, bottom-up demands for participation are the results of lessons from projects that have failed due to the non-inclusion of stakeholders (Rich 1994; Hunter 1996). Second, the more successful recent attempts to promote participation have encouraged local stakeholder involvement in project design, assessment, and implementation, rather than mere, *pro forma* use of public consultation exercises. Third, local governments now can find themselves pressured from outside (development assistance agencies and international NGOs), below (local actors), and within (government agencies closest to the targeted problems and affected populations). Fourth, the pressure often results from sincere, shared convictions that effective participation, sustainability, and economic development are compatible.

Why Participation?

The new conditionality is informed by the assumption of a positive relationship between democratic decision making and environmental sustainability also found in a great deal of the scholarly literature on sustainable development. But while there are sound theoretical and empirical bases for believing that democracy is better than authoritarianism for promoting "green" policies (Lipschutz 1996, 19–46; Janicke 1996, 71–72), insufficient attention has been paid to the particular kinds of democratic participation that best promote environmental sustainability in different social and political contexts.

Janicke notes that even in developed, politically liberal countries effective environmental policy is associated with new democratic forms that are more inclusive and participatory than established methods of national policymaking. Furthermore, he equates the ability to make effective environmental policy with capacity building and political modernization in already developed countries (1996, 79–81).

This raises interesting questions for the three countries considered below. All three are established parliamentary democracies with Westminster-style party government and hierarchical, top-down policy-making and implementation processes. None are highly developed in any conventional economic sense, but development assistance agencies have encouraged them to employ the same participatory methods aspired to by activists in highly industrialized countries. Can this be effective? And if so, will it constitute an advancement of democracy or a further acquiescence of poor, weak countries to forces of an evermore demanding, northern-dominated global economy?[3] Existing studies provide no easy answers, but suggest that successful participatory arrangements require careful, proactive methods of stakeholder identification and substantial capacity building for poor and politically marginalized stakeholders (Rosenberg and Korsmo 2001; Bass 2000).

Three Models of Participation

The cases included in this chapter were identified in the course of field research carried out in 1998 and 1999 in the Eastern Caribbean and Washington, DC. Selection was the result of a snowball sampling of government officials, officials of development assistance agencies, consultants, NGO officers, and local activists involved in sustainable development and the organization of stakeholders. The cases represent three basic organizational types, each one organized with the support of a different development assistance agency to facilitate participatory practices.

Independent Advisory Councils
These are bodies organized and convened by government officials with representation from local NGOs, businesses, community groups, activists, and government ministries and departments. All three of the small island states established Sustainable Development Councils (SDCs) as recommended by Agenda 21. They received initial funding under the United Nations' Capacity 21 program aimed at including underrepresented groups in participatory mechanisms and promoting public-private cooperation for environmentally and socially sustainable development (United Nations Environmental Programme 1994).

Government-Initiated Resource Management Policies
These are policies produced under the guidance of government departments, ministries or government affiliated agencies to manage natural resources and/or ecosystems using various methods of

stakeholder inclusion in planning, development, and implementation. They may be initiated by government, by individual government officials or agencies, or developed in cooperation with external funding agencies. The Grenada National Forest Policy is a particular example. It received support (grants, training, and equipment) from the British Department for International Development (DFID) and funding from the Government of Grenada and was assisted by an on-site DFID adviser. Both the policy-making process and the policy—although initiated, guided, and supported by the Forestry Department of Grenada's Ministry of Agriculture, Lands, Forestry and Fisheries—became products of stakeholder participation.

Autonomous Management Authorities
These are bodies established and run with limited government involvement for the purpose of creating and implementing management plans for particular locations, projects or resources. Ultimately, they are intended to be permanent, self-sustaining, representative, and vested with rule-making and enforcement authority. For this study I consider the Local Area Management Authority (LAMA) of the Scott's Head/Soufriere Marine Reserve in Dominica (SSMR), funded primarily by French Technical Cooperation (FTC), with support from the Organization of American States (OAS) and the Canadian International Development Agency (CIDA).

Explaining Effective Stakeholder Participation

Effective participation is an elusive concept. The mere inclusion of a group or individual in a process may be necessary, but it is certainly not sufficient. For participation to be effective it must be substantive as to process and outcomes, must allow serious consideration of the preferences of all stakeholders, and must provide mechanisms for reaching compromises and resolving conflict. It should include the creation of institutions or processes that can reflect stakeholder preferences in the making, implementation, and modification of plans and projects. Effective stakeholder participation also implies effective processes for identifying stakeholders, keeping them informed, preparing them adequately for participation, and facilitating participation of stakeholders of different backgrounds, cultures, and educational levels (Agarwal and Gibson 1999; Partridge 1994; and Chambers 1995, 1993). Therefore, we can consider effective participation to have taken place when we find (1) active inclusion of the local stakeholders most directly affected by the project or program; (2) stakeholder preferences reflected in the composition of the institutions established and the decisions made; and (3) direct input by local stakeholders in decisions taken.

In looking for explanations, typically, independent variables should be arrayed, quantitatively or qualitatively, along clearly defined continua. Unfortunately, this research does not support such clear, unambiguous generalizations. For example, we might expect substantive stakeholder participation to increase as management authorities become more autonomous of government. Instead, we find that while autonomy may be desirable, its relationship to effective participation depends on other factors, including the attitudes, actions, and abilities of government officials, the specific roles taken by the agents of development assistance agencies and the involvement of nongovernmental actors.

In short, explanations of effective and ineffective participatory methods must be sought in the details. How are stakeholders brought into the process? How is the input of each brought to bear on the design, implementation, and revision of particular projects? Are the conditions set by the development assistance agency, and the methods used to implement them, feasible and appropriate to the particular political contexts?

METHODS OF STAKEHOLDER IDENTIFICATION, PREPARATION, AND INCLUSION

Both in the scholarly literature and among practitioners one finds little principled objection to the use of participatory methods, but one also finds broad agreement that there is much left to be done in developing and implementing effective participatory methods. A substantial literature already exists on the dangers to the natural environment from unregulated public use (beginning with Hardin 1968). Stated or implied in much of this work is the recognition that all users need to be included in regulatory decisions if enforcement is to be effective (and cost-effective) (Ostrom 1990). There is also a small but growing literature at the intersection of theory and practice that deals specifically with participatory methods (Chambers 1993; Department for International Development 1999). Nevertheless, we still find resistance to participatory practices by some public officials based on the belief that not all political cultures support the effective inclusion of all stakeholders.[4] And still, some development assistance agencies continue to count public presentations on the findings of environmental impact studies as sufficient stakeholder participation.[5]

These beliefs raise critical, technical questions about participatory methods. In some cases these questions have been successfully addressed. In others the answers have yet to be worked out. Practitioners—including government officials, NGOs, community leaders, and activists—in the Eastern Caribbean are working on these issues as they attempt to comply with demands, both external and internal, for participation. A regional NGO based in St. Lucia, the Caribbean Natural Resources Institute (CANARI) uses a "functional" method of stakeholder identification intended to include all individuals and groups that affect or are affected by the activities and resources to be managed.[6] In Grenada a locally based consultant has used personal ties with affected communities to carry out stakeholder education and information campaigns. In Dominica local NGOs use a combination of educational programs and direct political action to mobilize citizens.[7] In still other cases, the representatives of development assistance agencies have been active in identifying, informing, and organizing stakeholders; although in such cases great care needs to be taken to avoid the appearance of outside interference or manipulation (Rosenberg and Korsmo, 2001, 297–299).[8]

THE CASES
Sustainable Development Councils (SDCs)

According to Agenda 21, Sustainable Development Councils were to be permanent bodies that brought together government, the private sector, NGOs, and user and consumer groups.[9] They were to be chaired by a government official who would also head a government sustainable development unit. Councils were to meet regularly to review new policies and programs, alert government to members' concerns about the sustainability of existing programs, and insure compliance with international agreements and the requirements of external funding agencies. In this regard, the SDCs were to have unique authority to affect decisions made by several ministries (United Nations Environmental Programme 2001).[10] To date the SDCs have been, at best, marginally successful, while the sustainable development units have yet to be fully established. The experience of Dominica is indicative of the problems.[11]

The National Sustainable Development Council of Dominica was created by an act of government in 1995. The majority of its 13 members came from individual businesses and business associations involved in tourism, manufacturing, construction, and services. Under its mandate to coordinate all development projects, all projects proposed by the cabinet or submitted to government by the private sector were to come through the council. In addition, the council was charged with monitoring and ensuring compliance with international environmental treaties and programs (such as Agenda 21, the Montreal Protocols on ozone depletion and UN conventions on desertification and biodiversity). But the council was weak, poorly funded and suffered from organizational problems from the beginning.

Politically, the National Sustainable Development Council was in a difficult position. To function as intended it would have to act as a virtual "superministry" with authority to review and revise any policy with environmental impact. The potential for conflict with senior agency heads and cabinet ministers was great. The council drew up Terms of Reference for distribution to the appropriate government ministries, but the document was ignored. Originally, the council was subsidiary to the preexisting National Development Council (NDC)—a statutory body concerned primarily with industry and tourism in whose building its office was located and from which it drew its coordinator and staff. NDC responsibilities not only overlapped those of the SDC, but its mandate—to promote growth—often contradicted SDC goals of sustainability and broader stakeholder participation. Relations between the functional ministries of the government and the NDC were well established. Neither the NDC nor the economic and planning ministries of government were willing to share responsibility with the SDC, a body headed by a junior administrator with the unenviable task of demanding that his seniors relinquish some of their control over development policy. At best, the SDC was able to review and make recommendations on specific projects directed to it by the NDC and the ministries. Otherwise, the SDC coordinator acted mainly as a liaison channeling information from international organizations to government.

Funding was also a problem for the SDC. Capacity 21 funds were quickly exhausted in the organizational work that set up the council. Nothing was left to actually carry out its sweeping mandate. The SDC became dependent on the limited amounts of external funding available for specific projects and initiatives distributed through the Organization of Eastern Caribbean States (OECS). By 1999, the SDC was moribund, awaiting reorganization as a new Environmental Coordinating Unit under the Ministry of Agriculture and the Environment, with support from an 18-month Global Environment Facility (GEF) grant.

The Grenada National Forest Policy

The Grenada National Forest Policy was developed by the Forestry Department of the Grenadian Ministry of Agriculture, Lands, Forestry and Fisheries to provide authoritative, long-range goals and implementation requirements for the sustainable use of Grenada's remaining forests.[12] The policy-planning process was initiated by the Forestry Department with the original intention of including local stakeholders at every step. The goal of the policy is sustainability through the inclusion of all users of forest resources in its design, revision, and implementation. The British Department for International Development (DFID) was the main source of funding.[13]

This case differs from the other two discussed in this chapter in important ways. First, its primary aim was to gather stakeholder input as part of a major and unprecedented departure from the normal policy-making process. Second, the process itself evolved as a result of stakeholder input. Third, although the process has led to some significant statutory and institutional changes, its effects on forest management have yet to be fully tested.

Officially, stakeholder participation was initiated at the request of the chief forestry officer after a two-day "visioning" workshop convened in May 1997. In his proposal he emphasized the inadequacies of the existing forestry policy, written in 1984, and cited Agenda 21 on the importance of consultation and participation.[14]

Although the plan was carried to its conclusion by the Forestry Department, under the leadership of the senior and chief forestry officers, DFID support and the activities of the DFID adviser were essential. For example, DFID provided the Forestry Department with new office computers, vehicles and a small operating budget to compensate for budgetary and staff cutbacks taken in the mid-1990s. DFID also provided funds for the chief forestry officer to pursue a Masters of Science in Forestry Extension at Reading University in the United Kingdom. This training (one of four advanced degrees for forestry officers funded by DFID as part of the project) became a key element in DFID's support of the policy process. The chief forestry officer gained increased technical knowledge of comprehensive forestry planning, and introduced the department to the ethos of participation and sustainability that is integral to Reading's forestry programs.[15]

In what follows, I will offer a few highlights indicative of the methods of stakeholder inclusion used.[16]

The visioning workshop identified the need for a new, comprehensive forest policy and suggested a set of goals and a methodology. Most importantly, it determined that consultations with the entire population and participation by forest stakeholders, broadly conceived, would be essential for a sustainable and practicable plan. The Forestry Department then identified a group of stakeholders to form a Forest Policy Process Committee and charged them with the design of the policy process. It was this committee that designed the process by which the policy would be formulated, including the use of participatory data gathering methods, and it was this committee that directed the Forestry Department's senior staff to produce the technical papers on various substantive areas as bases for discussions among stakeholders. The Policy Process Committee was made up of 19 members, 11 from the cognate functional ministries and agencies of government, 3 from local NGOs, and 3 from local producer and industry groups involved in forestry, tourism, farming, and furniture manufacturing. The two remaining members were the Chair Yves Renard of Caribbean Natural Resources Institute (CANARI), and the DFID Forestry adviser in the role of secretary.[17] At the same time the Forestry Department, with guidance and support from the Forest Policy Process Committee, began extensive and intensive public information campaigns and a series of public consultations.

In November 1997 local newspapers published Forest Policy Questionnaires that were also distributed by hand by committee members. Informative films were shown on television, and announcements were made on television and radio in support of the policy process. The questionnaires included several open-ended questions about forest use, problems facing the nation's forests, suggestions for remedies, the role of government and communities in forestry, and so on. To encourage return of the questionnaires, a prize drawing was held for respondents. The questionnaires served two immediate purposes: (1) they provided the committee with substantive input for developing the policy and the next steps of the policy-making process; and (2) they allowed the committee to identify additional stakeholders to invite to meetings and workshops. Individuals who took particular care answering the questionnaire received invitations to a Consensus Building Workshop. Thus the list of stakeholders expanded to include secondary school students, market women, sawmill operators, boat builders, craftspeople, tour guides, taxi drivers, teachers, and engineers, inter alia.

Forestry Department and committee members also solicited input through a series of direct community consultations and individual interviews with stakeholders. Over the next few months, 15 community consultations on forestry policy were held throughout Grenada, including one exclusively for women's groups. The department also sponsored four radio phone-in programs on ecotourism, land use policy, tree-planting and watershed management.

In April 1998, the committee met to discuss the results of the questionnaires, public consultations and radio phone-ins, and to plan the

Consensus Building Workshop. The new forest policy was drafted during the week of the workshop by a subcommittee of the Policy Process Committee consisting of the chief forestry officer, the senior forestry officer, the secretary-general of the Agency for Rural Transformation (a rural development NGO), a representative of the Ministry of Finance, and the head of CANARI. The draft was circulated to the participants in the July workshop, was revised accordingly, and was submitted to Ministry of Agriculture in November. In March the new policy was approved by cabinet. At the public launch of the policy, the prime minister called it an exemplar of participatory management planning.[18]

The ultimate proof of the policy will be its ability to promote sustainable forest use and to continue to incorporate stakeholders in the management of forest resources. The prospects appear to be favorable, and the success of the policy process has already manifested itself in a transformed Forestry Department. Grenada's Forestry Department is now the Department of Forestry and National Parks, representing its new responsibility as primary steward of Grenada's natural heritage. Prior to the policy-planning process, the department had emphasized "timbercentric," technical forestry and was unresponsive to stakeholders who lacked technical expertise or were not direct consumers of forest products. The reorganized department sees itself as service-oriented and makes responsiveness to stakeholders its prime responsibility. Implementation of the new policy has been distributed among senior officers with responsibilities in eight functional areas that define the department's expanded responsibilities: (1) mangroves and coastal woodlands; (2) forest conservation; (3) wildlife conservation; (4) upland watershed management; (5) environmental education; (6) tree establishment and management; (7) forest recreation; and (8) heritage conservation. Policy implementation will be reviewed by a board of 20 stakeholders, only 2 of whom are from the department.

The success of the process has increased the department's dedication to participatory methods and has given it new visibility within the Ministry of Agriculture. To support these developments, DFID has given its adviser in Grenada considerable flexibility and extended its support of the forest policy to the implementation phase.

Scott's Head/Soufriere Marine Reserve (SSMR) and LAMA

Of the three cases considered here, this is arguably the most ambitious since its goal was the formation of a fully autonomous management authority, comprised entirely of stakeholders, with full authority to make rules and enforce them. The area to be managed was a marine reserve encompassing Scott's Head/Soufriere Bay and adjacent coastline on the southeastern tip of the island. It is the primary source of livelihood for three fishing villages (Scott's Head, Soufriere, and Pointe Michel), provides fresh seafood for restaurants and markets in the nearby capital city of Roseau, and is used for recreation by locals and tourists. These direct uses along with run-off from the villages on the steep volcanic hillsides that surround the crescent-shaped bay impact the quality of its waters, the cleanliness of its beaches, its fisheries, and delicate coral reef. Therefore, stakeholders of the marine reserve include fishers, restaurateurs, hoteliers, merchants, dive operators, residents, tourists, and urban consumers.[19]

Funding to manage the marine reserve came from French Technical Cooperation (FTC), the Canadian International Development Agency (CIDA), and the Organization of American States (OAS) under its Inter-American Strategy for Public Participation in Environmental and Sustainable Development Decision Making in the Americas (ISP). FTC was, by far, the largest funding source. Its aid came with requirements for stakeholder inclusion and government accountability, and was supported by on-site advisers. CIDA aid was mainly of a technical nature for specific aspects of the project. The OAS offered the smallest amount but stipulated the most stringent requirements for stakeholder participation, demanding a fully autonomous statutory body of stakeholders, organized and authorized by the Government of Dominica according to a strict timetable.

The external funding came into a process that was already underway. The marine reserve and management authority began as the response of the Fisheries Division of the Ministry of Agriculture to complaints from local fishers that divers and pleasure craft were interfering with their fish pots and beach seining and damaging coral by dropping anchor in the bay. Fisheries Division decided to designate the area as a marine reserve and to establish rules for usage that would protect fishers while allowing other sustainable uses. The bay was declared a no-anchorage zone, was mapped, and was registered for particular uses. Fisheries Division then procured grants from FTC and CIDA to install mooring posts for visiting yachts and to fund educational and organizational activities among the local population. Since Fisheries Division determined that the most effective and cost-efficient way to manage the reserve and obviate conflict was to establish an independent management authority of stakeholders, by the time external funding was sought the Local Area Management Authority (LAMA) had already been conceived.

Fisheries intended that LAMA make all management decisions at the reserve, settle conflicts among stakeholders, and enforce rules and regulations. This latter function was to include the employment of armed wardens who could board watercraft, make arrests, and call in the coast guard when necessary.

Fisheries officers soon realized that the two biggest obstacles to a fully functioning LAMA were a lack of administrative infrastructure in the villages and the low levels of education and awareness of the village-level stakeholders. To address the first problem, the chief fisheries officer convened stakeholders meetings and chaired LAMA until its members could establish functional committees and elect their own officers.[20] In addition, the Fisheries Division offices in Roseau became the temporary "home address" for LAMA. All communications (regular and electronic mail, telephone, fax, and marine radio) to the LAMA board ran through the Fisheries office. The office also became a hub for communications among LAMA members and constituent groups. But by taking a central role in the formation and operations of LAMA, Fisheries raised doubts among local and outside observers about LAMA's autonomy and efficacy.[21]

Fisheries addressed the second problem through an educational program implemented primarily through the local schools, and by instituting a national SSMR Day celebration in Scott's Head village. Innovation and flexibility were required to engage stakeholders with various levels of education, knowledge, interest, and sophistication, including semiliterate fisherman, school children, businesspeople, professionals, and government officials.

Area students took an inventory of garbage found on local beaches to identify the sources of the problem and attended three sessions on conservation of the marine environment at their schools. The aim was to develop cadres of environmentally aware youth who could help change some of the nonsustainable behaviors of the community and convince their elders to cooperate in the management of the reserve.

Fisheries officers considered fishers the most difficult stakeholders to incorporate into the new management scheme. They were among the least educated groups in Dominica and had generally been neglected by government development programs. To address the communication problem created by low levels of literacy, Fisheries Division organized public meetings in the village squares on Sunday afternoons and gave secondary school students the task of coming up with slogans, sayings, or other ways of reaching the fishers, both in English and Creole Patois (the first language of many rural Dominicans). The students wrote and performed a skit. Fisheries

Division provided them with the equipment they needed and rum to coax the fishermen to attend.

This first public information campaign proved reasonably successful, and Fisheries Division has followed up with annual SSMR Day activities. Fisheries officers visit schools one month before the celebration to teach the students about the marine environment and issues concerned with fisheries. They hold a quiz competition on the radio. This event is funded by local businesses that donate money to cover expenses, and they also provide prizes. On SSMR Day all school children congregate at the marine reserve for the final quiz contest.

FTC took a keen interest in the educational activities. It assigned five officers over a period of four years and substantial funding to work with Fisheries on educational programs and oversaw much of the technical work related to protection of the marine environment. CIDA funds also helped in the production of TV and radio programs, pamphlets, slide presentations, and posters. As a result the public was barraged with information on the need for maintaining marine resources through environmental protection. Building on a relatively strong tradition of local government, Fisheries also made sure that the village councils got involved. But fisheries officers believe that the students were key to sensitizing the community.[22]

Despite the apparent success of the education programs, LAMA has experienced difficulties that it has thus far been unable to surmount. These difficulties, which had effectively incapacitated LAMA at the time that this research was completed, were the combined results of demands made by external funding agencies and a lack of trust between these agencies and the government, and between the government and LAMA.

By June 1998 LAMA had elected its first president and board of directors, all the functional committees were in place, and the chief fisheries officer was beginning to devolve his leadership role. LAMA represents eight categories of stakeholders: (1) fishermen's organizations; (2) village councils; (3) boy scouts and girl guides; (4) hospitality industry entities; (5) community groups; (6) the Dominica Watersports Association; (7) the Fisheries Division; and (8) the Dominica Police Force Marine Section. From these categories representatives of 15 different associations, departments, and businesses were elected to a management board (LAMA Management Board), which was broken down into four sector committees: (1) education; (2) operations and development; (3) scientific and research; and (4) finance. The management board elected a chair, vice chair, treasurer, and two trustees to one-year renewable terms. The first chair is a medical doctor and local dive operator.

Although the board and the committees met regularly and made significant progress in developing plans of action, thus far they accomplished little. The main obstacle is funding. Although FTC allocated sufficient funds for LAMA to begin its operations (approximately $225,000), and the OAS promised an additional $45,000, FTC has withheld the majority of its funds, and the OAS withdrew from the project in May 1998. This lack of funding has made it impossible for LAMA to recruit, train and hire wardens, arguably its most important function and the most tangible expression of its authority and autonomy. Without wardens LAMA can exist but not function. LAMA was designed to be self-financing. It would have to raise funds, including salaries, from the sale of the dive permits. Dominica Watersports Association members collect the permit fees from their clients. Wardens were to collect fees from independent divers entering the reserve.

The small grant, originally offered by the OAS (through ISP) early in 1998, was earmarked to support the legal and legislative process leading to the full official designation of LAMA as an independent management authority. Conditions were very explicit, requiring a completed legislative process according to a strict timetable (OAS 1998). The ISP project team quickly became frustrated with having to work through the Fisheries Division and felt that the government was dragging its feet on granting LAMA full legal authority. ISP staff monitored compliance with its guidelines with two short visits to Dominica. When, during the second visit, a scheduled meeting with LAMA failed to materialize the ISP project manager began to doubt LAMA's existence.[23] The Dominican government felt that the OAS was unrealistic and impatient, and set arbitrary standards of success that were inappropriate to the political context. The fisheries officers argued that the OAS refused to recognize anything short of full cabinet and parliamentary ratification LAMA's charter, and ignored the substantial progress made through *ad hoc* methods and informal channels. To further complicate matters for the OAS, FTC refused to work with any other international agencies. Frustrated with what they considered to be a lack of progress, the OAS withdrew, leaving considerable resentment among the fisheries officers, but making little impact on the other members of LAMA.[24]

OAS withdrawal was a minor setback; the impasse with FTC is a major impediment. FTC took on a more comprehensive role than the OAS, providing the major funding for most of the technical, educational and organization work. An FTC representative attended LAMA meetings, contributed to the planning process, reviewed LAMA proposals, and made inspection tours of the marine reserve. But in guiding the development of LAMA, FTC advocated a replication of a local management authority they had recently helped establish in St. Lucia; a point of contention for some fisheries officers and local stakeholders.[25]

To optimize compliance with its conditions, FTC planned to disburse funds to LAMA gradually over a three-year period. As this research was completed, the disbursement period had ended with more than half of the funds yet to be released; and LAMA had not met for six months. Both the Fisheries Division and LAMA agree that FTC's decision to suspend payments kept LAMA from fulfilling its mission. But they disagree as to why FTC took that action or who is to blame. Interestingly, neither fault FTC; instead they fault each other.

LAMA members characterize their relations with the Fisheries Division as constructive, but they emphasize one critical failure of government. Although the government authorized the levying of fees for dive permits and the SSMR Management Plan makes those fees the main sources of funding for LAMA, the government did not officially authorize LAMA's wardens to collect the fees. Without the ability to collect fees, LAMA remained dependent on government. LAMA officials believe that FTC insisted on full authorization for the wardens because it did not trust the government-of-the-day. The chair of the management board agreed with FTC, stating that "beyond a reasonable doubt, if the money had gone to *this* government, they would have spent it on something else, and the French know this."[26]

The official position of the Fisheries Division is that FTC objected to certain unspecified methods of operation used by LAMA, and is withholding funds until the situation can be remedied. Fisheries Division concurs that they have a good relationship with LAMA. Its officers remain optimistic that LAMA will soon be able to fulfill its mandate and maintain that all the necessary statutes have been gazetted for LAMA and that cabinet and parliamentary approval are imminent.

According to board members, LAMA still exists (although regular meetings have been suspended). In addition, the SSMR has been mapped and zoned, signs have been posted, rules and regulations for its use appear in the official gazette of the Government of Dominica, and SSMR Day continues to be popular annual event. The chair of the LAMA Management Board was reelected, and claims that LAMA is working with local organizations of fishers to improve their ability to participate in management decisions. In the meantime, the Dominica Watersports Association is attempting to accelerate the process of training and hiring wardens by donating the proceeds from its annual Dive Fest (an annual recreational and educational event promoting ecotourism) to LAMA.[27]

Summary of Findings

Conclusions based on three cases can only be suggestive. We can see that participatory methodologies clearly inform the efforts of certain development assistance agencies and that the policy content and methods of the new conditionality do affect the choice of participatory model used in recipient states. We can also say something about the relationship between the structural autonomy of participatory arrangements and their effectiveness. But our ability to generalize about the relationship between the policies and methods of these agencies and effective stakeholder participation is still limited.

In the following sections I summarize findings from each case study with respect to the three variables identified at the beginning of this paper: (1) the content and methods of conditionality; (2) methods of stakeholder inclusion; and (3) the structural autonomy of the participatory arrangements.

The Content and Methods of Conditionalilty

Agenda 21 provided impetus for broad-based participatory mechanisms that would not have developed (as rapidly) otherwise. In the case of the Sustainable Development Councils, local NGOs and government officials concerned with sustainability and participation valued the catalyzing effect of Agenda 21 and the funding available through Capacity 21. But that was not enough to establish viable institutions. The task set before the SDCs was virtually impossible with the available funding, and without a level of political authority that could not possibly be granted by, or achieved through association with, external funding agencies. Resistance from private sector and government interests vested in existing development policies delayed full institutionalization of the councils even though they were stipulated and supported by development assistance agencies and international agreements—an interesting contrast to the political effects of the old, neoliberal conditionality.

In Grenada, the influence of Agenda 21, DFID funding, and external training contributed to a highly participatory National Forest Policy. The previous forest policy process had not included participatory methods and had not led to a usable, let alone sustainable, approach to forest management. Although we may conclude that participation benefited from external support, we stretch the definition of conditionality too far if we characterize DFID's support for stakeholder participation as a condition of funding. DFID originally offered support for a forestry project, not a participatory policy process.

Nevertheless, DFID's activities in Grenada contain lessons for development assistance agencies wishing to make stakeholder participation a condition of their support. By contributing not just funding but also equipment, training and on-site advice, DFID nurtured a growing commitment to stakeholder participation among Grenadian foresters.[28] DFID, through the urgings of its on-site adviser, responded to Grenadian interest in a different kind of forest policy. The Grenada Forestry Department, in turn, used DFID support to cultivate support within government and make alliances with the private sector, NGOs, and interested communities. Thus, the commitment to participatory methods became authentically Grenadian, and the techniques developed and implemented by Forestry Department officials and the Forest Policy Process Committee were appropriate and effective. By attracting both external and domestic support the department was able to bring the government along, rather than be stifled by resistance from reluctant ministries, rival agencies, and their private sector allies.

In the Scott's Head/Soufriere Marine Reserve and the Local Area Management Authority we see some of the features of each of the other two cases. The idea for a marine reserve managed by local stakeholders was initiated locally, with the direct involvement of the responsible government agency and learning from a successful case in St. Lucia. But the external support needed for the project carried explicit conditions as to methods and outcomes.

The CIDA grant was earmarked for specific functions that had been determined by the Fisheries Division, and it seems to have been disbursed and spent effectively without undue influence by the funding agency. The OAS involvement, however, displayed a problematic combination of specific demands and weak support. The OAS commitment to substantive stakeholder participation was no less sincere than that of the DFID adviser in Grenada. But rather than providing sufficient support for the establishment of constructive alliances with stakeholders, OAS/ISP involvement came to be viewed by fisheries officers as a source of unwelcome pressure to accelerate and formalize a delicate process already underway. By attempting to monitor and support compliance with short site visits, the OAS failed to develop the necessary relationships of trust with local actors.

The conditions of FTC involvement, like those of CIDA, seem to have reflected the goals of the Fisheries Division and LAMA. While the OAS came in with a hemispheric initiative and a set of predetermined performance criteria, FTC provided funding for a project designed by Fisheries and LAMA. After that, FTC conditionality involved trying to assure that LAMA did, in fact, become a self-sustaining, fully empowered, and autonomous management agency.

FTC maintained an on-site presence and provided technical and financial support. In addition, it established itself as judge of the propriety of government actions, refused to work with other funding agencies, and maintained financial veto power over the project. Whether or not FTC mistrust of the Dominican government was well founded cannot be proven with the data available. But its decision to halt funding shows the negative side of the kind of relationship that worked so well in Grenada. Simply put, the agency providing support took too direct a role in pursuit of *its own* goals.

Methods of Stakeholder Inclusion

Effective methods of stakeholder identification and preparation are essential. In addition, the organizational structures and procedures used must be appropriate to local political conditions. Agenda 21 recognizes the importance of careful stakeholder identification and education, but in the case of the SDCs, Capacity 21 funding was not adequate to the task. Dominica had two advantages that should have helped make its SDC viable: (1) a relatively well-developed system of local government; and (2) a National Association of Nongovernmental Organisations (NANGO) ready to participate in the SDC. However, neither proved adequate to compensate for the shortcomings of SDC methodology. NANGO was understaffed and not considered adequately representative by the entire NGO community. Local governments could not help overcome the resistance from the national ministries and governmental agencies that refused to cooperate with the SDC. In short, grassroots actors lacked the capacity to participate in formal venues that could be easily dominated by government and business interests, and support for building such capacity was missing from Capacity 21.

The Grenada National Forest Policy contains important lessons about methods of stakeholder inclusion. The planning process took a broad approach to stakeholder identification and allowed opportunities for stakeholders to identify themselves. The Forest Policy Process Committee was not particularly successful in its school-based educational activities, which is usually critical to successful participatory processes, but it compensated by using the media, public consultations, capable consultants, churches, and local NGOS, and offering incentives for participation. Overall, the committee succeeded in garnering wide input and establishing trust.

The policy-making process created opportunities for substantive stakeholder input at the earliest stages. Stakeholders could affect the process before it affected them. The support and influence of DFID and CANARI were important for developing goals and methods, but it was the efforts of the Forestry Department that did most to spread a participatory ethos among stakeholders. Participation also included opportunities to revise both the policy and the process as they developed, and promised opportunities for participatory management of the policy once implemented.

The Dominican Fisheries Division had its greatest successes at SSMR with stakeholder identification and preparation. Educational programs made effective use of existing resources, especially the schools. Fisheries supported efforts by village youth to develop effective programs aimed at their communities. The roster of member organizations in LAMA appears comprehensive. LAMA officials reported fairly good working relationships among people of various backgrounds and from various walks of life. Cooperation between the dive operators and the fishers, the two groups with the greatest potential for conflict, proved difficult but some progress was made. It also seems that the chief fisheries officer allowed leadership to devolve to the LAMA Management Board and committees in a timely manner.

THE STRUCTURAL AUTONOMY OF PARTICIPATORY ARRANGEMENTS

By design and intent, the SDCs should rank high on a scale of autonomy from external and government control. They were situated outside of regular departments, ministries, and agencies and were made up of a majority of private sector and NGO members. Capacity 21 and ancillary funding came with minimal oversight. But the SDCs' autonomy from government actually seems to have undermined their ability to act as venues for effective stakeholder participation. In the Westminster-style parliamentary systems of the Eastern Caribbean, the inability to affect decisions at the cabinet level is debilitating. SDC directors found little support for their efforts to insert themselves into the policy-making process. And unlike the Grenada case, training and in-kind support for grassroots activities was not available to counter political marginalization.

There may be hope for greater effectiveness if SDCs can be converted into sustainable development units. These units (one is currently in operation in St. Lucia) are located within ministries that have substantive responsibility for development policy and have official standing on par with other ministerial departments. Thus, the units may have greater ability than the SDCs to "mainstream" considerations of sustainability and stakeholder participation in the overall policy-making processes of their governments.

The Grenada National Forest Policy ranks relatively low on any measure of autonomy. It was, after all, a policy-making process initiated by and for government. It worked, however, because the responsible government department internalized the values of sustainability and participation and used participatory methods to gain allies within government, the private sector, and the NGO community. The cabinet and prime minister neither supported nor interfered with the process as it unfolded. The Forestry Department eventually won their support through persuasion, success in obtaining external support, and by gaining the recognition of international organizations, regional NGOs, and noted environmental scientists. DFID provided substantial support that helped build local capacity for effective participation. The presence of a DFID adviser may be taken as an indication of a low level of autonomy from the development assistance agency as well. But the adviser did not direct, evaluate, or intercede in the process; he merely facilitated.

If LAMA had been able to collect fees and employ wardens, then it would have been the most autonomous of the cases examined in this chapter. In addition, the plan to disburse FTC funds incrementally, according to a flexible, multiyear schedule would have allowed LAMA to increase its autonomy as it increased its capacity. But autonomy has little meaning without capacity.

Similar to the Grenadian Forest Policy, a close and tutelary relationship with a government agency was essential in creating the conditions for effective participation. Without the support and guidance of the Fisheries Division, LAMA would not exist. However, the continued ability of the government to deny LAMA full statutory responsibility for fee collection and enforcement—after stakeholders were identified, prepared, and included in a participatory process—has jeopardized the ability of local stakeholders to manage the reserve. The government's failure increased LAMA's already substantial dependence on FTC funding and decision making.

Conclusions

Conditions established by development assistance agencies are having noticeable effects on the use of participatory methods for sustainable development. While there is still cause to doubt the sincerity and efficacy of agencies that demand stakeholder inclusion, there is also reason to believe that they can play a positive role. Support for effective stakeholder participation can be found in a range of development assistance agencies, including the OAS, French Technical Cooperation, British DFID, the GEF, and the World Bank.

But there are effective and ineffective ways of promoting participation. Efficacy depends a great deal on how the conditions for participation are set, presented, supported, and monitored, and on the distribution of power, levels of education and state-civil society relations in the recipient country.

Four explanatory variables stand out. Three were identified at the beginning of this chapter: (1) conditionality; (2) methods of stakeholder identification, preparation, and inclusion; and (3) the structural relationships among stakeholders, the recipient government, and the funding agencies. A fourth, which appears in all three cases examined here, is leadership. Perhaps because of the small populations of St. Lucia, Dominica, and Grenada, and the limited human resources to lead transformation processes, critically placed individuals can make a difference. But effective leadership in these cases is quiet leadership.

Identifying the critical variables, of course, mainly locates the areas of uncertainty associated with the new conditionality and does not necessary provide a formula for overcoming uncertainty. The positive changes noted above could prove fleeting. Under the presidency of James Wolfensohn (1995–2005), the World Bank allowed task teams to exercise some discretion in applying formal, but vague, environmental and participatory conditionalities. The World Bank's role as funder of IMF structural adjustment packages put it in a position to provide capital for more sustainable projects and to mitigate some of the environmental effects of structural adjustment. The World Bank also tended to set the tone for regional development banks and some bilaterals. Thus, to the extent that the World Bank supported environmental and participatory conditionalities, the uncertain effects of neoliberalism on the environment and democracy were made even more uncertain but potentially less harmful. As this chapter is being written, however, a new president takes the reins at the World Bank. Paul Wolfowitz comes to the bank as the selection of the U.S. President George W. Bush, whose administration has refused to accept global warming as scientific fact, has opted out of the Kyoto treaty on climate change, and has weakened enforcement of federal environmental law in the United States. Whether Mr. Wolfowitz will bring this orientation to the World Bank or build on the legacy of his predecessor is unknown at this time.

Furthermore, neither new conditionalities nor globalization have erased the structural uncertainties faced by small island developing states in the Caribbean. Any successes catalyzed by the new conditionalities could be quickly affected by a number of persistent factors. For example, populations in the English-speaking Caribbean tend to be highly mobile. Principals in local stakeholder groups, therefore, may leave to pursue employment opportunities in other parts of the Caribbean, Canada, the United States, and the United Kingdom. On the other hand, members of diaspora communities do frequently return home bringing with them political ideas and skills relevant to participatory practices and sustainability. The region also continues to experience a great deal of uncertainty from the interaction of global ecological and economic trends. Sea level rise associated with global climate change threatens sensitive coastal areas. Local observers note increasingly intense storm surges eroding beaches and accelerating the destruction of already threatened coral reefs (Grenada National Climate Change Committee 2001, 21–36). Such developments challenge the ability of Caribbean states to generate revenues from highly competitive tourism markets (both conventional and ecotourism), cause agricultural and infrastructural damage, discourage private investment, and divert resources from participatory environmental management and sustainable development to disaster relief and mitigation.[29]

The new conditionality promises substantive changes in the connections between development assistance and environmental sustainability. But for the natural environmental and grassroots democracy in the Eastern Caribbean, uncertainty has been changed, not eliminated. Under globalization the potential for environmental disasters and the failure of grassroots democracy are enhanced. At the same time, environmental considerations are no longer ignored in development assistance; and grassroots, participatory practices may receive direct support for the contribution they can to the sustainable management of natural resources. Whether these trends are sufficient to positively affect the ecology and the economy of the Eastern Caribbean remains to be seen.

Finally, the cases examined above add nuance to but do not undermine the suggestions of Latin American and Caribbean exceptionalism made by López-Alves and Johnson in their introduction to this volume. Taken as a whole, they observe, the effects of globalization seem to have been less dramatic and the responses more rooted in local political realities in the Americas than in other parts of the erstwhile second and third worlds. This exceptionalism, in fact, is more clearly seen in the Caribbean than in Latin America per se precisely because the region has been embedded in processes of global economic, political, and cultural integration, and ecological transformation for so long. Simply put, the Caribbean is where Columbus landed. The ability of modern Caribbean states and societies to adjust to global uncertainties, therefore, is conditioned by long experience at absorbing, responding to, and domesticating the effects of high volumes of foreign trade and investment, cultural hybridization, and democratic aspirations. Late twentieth-century neoliberalism, the end of the cold war, and new global social movements converged to create new types of uncertainty for Caribbean states. Small states, still dependent on official development assistance for significant portions of their financial flows, are being pulled in new political directions by external and internal pressures to take the environment into account. Globalization and environmental catastrophe may yet undermine the democratic polities of the Eastern Caribbean but thus far, as in the rest of Latin America, political leaders and grassroots actors have shown themselves capable of realizing opportunities as well as threats from the new challenges.

Notes

1. Portions of the research for this chapter were supported by the National Science Foundation under grant no. OPP-9725600. Any opinions, findings, and conclusions or recommendations expressed in this material are those of the author and do not necessarily reflect the views of the National Science Foundation.
2. One informant suggested that World Bank requirements for public consultations were no less a form of conditionality than International Monetary Fund Structural Adjustment Programs (interview with Dr. Vasantha Chase, Director, Natural Resources Management Unit, Organization of Eastern Caribbean States, Castries, St. Lucia, May 29, 1998). Another agreed that his government was looking carefully at "tied" aid and was inclined to reject funding that came with too many conditions. He also noted that there was still a tendency among ministers and technical officers to view public consultation as interference in the timely execution of needed projects (interviews with Christopher Corbin, Ministry of Planning, Development and Environment, Government of St. Lucia, Castries St. Lucia, May 29, 1998 and May 31, 1999).
3. Interviews with David Simmons Manager, Waste Management Project, Organization of Eastern Caribbean States, Castries, St. Lucia, May 28, 1999 and Rolax Frederick, Senior Forestry Officer, Forestry Department, Ministry of Agriculture, St. George's, Grenada, June 9, 1998.
4. While globalization and democratization are not mutually exclusive, sovereignty is a necessary component of democracy. See Phillippe C. Schmitter and Terry Lynn Karl, "What Democracy Is . . . and Is Not," *Journal of Democracy* 2 (8) (Summer 1991): 75–88.

5. Interview with Dr. Vasantha Chase, Director, Natural Resources Management Unit, Organization of Eastern Caribbean States, Castries, St. Lucia, May 29, 1998.
6. Interview with Ussamah Dabbagh, Task Manager, OECS Solid Waste Management Project, World Bank Environmental Department, Washington, DC, March 19, 1998; telephone interview with Ussamah Dabbagh, Washington, DC, February 17, 1998.
7. Telephone interview with Yves Renard, Director, CANARI, Vieux Forte, St. Lucia, June 2, 1998.
8. Interviews with Valma R. Jessamy, CEO, Jessamy Environmental Consulting and Research, Concord, St. John's, Grenada, June 8, 1998; Henry Shillingford, Programme Director, Dominica Conservation Association, Roseau, Dominica, June 8, 1999; and Atherton Martin, Director, Dominica Conservation Association, May 26, 1998.
9. Interviews with Paul Butler, Director, Environmental Education, RARE Center for Tropical Conservation, Castries, St. Lucia, May 31, 1998 and June 3, 1999 and George Ledec, Senior Ecologist, Environmentally and Socially Sustainable Development Latin America and Caribbean Region, Washington, DC, May 20, 1999.
10. A more detailed examination of the Eastern Caribbean experience with Sustainable Development Councils can be found in Jonathan Rosenberg and Linus Spencer Thomas, "Participating or Just Talking? Sustainable Development Councils and the Implementation of Agenda 21," *Global Environmental Politics* 5 (2) (2005): 61–87.
11. The SDCs and sustainable development units in Dominica, St. Lucia, and Grenada were designed to conform to Agenda 21 specifications. Interviews with Christopher Corbin, Castries, St. Lucia, May 29, 1998 and May 31, 1999; Gerard Hill, Coordinator, Sustainable Development Council, Roseau, Dominica, May 21, 1998; and the author's observation of a meeting of the Grenada Sustainable Development Council, St. George's, Grenada, June 18, 1999.
12. The following discussion is based on interviews with Gerard Hill cited above and the "Terms of Reference for the Sustainable Development Council," unpublished government document (Roseau: Government of Dominica, n.d.).
13. The Grenada National Forest Policy process and the Scott's Head/Soufriere Marine Reserve are also examined in Jonathan Rosenberg, "Sustainable Development of Biodiversity Resources in the Eastern Caribbean: Triple Alliances and Policy Implementation," *Journal of International Wildlife Law and Policy* 9 (2006): 1–17.
14. The National Forest Policy was jointly funded by DFID and the Government of Grenada. Since no breakdown of costs has been made, it is difficult to determine which source contributed more (e-mail correspondence with Robert Dunn, DFID Forestry Adviser, Forestry Department, St. George's, Grenada, May 31, 2000).

TOWARD A NEW CONDITIONALITY? 173

15. Forestry Department, "Grenada's Forest Policy Development Process," St. George's, Grenada (photocopy), n.d.; Forestry Department, "Non-Legally Binding Authoritative Statement of Principles for a Global Consensus on the Management, Conservation and Sustainable Development of All Types of Forests," St. George's, Grenada (photocopy), n.d.
16. Interview with Robert Dunn, St. George's, Grenada, June 23, 1999.
17. Unless otherwise noted, the following description of events comes from the following interviews and documents: interview with Rolax Frederick, Acting Chief Forestry Officer, St. George's, Grenada, June 9, 1998; interview with Alan Joseph, Chief Forestry Officer and Robert Dunn, DFID Forestry Adviser, St. George's Grenada, June 15, 1999; interview with Robert Dunn, St. George's, Grenada, June 23, 1999; Forest Policy Drafting Committee, "Forest Policy for Grenada, Carriacou and Petit Martinique," St. George's, Grenada, Forestry Department (photocopy), 1998; Robert Dunn, "Grenada's Participatory Forest Policy Development Process: Empowerment through Appropriate Support," St. George's, Grenada (photocopy), n.d.; and Forestry Department, "Proposed 10-year Strategic Plan for the Forestry Department: 1st January, 2000 to 31st December, 2009," St. George's, Grenada (photocopy), 1999.
18. CANARI is a regional NGO and a leader in the use of participatory methods of natural resources management. Mr. Renard's participation was funded by DFID (e-mail correspondence with Robert Dunn, May 30, 2000).
19. *The Grenadian Voice Internet Edition*, April 16, 1999, "New National Forestry Policy approved by Cabinet," 18 (6).
20. This and the following description of events come from an interview with Harold Guiste, Fisheries Officer, Fisheries Division of the Ministry of Agriculture and the Environment, Roseau, Dominica, June 22, 1998 and from Nigel Lawrence, Andrew Magloire, and Harold Guiste's "Soufriere/Scott's Head Marine Reserve Management Plan," unpublished government document(Roseau, Dominica: Fisheries Division of the Ministry of Agriculture and the Environment, n.d.).
21. Interview with Kris Simelda, Chair, LAMA Education Committee, Scott's Head, Dominica, June 12, 1999.
22. This view was expressed by informants outside of LAMA and the Fisheries Division (interview with Henry Shillingford, Programme Director, Dominica Conservation Association, Roseau, Dominica, June 8, 1999; telephone interview with Zoila Girón, Project Manager, ISP, OAS, Washington, DC, April 16, 1998 and personal interview, May 19, 1999). One LAMA member confirmed that this impression may have been warranted in 1998 (interview with William Lawrence, Executive Secretary, Dominica Watersports Association, Roseau, Dominica, June 10, 1999).
23. Interviews with Harold Guiste, William Lawrence, and Kris Simelda confirm this assessment. But in 1999, the Programme Director the Dominica Conservation Association was unaware of SSMR Day.

24. Telephone interviews with Zoila Girón, April 16, 1998 and personal interview, May 19, 1999.
25. Interviews with Harold Guiste, June 22, 1998 and June 7, 1999. The fisheries officer's assessment of OAS handling of the situation was confirmed by an OAS official familiar with the situation who has requested anonymity.
26. This marine protected area, also called Soufriere, is managed by an autonomous stakeholders' association that was developed under the guidance of Yves Renard of CANARI and is considered a model of its kind for the region.
27. Interview with Dr. V. Moise, Chair of Management Board, LAMA, Soufriere, Dominica, June 12, 1999. This negative assessment of the government, including accusations of corruption was echoed by three other well-positioned informants who prefer to remain anonymous.
28. Interview with William Lawrence, Executive Secretary, Roseau, Dominica Watersports Association, June 10, 1999.
29. The extent to which commitment developed independent of, or prior to DFID involvement cannot be fully determined from the research done for this paper.

References

Agarwal, Anil, and C. C. Gibson. 1999. "Enchantment and Disenchantment: The Role of the Community in Natural Resource Conservation." *World Development* 27 (4): 629–649.

Bass, Stephen. 2000. *Participation in the Caribbean: A review of Grenada's forest policy process.* London: International Institute for Environment and Development.

Bryner, Gary C. 1999. "Agenda 21: Myth or Reality?" In *The Global Environment: Institutions, Law, and Policy,* edited by Norman J. Vig and Regina S. Axelrod. Washington, DC: Congressional Quarterly Press.

Chambers, Robert. 1993. *Challenging the Professions: Frontiers for Rural Development.* London: Intermediate Technology Publications.

———. 1995. "NGOs and Development: The Primacy of the Personal." *Institute of Development Studies Working Paper 14.* Brighton: University of Sussex.

Department for International Development. 1999. *Shaping Forest Management: How Coalitions Manage Forests.* London: DFID.

Ferguson, James. 1990. *Grenada: Revolution in Reverse.* London: Latin American Bureau.

Fiorino, Daniel J. 1996. "Environmental Policy and the Participation Gap." In *Democracy and the Environment: Problems and Prospects,* edited by William M. Lafferty and James Meadowcroft. Cheltenham, UK and Brookfield, US: Edward Elgar.

Global Environment Facility (Fondo para el Medio Ambiente Mundial, FMAM). 1996. *Participación del Público en los Proyectos Financiados por el FMAM*. Washington, DC: Fondo para el Medio Ambiente Mundial.
Grenada National Climate Change Committee. 2001. *First National Communication on Climate Change*. St. George's, Grenada: Caribbean Planning for Adaptation to Global Climate Change Project.
Hardin, Garrett. 1968. "The Tragedy of the Commons." *Science* 162 (3859): 1243–1248.
Hunter, David. 1996. "The Role of the World Bank in Strengthening Governance, Civil Society, and Human Rights." In *Lending Credibility: New Mandates and Partnerships for the World Bank*, edited by P. Bosshard, C. Heredia, D. Hunter, and F. Seymour. Washington, DC: The World Wildlife Fund.
Janicke, Martin. 1996. "Democracy as a Condition for Environmental Policy Success: The Importance of Non-Institutional Factors." In *Democracy and the Environment: Problems and Prospects*, edited by William M. Lafferty and James Meadowcroft. Cheltenham, UK: Edward Elgar Publishing, Ltd.
Keily, Ray. 1998. "Neo-Liberalism Revised? A Critical Account of World Bank Concepts of Good Governance and Market Friendly Intervention." *Capital and Class* (64) (Spring): 63–88.
Lipschuz, Ronnie D. 1996. *Global Civil Society and Global Environmental Governance: The Politics of Nature from Place to Planet*. Albany: State University of New York Press.
Miller, Marian A. L. 1998. "Sovereignty Reconfigured: Environmental Regimes and Third World States." In *The Greening of Sovereignty in World Politics*, edited by Karen T. Litfin. Cambridge, MA and London: MIT Press.
OAS (Organization of American States). 1998. *Draft Implementation Plan: Inter-American Strategy for Public Participation in Environment and Sustainable Development Decision-Making in the Americas (ISP)*. Washington, DC: Organization of American States.
Ostrom, Elinor. 1990. *Governing the Commons: the Evolution of Institutions for Collective Action*. Cambridge, UK: Cambridge University Press.
Partridge, William L. 1994. *People's Participation in Environmental Assessment in Latin America: Best Practices. LATEN Dissemination Note #11*. Washington, DC: World Bank Latin America Technical Department, Environment Unit.
Rajagopal, Balakrishnan. 2000. "From Resistance to Renewal: The Third World, Social Movements, and the Expansion of International Institutions." *Harvard International Law Journal* 41 (2) (Spring): 529–578.
Reed, David. 1997. "The Environmental Legacy of Bretton Woods: The World Bank." In *Global Governance: Drawing Insights from the Environmental Experience*, edited by Oran R. Young. Cambridge, MA and London: MIT Press.
Rich, Bruce. 1994. *Mortgaging the Earth: The World Bank, Environmental Impoverishment, and the Crisis of Development*. Boston: Beacon Press.

Rosenberg, Jonathan, and Fae L. Korsmo. 2001. "Local Participation, International Politics, and the Environment: The World Bank and the Grenada Dove." *Journal of Environmental Management* 62 (July): 283–300.

Singh, Kelvin. 2002. "Globalisation and the Caribbean: A Five Hundred-year Perspective." In *Caribbean Survival and the Global Challenge*, edited by Ramesh Ramsaran. Boulder CO: Lynne Reinner.

United Nations Environmental Programme. 2001. *Agenda 21: Environment and Development Agenda*, http://www.unep.org/Documents/Default.asp?DocumentID=52.

United Nations Environmental Programme. 1994. *Report of the Global Conference on the Sustainable Development of Small Island Developing States*, http://www.unep.ch/islands/dsidschf.htm.

World Bank. 1996. *The World Bank Participation Sourcebook*. Washington, DC: World Bank.

———. 1998. "Operational Policy 4.01: Environmental Assessment." In *The World Bank Operational Manual*. Washington, DC: World Bank, 1998.

PART 3

UNCERTAINTIES ABOUT HUMAN RIGHTS AND JUSTICE

In this final section, the authors consider how globalization can alter our understandings of critical concepts in significant ways. The chapters focus on two of the most important themes in contemporary political discourse: the notions of human rights and justice.

Steven Cassedy examines the ways in which globalization has led to changes in our conception of human rights. Like David Rock in part 1, Cassedy takes a long-term view of globalization, starting in the late nineteenth century. During that period, the notion developed that rights flow to individuals as members of the human family, and are guaranteed and enforced both by their own nation and ultimately the international community. Moreover, Cassedy contends that Latin America played a key role in this process. He connects the overall historical and theoretical evolution of human rights to the history of Latin America and provides a framework of analysis that allows us to relate this crucial topic to globalization and uncertainty.

In the final chapter, Thomas Siemsen reevaluates our ideas of justice in light of the changes wrought by globalization. He argues that global markets impose their own order on societies. Specifically as globalization has progressed, the notions of crime and punishment have taken on new meanings. Siemsen stresses that this development has occurred in the context of growing uncertainty. Along with other contributors to this volume, he notes that while it seems clear that the old rules have changed, the new rules are not always evident—creating further uncertainty. In this case, the game's players are not always sure what behavior will bring about punishment or reward.

7

GLOBALIZATION AND THE MODERN CONCEPTION OF HUMAN RIGHTS

Steven Cassedy

The first wave of globalization, as other chapters in this volume show, has as its material base the revolutions in transportation and communication that marked the increasingly industrialized West in the nineteenth century. Whether the term globalization refers to international markets or to ideas, it is inconceivable in its modern sense without the movement of people, goods, words, and eventually images at speeds unimaginable before the first half of the nineteenth century. So it is not surprising that the modern conception of human rights, international to the core, took shape in an era when the first wave of globalization reached its peak: in the last years of the nineteenth century and the early decades of the twentieth.

I think it is safe to say that, in modern political and diplomatic discussions of human rights, no document is regarded as more foundational than the *Universal Declaration of Human Rights*, ratified by the General Assembly of the fledgling United Nations in December 1948. For purposes of this chapter, let us consider the modern conception of human rights to be the one set forth in that document. The conception emerges in three stages.

The initial stage in the process is *cosmopolitan individualism*, in which the individual is defined in relation to the polity (commonwealth, body politic, civil society); in which membership in the polity is (at least in theory) independent of race; and in which individual rights are defined in relation to cosmopolitan principles, that is, they flow from the fact of *being a man* (the gender-specific term was always in use in this era).

The second stage in the process is *nationalism*, in which ideally the individual is defined by race; in which polity and race are coextensive (and called a *nation*), so that membership in the polity is dependent on race; and in which individual rights are defined exclusively in relation to the nation.

The third stage, occurring during the first wave of globalization, is *internationalism*, in which individuals are defined no longer by race but by the transnational category of "human family" (human society); in which nation and race are distinct; and in which the rights that flow to individuals as members of the human family are guaranteed and enforced in the first instance by the nations to which they belong but ultimately (and perhaps only ideally) by the international community. I use the term transnational to mean existing or acting across, or without regard to, recognized national boundaries, and I use the term international to mean existing or operating among and throughout many nations.

Many writers have described the stages, but none have described in any detail the transition from the second to the third.[1] This is the part of the story that illustrates how the emergence of the modern conception of human rights is truly part of a process of globalization. Latin America played a vital role in the process, primarily in the third stage.[2]

I start this chapter by describing the *Universal Declaration of Human Rights* as the culminating moment of the process. I then move on to describe the three historical stages that led to this modern conception.

THE MODERN CONCEPTION AND THE *UNIVERSAL DECLARATION*

The *Declaration* was the work of many groups and of many individuals from many backgrounds. Eleanor Roosevelt, as head of the UN Human Rights Commission, which was charged with creating a document concerning human rights, saw to it that the process would be pluralistic and representative of a broad array of national, political, and cultural traditions. But if we examine the various materials that reveal both the sources of the ideas that found their way into the final document and the process by which it came into being, we can see the emergence of certain themes that took on sufficient strength to survive the lengthy and often rancorous deliberations leading to that final document.[3] In the interest of simplification, I will list three of these themes. In each case, I will describe the form in which the theme occurs in the final document and then comment on how it took shape:

1. While including reference to *peoples* and *races*, the *Universal Declaration* nonetheless largely uncouples these two terms from *nations*, *states*, and *countries* in order to speak of membership in a

"human family." The very first paragraph of the Preamble speaks of "members of the human family." Article 2 announces the entitlement of everyone to the fundamental rights listed in the *Declaration* without distinction of, among other things, race or national origin. In fact, the words race and racial never occur in the *Declaration* except in proximity to the words such as nation, national, or nationality, showing, in their three appearances, a vestigial nationalist association of ethnicity and state. Nation and nationality, however, occur by themselves in a sense apparently synonymous with state (as in member states) or country (as in member countries). Thus the words nation, national, and nationality have taken on a measure of ambiguity, hesitating between an older meaning connecting them with some form of group solidarity (presumably racial or ethnic) and a newer, neutral one. Of the two meanings, the second is certainly the dominant.

One can already see the shift away from nationalism in the planning stages of the *Declaration*. There was virtually unanimous agreement, for instance, on the notion that rights should no longer flow either purely from one's birth as a "man" (since this left vague the larger context of one's status as a "man") or from one's citizenship in an actual sovereign nation, though different documents and different individuals had slightly different notions about exactly where rights should flow from. This is one area in which Latin America made a signal contribution. When the newly formed Organization of American States (OAS) met in Bogotá, Colombia, in 1948 (before the *Universal Declaration* was adopted) and issued the *American Declaration of the Rights and Duties of Man*, the document's framers were careful to state at the outset that "the essential rights of man are not derived from the fact that he is a national of a certain state, but are based upon attributes of his human personality."[4] The *American Declaration*, in its drafting stages, was an important model for the *Universal Declaration*.

The *Universal Declaration* went through six major drafts before the final version was adopted. All but one contains a statement locating the individual in a community that transcends the sovereign nation (though in some cases locating the individual at the same time in the sovereign nation). The draft by John Humphrey, the first director of the Human Rights Division of the UN Secretariat, includes this statement: "Man is a citizen both of his State and of the world." French jurist René Cassin, one of the principal authors of the final document, refers in his draft to "the community of nations" as the protector of fundamental rights and freedoms.

2. Despite this uncoupling, the *Declaration* makes *nationality* a right of the individual. In Article 15, which asserts this right, the word nationality appears to mean little more than country of citizenship. Articles 13–15, which arose in connection with concern over the plight of refugees in the years following World War II, appear to use the words country, "state," and nationality almost interchangeably.

In the drafts of the *Declaration*, there was even wider agreement on the issue of nationality than on the source of the individual's rights. Every document includes the right of the individual to a nationality, though both the discussions that gave rise to the inclusion of this right and the contexts in which the right is asserted in the various documents make clear that nationality means something very different from what the word nation had meant in a nineteenth-century nationalist world (I will discuss this later). To the drafters of the *Declaration*, writing in the aftermath of World War II, nationality had to do with the right to asylum, thus with protection from oppressive regimes and from statelessness. Cassin made this clear when he wrote about the *Declaration* three years after its adoption. He explained the right to nationality by using the French terms *foyer* (place to live), *domicile* (home), *asile* (asylum), *cité* (collectivity, community), and *pays* (country). Nationality, severed from group solidarity in ethnicity or race, was now simply one in a list of places where the individual could belong and be safe.[5]

3. The *Declaration*, owing in large part to Latin American influence, includes "second-generation" rights, that is, social, economic, and cultural rights. In the *Universal Declaration*, the various social and economic rights are defined in connection with "national effort and international co-operation" and "the community." They are never defined in connection with particular nations.

Most accounts of the genesis of the *Universal Declaration* give credit to John Humphrey for introducing these rights, because he included them in his own draft. Articles 35–44 of the Humphrey Draft, which include the right to medical care, education, "socially useful work," good working conditions, an equitable share of the national income, public help, social security, good food and housing, leisure, and participation in cultural life, formed the basis for Articles 22–27 of the final document. Articles 22 through 27 assert the rights to social security, work, equal pay for equal work, just remuneration for work, membership in trade unions, rest and leisure, an appropriate standard of living, "special care and assistance" for mothers and children, education, the use of education for "the full development of the human personality," the right of parents "to choose the kind of education that shall be given to their children," participation in the cultural life of the community, and copyright protection.

But Humphrey did not invent these rights. Credit here goes clearly to Latin America, and the inclusion of the second-generation rights in the final version of the *Universal Declaration* may well represent that region's most significant contribution to modern thinking about human rights. Beginning in early 1945, a group of Latin American nations had been working on rights declarations that culminated in the 1948 Bogotá *Declaration* and in a set of bills presented to the Human Rights Commission. The tradition on which these declarations were based was strongly socialist, and since Humphrey himself was a moderate socialist, he was sympathetic to their provisions. Johannes Morsink has shown that Humphrey found essentially all the ideas for the economic, social, and cultural articles in his draft—and much of the wording as well—in three Latin American documents (from Panama, Chile, and Cuba), in addition to one submitted to the commission by the American Federation of Labor.[6] All four documents formed part of an ultimately unsuccessful effort to include a bill of rights in the overall Charter of the United Nations. In his study, Morsink includes a chart demonstrating the high degree of correlation between the four documents and the Humphrey Draft.[7] And one can easily see by comparing articles 35–44 of the Humphrey Draft with Articles 22–27 of the *Universal Declaration* and with Articles 11–16 of the Bogotá *Declaration* (which, though written after the Humphrey Draft, is the fruit of the same effort that produced the Latin American documents on which Humphrey relied) that there is almost complete agreement among the principles set forth in *these* three documents.

The Latin American documents of the 1940s were themselves founded on a tradition that was a generation, or two, old. Morsink rightly mentions the Mexican constitution of 1917 as an inspiration for later documents that would include social and economic rights.[8] The constitution reflects the ideas of a variety of individuals, but its emphasis on economic and social rights is owing largely to the influence of Ricardo Flores Magón and the Partido Liberal Mexicano (PLM, Mexican Liberal Party). Eleven years before the promulgation of the constitution, this party issued a *Program and Manifesto*. Flores Magón, the president of the party, was very much a product of recent trends in international leftist politics, among them international socialism and the antistatism of Russian anarchist Mikhail Bakunin. One can easily see Flores Magón's hand in the document. The strictly constitutional reforms that the *Program* proposes are without exception designed to limit the power of an oppressive government, something that Bakunin would have favored. But what smacks of socialist thought at the turn of the century are the provisions having to do with education and labor. The party calls for compulsory and universal primary education, education that will be strictly secular, and an increase in the number of schools. It calls for an eight-hour workday, a minimum wage, a ban on labor for children under the age of 14, responsible conduct among employers, Sunday as a day of rest every week, and a number of other reforms. Every single provision under education and labor either found its way into the 1917 constitution or actually called for more than that constitution granted.[9] In his 1993 study of human rights in Mexican constitutionalism (i.e., from 1824 to the end of the twentieth century), Rodolfo Lara Ponte, the fourth commissioner of the Human Rights National Commission of Mexico and one of Mexico's most prominent experts on human rights, identifies the *Program* of the PLM as the source of the ideological tendencies that produced the constitution of 1917.[10]

For each of the social and economic rights contained in the *Universal Declaration*, except the two in Article 27 (cultural life and copyright protection), we can find a close equivalent, if not the identical right, in the Mexican document.[11] The drafters of the *Universal Declaration* do not clearly define the "social security" that appears in Article 22, except to say that it entitles each individual "to realization . . . of the economic, social and cultural rights indispensable for his dignity and the free development of his personality." But if we take Article 22 as enunciating the general principle that underlies Articles 23–27, then we get a good idea of what the phrase social security embraces. The original Mexican constitution does not use the phrase *seguridad social* (social security), but section 123 bears the rubric "Del Trabajo y de la Previsión Social." The phrase is officially translated into English as "Labor and Social Security." Literally translated, it means "Labor and Social Foresight," and it suggests government *planning* (*previsión*) for what will become, from the *recipient's* point of view, social security (in the broad sense of this phrase). The constitution lists a series of rights that we might easily see as equivalent to the rights that Article 22 of the *Universal Declaration* intends by the phrase social security.

Though the rights listed in Articles 23–26 of the *Universal Declaration* do not all appear in exactly the same form in the Mexican constitution, all are present there in at least a similar form. For example, the Mexican constitution does not offer a general right to rest and leisure, but section 123 includes the right of workers to Sunday as a day of rest. It does not explicitly mention an adequate standard of living to which every citizen shall be entitled, but almost all of section 123 is essentially about the right to a decent standard of living for workers and their families. The Mexican constitution also provides for education that is free both in the sense of "free of charge" (*gratuito*) and in the sense of "unconstrained" (*libre*). Naturally this document is a *constitution* and is therefore applicable to a particular state. Some of its provisions, especially the most anticlerical, have as their source circumstances peculiar to revolutionary Mexico. But the social and economic rights reflect a trend that was international in 1917. The specifics about working conditions especially—and, for that matter, the simple fact that social and economic rights are so clearly grounded in the world of wage-labor—show a huge debt to international socialism. One can find the same language and the same demands in countless socialist documents worldwide at this time.

Stage 1: Cosmopolitan Individualism

This stage occurs in the Enlightenment era of social contract theory. For social contract theorists, from Thomas Hobbes to Thomas Jefferson, rights come from nature, which means they are *innate*, which in turn suggests they are universal. But rights are asserted and guaranteed only in the state (commonwealth, civil society, body politic), which arises out of the contractual agreement under which individuals renounce a share of their freedom in order to empower a ruling body, with their consent, to protect them and maintain peace. For these theorists, the state is something quite different from a nation, as that term will be understood in the nineteenth century. While the nation—not in reality, of course, but only ideally—arises naturally as an expression of the character of a people (folk, ethnic group), the state that the Enlightenment philosophers envisioned is, by contrast, an artificial construct—not in the sense that it is accidental and without foundation, but in the sense that it arises out of art or artifice. Hobbes says this quite explicitly at the very beginning of his *Leviathan*, where he likens the commonwealth to a human body: "For by Art is created that great LEVIATHAN called a COMMON-WEALTH, or STATE (in latine, CIVITAS), which is but an Artificiall Man, though of greater stature and strength than the Naturall, for whose protection and defence it was intended; and in which, the *Soveraignty* is an Artificiall *Soul*, as giving life and motion to the whole body."[12] In theory, at least, one may infer from this claim that the commonwealth is independent of race, nation, and ethnicity in the sense in which we understand these terms today.

When Hobbes speaks of a *nation*, as he does at the very end of the introduction to the *Leviathan*, it is clear that he sees nothing more than a gathering of individuals without regard for what the nineteenth century will view as their *national* characteristics. "He that is to govern a whole Nation, must read in himself, not this, or that particular man; but Man-kind."[13] The classic documents of social contract theory are relatively free of references to characteristics of actual nations. Hobbes, for example, mentions the Germans only in order to make a trivial point unrelated to the theoretical concerns of the *Leviathan*.

Among the social contract theorists, there was hardly unanimity on the precise definition of rights and their source. But if one principle was constant, it was that rights, even when they were seen as stemming from nature, were ultimately asserted, defended, and validated within the commonwealth. For Hobbes, the commonwealth comes into being as soon as individuals take their right to govern themselves and give it to a sovereign.[14] Locke distinguishes between the compacts that exist among men in the state of nature and the compact that serves as the foundation of a civil society. But where protection is required beyond what the state of nature can provide is above all in matters of property, for here more power is needed to punish offenders than an individual in the state of nature, serving as "Judge for himself, and Executioner," possesses. And so in civil society we resign "into the hands of the community" our natural power to protect ourselves and our property.[15] Rousseau is quite explicit about the rights we enjoy in a civil society: the social contract is the basis of all rights in the civil state, which, for its part, is the master of all the goods of its members.[16]

The rights that social contracts guarantee are thus *civil* rights, not *human* rights in the modern sense. They may very well already exist in the natural state that precedes the social contract, and they may be fairly specifically spelled out by a given theorist. However, after the institution of the social contract these rights are so closely bound up with the particular civil society in question (even though such a civil society is almost always a pure abstraction for the social contract theorists) that one can hardly speak of a list of specific rights *in civil society* that are universal in the sense of being enforceable outside that society. And yet the rights are *cosmopolitan*, in the sense that they are never bound to a particular, existing *nation*, with its peculiar characteristics (I am distinguishing *cosmopolitan*, as operating outside any national system, from *transnational*, as operating within a national system but cutting across or disregarding boundaries within that system). And they are designed to protect *individuals*, not specially defined groups, even though individuals collectively enter into the social contract.

Social contract theorists did not speak about nations in the nineteenth-century sense of the term, but for those who do they left at least the implicit idea that it is always the business of the particular civil society to make good on rights. For many generations of nationalists, this idea will be explicitly stated at the same time as *nation* both supersedes civil society and takes on its intimate association with race (folk, people).

Stage 2: Nationalism

No one gave stronger and clearer expression to this new trend than Johann Gottlieb Fichte in his *Addresses to the German Nation* (given in occupied Berlin in 1807 and 1808). A decade earlier, in the *Foundations of Natural Right, According to Principles of the Science of Knowledge* (1795–1796), while he had identified certain natural rights that all individuals possess, Fichte had been quite explicit in his insistence that states never have the right to interfere in the affairs of another state in connection with that state's treatment of its own citizens. "Thus every state has the right to judge the legality of another state with whose citizens its own enter into association. This right does not, however, extend—and this is worth remarking—farther than the issue of whether the neighboring state is in a position to enter into an external relation. The inner constitution is of absolutely no concern to another state, and no state has any right of judgment over such a constitution." This is the "reciprocal independence of states."[17]

In the eighth *Address to the German Nation*, Fichte has left behind any eighteenth-century notion of abstract civil societies in which men of indifferent nationality live by the terms of a social contract. A *Volk* is "the totality of men living together in society and constantly engendering themselves from themselves naturally and spiritually, this totality of men existing all together under a certain particular law by which the divine develops out of them."[18] As Fichte had concluded in the fourth *Address*, the Germans are peculiar because, unlike other peoples, they remained in their fatherland instead of migrating, and they speak an unborrowed language uniquely reflective of their character. So his description of fatherland will not strike us as excessive. *Volk* and fatherland, he says, "lie way beyond social order in the ordinary sense of the word," since social order implies little more than "certain rights and internal peace." Social order in this sense is merely a means to what love of fatherland seeks, namely "the blossoming of the eternal and divine in the world." Love of fatherland "must itself govern the state as highest, final, and independent authority," he says, and because this authority needs to bring about internal peace within the state, the natural freedom of individuals will in many respects have to be limited.[19]

How this sentiment (sometimes without the intention of raising racial elements to a dominant position) shaped the political history of Europe in the nineteenth century is a familiar story. Love of fatherland as the "highest, final, and independent authority" is what led to movements of unification, as in Germany and Italy, and movements of secession, as in the Balkans. Fichte's formula—internal peace in the name of the fatherland, even at the cost of individual rights, plus national sovereignty relative to other states, implying noninterference in the internal affairs of other states, even in questions of essential rights—is the ideal toward which nationalism strives, whether it has gathered together a nation/race across existing political borders or whether it has created a new border in order to sever a nation/race's ties with an ethnically/racially foreign regime.

Nation and Race in Transition

The process of globalization by which rights become international requires a transitional phase in which the terms nation and race become unstable, in advance of losing their earlier meanings almost entirely. This phase has its own set of subphases. Initially the connection between race and state becomes more intimate, as the terms *nation, race, people* (*Volk* in German), and (later on) *ethnic group* become increasingly interchangeable. By the late nineteenth century, when racialist thinking was entering what might be described as its pinnacle phase in the West, a state of affairs had emerged in which the use of *race* (or *people*) and *nation* as near synonyms oddly coexisted with the attempt to distinguish them from each other. This was especially true of the group in the West that most clearly exemplified all the ambiguities and complexities of the race/nation issue (and that, as we will see, for this very reason would shortly be one of the groups at the center of the debate over human rights): the Jews. In Russia, which was a glaring example of what we might call today a multiethnic state, the Jews regarded themselves and were regarded by others both as a separate *nation* and as a separate *people*, often without distinction between the terms. In the 1870s, in his personal periodical publication called the *Diary of a Writer*, an older and very cranky Dostoevsky made a number of nasty comments about Russian Jews. When he came to speak of equal rights for Jews (which he oddly both supported and opposed), he insisted that even with such equal rights this group was never likely to give up its *"status in statu"* ("state within a state," or "nation within a nation")—all this in a context in which he unabashedly speaks of the Russian people (*narod*) as distinct from the Jewish people (*narod*).[20]

Four years after Russia's great nationalist writer made these remarks, and only months after he died, circumstances forced the Jews of Russia to confront the race/nation issue with an unwelcome sense of urgency: starting in April 1881, a series of devastating pogroms brought home to the members of this group just how vexed was the question of their racial, national, and civil status. The ideas that resulted from these terrible times and that became snarled together in a bafflingly complicated knot were the necessity to distinguish between *people* and *nation* within Russia, the necessity to establish nationhood or nationality for the Jews either within Russia or elsewhere in the world, and the necessity to obtain equal rights for the Jews in Russia. In one of the few highbrow Russian-language newspapers published in St. Petersburg by and for members of the tiny Jewish intelligentsia, one writer, about a half year after the outbreak of anti-Jewish violence, urges his readers to distinguish between *people* (*narod*) and *nation* (*natsiia*) and laments the situation wherein Jews are reproached for their separateness (for allegedly forming a nation within a nation) while being deprived of legal rights.[21]

Nowhere, perhaps, is the tendency clearer both to link and to distinguish *race* and *nation* than in the bible of racialism, Houston Stewart Chamberlain's *Foundations of the Nineteenth Century*, published in German in 1899 and in English translation in 1910. To begin with, lest there be any doubt about the esteem in which Chamberlain holds the concept, consider this passage, from the section titled "The Meaning of Race": "Race lifts a man up above himself; it confers upon him extraordinary, one might even say supernatural abilities, so greatly do these abilities set him apart from an individual who has emerged from a chaotic jumble of various and sundry peoples."[22] Though Chamberlain is famous, and much vilified, for his contribution to Nazi ideology, in his treatment of race he singles out the Jews for praise, since despite their flaws they have made purity of race their "unshakable fundamental law."[23] But races do not spring from the ground pure and fully formed; they undergo *formation* over time. This is where the concept of *nation* comes in: "Almost always it is the nation, as a political structure, that creates the conditions for the formation of race, or that at least leads to the highest, most individual activities of a race," he says.[24] Race is "an organic living being," so "a strong national union is the safest means of protection against going astray."[25]

Thus in an era when nation-states are increasingly asserting their own sovereignty and, with European colonial penetration into Africa in the 1880s, asserting their sovereignty over non-Europeans regarded as racially inferior, the ideas of race and nation are becoming increasingly unstable. As we will see shortly, rights are the reason, and globalization is the vehicle for this process.

Stage 3: Internationalism, Phase 1

The late eighteenth and nineteenth centuries had already witnessed the rise of at least two rights movements that were, in a restricted sense, international: the women's rights movement and the antislavery movement. In both cases, the victims of rights abuses enjoyed a national or civil status that was, either in reality or by the claims of their champions, ambiguous. The key events of the women's rights movement in Europe and the United States are well known, as is the peculiar history in the United States that brought the women's rights advocates from their intimate association with abolitionism, to a post-Civil War position of relative independence from and even hostility to the Negro rights movement, to an almost exclusive focus on women's voting rights from the end of the nineteenth century till the ratification of the Nineteenth Amendment in 1920.

Bonnie Anderson has recently shown that even in the first half of the nineteenth century the movement was international. Between 1830 and 1860, the years on which her study focuses, there were feminists in the United States and an impressive number of European countries. Globalization, at least in a fairly rudimentary stage, played a large role. Many of the movement's leaders corresponded with each other, something that was now easier to do than in the past owing to improvements in transportation (railroads, steamships) and communication technology (telegraphy, more efficient postal service). Women traveled abroad in connection with the movement, something possible only with improvements in transportation. What is perhaps most significant for the internationalism of the movement, Anderson shows, is that so many of the women involved in it had gotten their start in other movements that were themselves internationalist, chief among them socialism and the antislavery movement. But Anderson also shows how restricted was the internationalism of the women's movements in these early years. Even though feminists from different countries occasionally gathered at conferences and even though there was a great deal of contact between feminists living in different countries, there were no truly international organizations. Moreover, as the movement devoted itself with increasing single-mindedness later in the nineteenth century to the issue of suffrage, it actually became less internationalist, as women focused on voting rights, which is to say *civil* rights in their own countries.[26]

The older movement, and the one that best serves as a transition to the history of human rights in the twentieth century, is the antislavery movement. As early as the mid-eighteenth century Quakers and other groups were meeting in England to speak out against slavery. In 1830, the British and Foreign Anti-Slavery Society was founded. This organization was subsequently renamed the Anti-Slavery International for the Protection of Human Rights, which describes itself today as "the world's oldest human rights organisation."[27] The annual meeting of the British and Foreign Anti-Slavery Society in 1840 featured rhetoric that very much looks forward to what we find in the *Universal Declaration* a century later. The duke of Sussex, speaking as chair of the meeting, referred to the antislavery cause as one that "combined all nations, all religions, and all colours."[28]

The story of the antislavery movement in its early phases contains elements that we find at the turn of the twentieth century, many showing the increasing impact of globalization. Betty Fladeland documented the international character of the movement in her 1972 study of Anglo-American antislavery cooperation.[29] Starting at the end of the eighteenth century, Fladeland shows, there were extensive contacts between Great Britain and the United States. Even in an era before modern means of transportation and communication had emerged, participants in the movement exchanged information across the Atlantic Ocean. Newspaper accounts, lecture tours, and political pamphlets helped spread the word in both nations. Travel between these two nations was common among leaders in the movement. A series of treaties—not all successful in their practical application, to be sure—addressed the national sovereignty problem by authorizing the signatory nations to patrol the seas and enforce bans on the slave trade. The greatest measure of the entire movement's success was the abolition of slavery and the emancipation of slaves (in some cases after the period that Fladeland covers in her book) in Spanish America, French and British colonies, and the United States.

The transition from this movement to, say, the international movement to condemn Belgian atrocities in the Congo at the turn of the twentieth century (which I will speak about later) is easy to see. Slavery was the rights issue, African natives or, to use the term of the day, "negroes" were the victims, moral and religious outrage was the response, and revelation and persuasion were the tactics. The element that was missing, to give the story its full international dimension, was the quantity, immediacy, and type of images of suffering. The primary propaganda tools of the antislavery movement were travelers' accounts and newspaper accounts of atrocities in the West Indies and the Southern United States.[30] Of course, written newspaper accounts of events that had taken place months earlier did not have the impact of photographic images, as in the time of the Belgian occupation of the Congo. This required further technological advances of the sort that gave globalization a major push.

Stage 3: Internationalism, Phase 2

Human rights truly began to be an international issue during the period from the end of the nineteenth century to the first few decades of the twentieth. During these years, the women's rights movement gained international attention as newspapers around the world offered photographic images of British police arresting militant suffragists or printed reports about the brutal forced feeding of suffragists on hunger strikes. In the teens, Europeans could read about the U.S. Congress's efforts to exclude undesirable groups through immigration restrictions. During the entire period, readers around the world could learn of the dozens of lynchings carried out each year in the Southern United States, and in 1915 the London *Times* carried a report of the lynching of a Jew in Georgia. During World War I, readers around the world were treated to gruesome reports of genocide carried out by Ottoman troops against ethnic Armenians. This is also the period when the new revolutionary regime in Mexico promulgated the constitution that clearly reflected, in the many social and economic rights it lists, the principles of international socialism, as I described earlier.

Three cases stand out in this period as particularly emblematic of the dramatic shift taking place in the terms in which human rights were conceived internationally. All three involved conflicts between race and nation, all aroused the passions of an international community, all involved rights that, in the circumstances, had to be defined as human rather than purely civil, and all were transmitted to the Western world through newspapers and other media as burning issues of immediate import. They were the Dreyfus Affair in France, the Belgian occupation of the Congo, and the Mendel Beilis blood libel trial in Russia.

What made the coverage of all this possible was, in a word, globalization, in particular the globalization brought about by advances in communication and journalism technology. Among these advances were the development of the high-speed cylindrical rotary press (1865), the introduction of electricity into the printing process (1884), and the invention of linotype (first used in 1886), all of which aided in increasing the circulation of newspapers. The introduction of the cinema in 1895 provided a new medium for the dissemination of images. It is certainly worth noting incidentally that the film said to be the world's first docudrama, *L'Affaire Dreyfus* by pioneer French Director Georges Méliès (probably best known for his fanciful *Trip to the Moon*, 1902) and the early full-length feature films by D. W. Griffith, *Birth of a Nation* (1915) and *Intolerance* (1916), were expressly devoted to the subject of race and nation.

Dreyfus

The Dreyfus case officially lasted from October 1894, when Captain Alfred Dreyfus was arrested and charged with treason, to July 1906, when the Court of Appeals finally exonerated him, reversing all earlier convictions. Its status as "l'Affaire" and an international human rights scandal, however, did not truly emerge till the publication in *l'Aurore* of Emile Zola's public letter to President Felix Faure, the celebrated "J'accuse," in January of 1898.

Zola himself focused on legal issues in this indictment and saved his greatest scorn for members of the military establishment and their role in condemning an innocent man. He gave the topic of anti-Semitism relatively brief, though powerful treatment (mentioning, for example, "odious anti-Semitism, of which great, liberal France of the rights of man will die"). The rest of France, however, was not so narrow in its understanding of the Affair. There is no need to review the familiar story of how a legal case involving a completely unknown and unprepossessing Jewish army officer turned into a referendum on the Jews themselves and their position in French society. Though there were many gradations in public opinion, for many, to be an anti-Dreyfusard meant not simply to be dispassionately persuaded of Dreyfus's guilt in this legal case but to be an enemy of the Jews in general; conversely, for many, to be a Dreyfusard meant not to be dispassionately persuaded of Dreyfus's innocence but to be a champion of Jewish rights in general.

By the time the Dreyfus case came before the military court and the court of public opinion, all the elements were in place for a crisis in the conception of rights. The firmly entrenched view that the Jews were a race conflicted with the powerful sense that race and nation ought to be coextensive. The charge, after all, was treason, which means a crime against the nation. No one expressed the conflict more bluntly than the anti-Dreyfusard writer Maurice Barrès, when he said, "I need no one to tell me why Dreyfus committed treason. . . . That Dreyfus is capable of treason, I conclude from his race."[31]

The Affair helped create collective intervention at the international level, as societies formed, protest meetings were held, and editorials were written around the world in response to the events in France. One small measure of the international dimension of the case is the rise in newspaper coverage, in countries other than France, after Zola published "J'accuse." To take only one example, in the *New York Times*, from January to June 1898, overall news coverage of the Dreyfus Affair is fully double what it was in the preceding six months, and editorial coverage is triple. The Yiddish press in the United States reported every detail of the affair and provided strong editorial commentary at key moments.[32]

The Congo

Adam Hochschild has written about this episode in *King Leopold's Ghost*. Hochschild's book is largely a journalist's exposé-style indictment of Leopold II, the Belgian king who acquired the Congo territory as his personal property in 1885 and then oversaw the creation of a business empire from it. The raw products of this empire were ivory and rubber, its labor force was the native African population (generally working without pay and under threat of mutilation or death), and its profits allegedly flowed into the king's own pockets. The story is striking partly because, when Hochschild published his book in 1998, the Western world seemed to have forgotten about it altogether.

But if the world had forgotten the story by 1998, Hochschild maintains, it certainly knew about it at the turn of the twentieth century. This was largely thanks to the efforts of Edmund Morel, an Antwerp-based employee of a British shipping company who was able to piece together evidence to support the claim that the king of Belgium was using his personal colonial holding to run a business powered by slave labor. Morel dedicated years of his life to investigating and exposing Belgian abuses in the Congo. His campaign led to what Hochschild calls "the first great international human rights movement of the twentieth century," a movement that came to include such figures as Booker T. Washington, Anatole France, Arthur Conan Doyle, the archbishop of Canterbury, and Mark Twain.[33]

One might easily dispute the claim that this was "the *first* great international human rights movement of the twentieth century" (what about the Dreyfus Affair, for example?), but there is no doubt that it had to do with human and not purely civil rights, that it was international, and that, if we are speaking of size, then by any reasonable measure it was "great." That it had to do with human rights Morel says explicitly in the *History of the Congo Reform Movement*, his own account of the movement he had helped found. Writing in 1914, Morel describes the much lionized Henry Morton Stanley as "the unconscious instrument of the most colossal invasion of human rights the world has ever witnessed" (because Stanley had led a brutal five-year exploratory expedition to the Congo for King Leopold, beginning in 1879). That nationality (at least in the sense of sovereignty) and race were issues in Morel's mind is just as clear. Chapters 2 and 3 of Morel's book are titled "The Native Races of the Congo," and the author's aim in them is to show a gradual transformation of attitudes regarding nation and race from the beginning of Leopold's Congo involvement to the period when abuses began to reach their height. When European delegates convened in Berlin in 1884–1885, at the invitation of Bismarck, to establish spheres of colonial influence in Africa, Leopold had already made the claim that the Congo was a vast territory in which legitimate local rulers enjoyed the sovereign rights that European powers were accustomed to recognize. Morel quotes the French delegate to show that sensitivity at the Berlin Conference was high for the rights of African natives: "Everytime that a vote or a single proposal raised the interests of the African races, the Assembly at Berlin showed that it did not look upon them as purely accidental associations, without juridical rights, or outside the community of the rights of men." Furthermore, Morel says, delegates emphasized the admirable qualities of precisely these "African races."[34] Morel shows, however, that 15 years later, when it served Leopold's interests to defend the behavior of the colonial government in the Congo Free State, he and others resorted to a frontal assault on the racial character of the natives in order to argue that they were not entitled to any of the rights that the Berlin Conference had recognized.[35]

That the movement was international is certainly clear from its cast of characters. Contemporary newspapers will show just how international not just the movement but the case itself became. Between 1901 and 1908, when Belgium formally "annexed" the Congo, making it a colonial territory instead of the personal property of King Leopold, the *New York Times* and the *Times* (London) ran numerous articles not only about atrocities in the territory but also about Morel, the protest movement, efforts by various governments to investigate Belgian conduct in Leopold's territory, and the responses that these efforts elicited from Leopold and his defenders.

Race got its share of press in the United States. For example, in 1904, *The Outlook* published an article titled "Cruelty in the Congo Country" with Booker T. Washington as the author.[36] Though Washington apparently wrote little of the article attributed to him, he agreed to lend his name and support to the ideas in the article and to the Congo reform movement. As one would expect from something truly written by the author of *Up from Slavery*, the article makes race a dominant issue in the Congo affair. "The oppression of the colored race in any one part of the world means, sooner or later, the oppression of the same race elsewhere," we read.

Finally one should mention that, even though the Congo case did not create the same profusion of visual images in the press that the Dreyfus case did in France and even though the newspapers themselves seldom carried photographs of abuses or victims of abuses, the case did generate its share of such images. Morel's exposé *King Leopold's Rule in Africa* (1904), for example, contains gruesome photographs of mutilated children. Hochschild reproduces in *King Leopold's Ghost* a set of similar photos gathered by Anti-Slavery International, in addition to a collection of contemporary cartoons designed to expose the cruelty and hypocrisy of the ivory and rubber regimes in Africa.

Mendel Beilis

The facts of the Beilis case are fairly simple. They also perfectly qualify the case for a chapter in the history of the modern conception of human rights. In 1911, a young Christian boy was found murdered in Kiev. After some months, Russian authorities arrested Mendel Beilis, a local Jew who worked at a brick factory, and charged him with ritual murder (the murder of Christians in order to use their blood for religious purposes). Beilis was held for two years. The Tsar's government fabricated evidence against him, confident that the prevailing hostile attitudes toward Jews in Russia would lead to the defendant's conviction. The true culprit was found, but the government persisted in its campaign against Beilis. In the end, a jury made up mostly of peasants voted to acquit him.

I have already mentioned that *race* and *nation* were particularly charged concepts for the Jews of Russia, often used interchangeably but always pointing to the Jews' impossibly complicated legal and social status in their home country. Since it had already been common in the second half of the nineteenth century for both Jews and their enemies in Russia to speak of a Jewish race and a Jewish nation (or nation within a nation), it is not surprising to see these terms emerge in 1911, as an accusation reminiscent of the Middle Ages is leveled at a Russian subject. In his own memoirs (written in Yiddish) about the trial, Beilis tells of a group of scientists that the authorities consulted in order to establish a learned view of the murderer's motives. One of them was Professor Sikorsky of Kiev University, a psychologist that the government had engaged for his expertise on the psychological motives of the crime. The professor was asked a question that, as Beilis reports it, is itself significant, namely "to what sort of *nation* the murderer belonged and what sort of motives he might therefore have had." His answer, as Beilis himself transcribes it, "The murder was committed by Jews and the intent of the murder was *racial* vengeance, or the 'vengeance of the children of Jacob.' "[37]

The case soon attracted national and international attention.[38] Beilis himself writes that a huge number of spectators was in attendance at the trial, "as if there were supposed to be a parade."[39] Many newspapers in the Western world sent correspondents to the trial, reporting both the details of the case and the public responses to it, in addition to offering editorial comments.[40]

From details of the trial and the coverage it received, we can see how the Jews were regarded as a distinct race and a separate *nation*. Beilis's enemies repeatedly highlighted the divide between Russia and the accused by suggesting that the Jews themselves, for their own religious reasons, followed legal principles that were at odds with those of their host country. If Jews were a separate nation, then they were not entitled to the same civil rights as those who belonged to the Russian nation. And if the Jews were not entitled to civil rights, then all the international community could do was claim either that they *should* be entitled to these rights or that they were entitled to rights of a higher order.

African Americans and Jews: The Final Uncoupling and the Transnational National

It goes without saying that the Beilis trial aroused the concern of Jews around the world. The most inspired comment that I know of on the Beilis affair and its implications for the evolution of human rights was one that appeared in a publication that only a handful of people regularly read, though the author was widely known in Jewish immigrant communities in England and the United States. He was Morris Winchevsky (1856–1932), the Russian Jewish socialist who became one of the towering figures in the British and American Jewish labor movements around the turn of the century. In an article titled "Race and Class," published in the highbrow Yiddish-language New York monthly *Di Tsukunft* (The Future), Winchevsky explained why the Beilis trial had caused him to rethink some of his most deeply held political views. He had never believed that race and nation ought to be a concern for socialism, which, as an international movement, promised benefits for all. In 1913, before the Beilis affair ended in the defendant's acquittal, Winchevsky writes that the case has made him change his mind on this subject. In response to a hard-line socialist pamphlet he has just read that cautions Jewish readers to remember, in connection with the trial in Russia, that only socialism can guarantee justice, Winchevsky now exclaims that the Beilis case shows race does make a difference.

He then introduces an essential distinction: that between *cosmopolitan* and *international*. To Winchevsky, the first of these means "citizen of the world," something, he says, that today applies only to Gypsies. The second, however, suggests to him activity that ignores national boundaries (and thus comprises the meanings of both *transnational* and *international* as I have defined these terms). Socialism, he argues, must seek to be international, in accordance with its own most sacred principles, but at the same time it must recognize the existence of individual *nations* (a term that, as was typical for the era, included *races* and *religious groups*) and thus contain an element of nationalism in this favorable sense. "Internationalism is unthinkable without nations," he says. To put it differently, internationalism must be built on the primary existence of nations but then must supersede and transcend those nations while also incorporating them (Winchevsky appears to be something of a Hegelian in his analysis).

This conception may be applied to human rights as well as to socialism. An individual has, among other rights, the right to be the national of a nation, but that nation may have to be construed as a race or a religious group—something, in other words, that does not correspond to any existing sovereign political state. But owing precisely to the failure of the nation-state system, the rights that the individual enjoys can be guaranteed only in an international context. The individual thus becomes, to coin a phrase, a transnational national (once again, to use the word *transnational* in the sense I gave earlier, that of existing or operating across, or without regard to, recognized national boundaries).

This is why African Americans and Jews must figure so prominently in the story of the modern idea of human rights. In the 1920s, the chief intellectual architects of the Harlem Renaissance saw and expressed more clearly than anyone else the significance of these two groups. In fact, I think there is good reason to regard *The New Negro* (1925), that bible of the Harlem Renaissance edited by the Harvard- and Oxford-educated philosopher Alain Locke, as *the* text marking the transition between what I have called stage 2 and stage 3 in the evolution of the human rights idea. The book, designed to showcase the talents of what Locke called, as in his title, the "New Negro," is an anthology of learned commentary on African American culture and examples of that culture (fiction, poetry, drama, visual art, and music). The terms *race, nation, nationality,* and *international* are ubiquitous in this collection.

We read that Harlem is a "race capital" but that the effort to rehabilitate the "race" has made that urban neighborhood the home of the Negro's "Zionism." Locke's inference from this is perfectly attuned to the transitional moment in which he writes: "As with the Jew, persecution is making the Negro international." *International,* not national. Or better, as Winchevsky might have put it, national and *then as a consequence* international. If one reads the book straight through, after being exposed to examples of the Negro's "race genius," "pride of race," and "racial art," one comes to the book's final selection, "The Negro Mind Reaches Out," by W. E. B. DuBois. Having spent the bulk of his article giving a survey of the current international status of the color and the labor problem, DuBois makes this statement:

> Above all this rises the shadow of two international groups—the Jews and the modern Negroes. The Jews are, in blood, Spanish, German, French, Arabian and American. Their ancient unity of religious faith is crumbling, but out of it all has come a spiritual unity born of suffering, prejudice and industrial power which can be used and is being used to spread an international consciousness. . . . And toward this same great end a new group of groups is setting its face. . . . This hundred and fifty millions of [Negroes] are gaining slowly an intelligent thoughtful leadership. The main seat of their leadership is to-day the United States.[41]

He expresses confidence that "the day faintly dawns when the new force for international understanding and racial readjustment will and must be felt."[42] The specific arena in which this readjustment will be felt is the arena of human rights. The American Negro is now speaking for himself, DuBois says, and two concrete results of this phenomenon are a reduction in the number of lynchings in the United States, through the activities of the NAACP (National Association for the Advancement of Colored People), and the establishment of the international Pan-African Congress.

And this brings us back to Eleanor Roosevelt and the *Universal Declaration*. Roosevelt's association with the NAACP went back to 1934, when she joined the Washington, DC, chapter of both that organization and the National Urban League. From then till her work on the *Declaration*, she remained involved in the Negro rights movement, joining the NAACP board of directors and becoming a lifetime member of the National Council of Negro Women in 1945. In 1942, she contributed to the *New Republic* a short piece titled "Race, Religion and Prejudice," in which she made a plea for the "fundamental rights of a citizen" without regard for race, color, or religion.[43]

LATIN AMERICA, RIGHTS, AND DISCIPLINARY GLOBALIZATION

From the Mexican constitution of 1917 to the *American Declaration of the Rights and Duties of Man* issued in Bogotá in 1948, Latin America has shown a consistent tendency to recognize basic social and economic rights as among those that belong internationally to each member of the human family and to incorporate those rights into constitutions, international declarations, and political manifestos (though, as everyone knows, practice has often diverged sharply from theory). Its constitutions have consistently adopted basic human rights, defined internationally, as the founding principles for individual nations. In fact, the introductory statement to the Bogotá *Declaration* both asserts the basic rights and gives their history in Latin American constitutionalism. It reads, "Its [Latin America's] national constitutions recognize that the judicial and political institutions that govern life in society have as their principal end the protection of the essential rights of man." "The international protection of the rights of man must be the principal guide of [Latin] American law in its evolution."[44] The Mexican constitution came along at a moment when human rights were already being viewed from an international perspective, both because they were transnational and because they were more and more frequently the focus of international attention.

The clearest distinction between first-generation and second-generation human rights is that the first have to do with the individual as a member of a political entity (commonwealth, body politic, state), while the second have to do with the individual as a member of a social entity. As a consequence, second-generation rights are more closely connected with social conduct than are first-generation rights and are thus more likely to involve forms of discipline. To be sure, the first-generation right to life implies that the state must watch for and punish willful conduct that results in the deprivation of life. But this is something quite different from the second-generation right to a compulsory and free education, which requires not only that the state establish schools but that it pay for them, too. The second-generation right to an eight-hour workday requires not only that the state watch for and punish willful conduct that results in the exploitation of workers but that it establish *this* specific standard and provide for its enforcement. Needless to say, this suggests a much higher level of social control and discipline than does the simple prohibition of murder. In one instance the state is often actively controlling behavior *and* remaining vigilant, while in the other it is (at least in theory) merely remaining vigilant.

Ultimately this form of discipline arises from the same process of globalization that produced other essential features of the modern conception of human rights (such as grounding these rights in the international community and in transnational principles, while paradoxically making nationality a right). To the extent that the Mexican constitution of 1917 inaugurates a trend in Latin America, we can see that socialism, itself intrinsically international, had bequeathed to that document a set of specific principles designed to apply to working people from all nations. Other rights in the *Universal Declaration*, besides those enunciated in Articles 22–27, as we have seen, arose in a process of globalization that involved (partially) abandoning the received idea of nation and race in order to enthrone the individual as a new transnational, transracial being whose rights are, at least in an unofficial sense, guaranteed by the international community.

Notes

1. The standard literature on the subject includes the following works: Karel Vasak, ed., *The International Dimensions of Human Rights* (Paris: UNESCO, 1982); Paul Sieghart, *The International Law of Human Rights* (Oxford: Clarendon, 1983); Robert F. Drinan, *Cry of the Oppressed: The History and Hope of the Human Rights Revolution* (San Francisco: Harper and Row, 1987); Louis Henkin, *The Age of Rights* (New York: Columbia University Press, 1990); Walter Laqueur and Barry Rubin, eds., *The Human Rights Reader* (New York, 1979; rev. ed, New York: Meridian, 1990); Scott Davidson, *Human Rights* (Buckingham and Philadelphia: Open University Press, 1993); and Paul Gordon Lauren, *The Evolution of International Human Rights: Visions Seen* (Philadelphia: University of Pennsylvania Press, 1998).
2. For a slightly different historical formulation, one that takes into account the world after the *Declaration*, see Karel Vasak, "A 30-Year

Struggle: The Sustained Efforts to Give Force of Law to the Universal Declaration of Human Rights," *Unesco Courier*, November 1977, 29.
3. Mary Ann Glendon has provided a highly readable and human account of the process in *A World Made New: Eleanor Roosevelt and the Universal Declaration of Human Rights* (New York: Random House, 2001).
4. For the Spanish text of the declaration, see Máximo Pacheco Gomez, *Los Derechos Humanos: Documentos Basicos* (Santiago, Chile: Editorial Juridica de Chile, 1987), 53–58. The English translation may be found in Ian Brownlie, *Basic Documents on Human Rights* (Oxford: Clarendon, 1971), 488–494. A more accurate rendering of the Spanish text would be "the essential rights of man do not arise from the fact of his being a national of a particular State but have as their foundation the attributes of the human person [not personality]" ("los derechos esenciales del hombre no nacen del hecho de ser nacional de determinado Estado sino que tienen como fundamento los atributos de la persona humana"). All translations in this chapter are mine.
5. René Cassin, "La Déclaration universelle et la mise en oeuvre des droits de l'homme" (The *Universal Declaration* and putting into effect the rights of man), *Recueil des cours de l'Académie de Droit International*, 79 (1951): 278.
6. Johannes Morsink, *The Universal Declaration of Human Rights: Origins, Drafting, and Intent* (Philadelphia: University of Pennsylvania Press, 1999), 130–134.
7. Ibid., 132.
8. Ibid., 130.
9. On this point, and for an English translation of the program, but not the manifesto, see James D. Cockcroft, *Intellectual Precursors of the Mexican Revolution 1900–1913* (Austin and London: University of Texas Press, 1968), 239–245.
10. Rodolfo Lara Ponte, *Los Derechos Humanos en el Constitucionalismo Mexicano* (Human Rights and Mexican Constitutionalism) (Mexico City: Universidad Nacional Autónoma de México, 1993), 130–132.
11. The original text of the Mexican Constitution of 1917 may be found at http://www.juridicas.unam.mx/infjur/leg/conshist/pdf/1917.pdf (accessed August 27, 2006).
12. Thomas Hobbes, "Introduction," in *Leviathan*, ed. Richard Tuck (Cambridge: Cambridge University Press, 1991), 9.
13. Ibid., 11.
14. Ibid., 120.
15. John Locke, *Two Treatises of Government*, ed. Peter Laslett (Cambridge: Cambridge University Press, 1967), 342.
16. Jean-Jacques Rousseau, *Oeuvres complètes*, ed. Bernard Gagnebin and Marcel Raymond (Paris: Gallimard, 1959–1995), 3:365.
17. Johann Gottlieb Fichte, *Sämmtliche Werke*, ed. J. H. Fichte (Berlin: Veit und Comp, 1845), 3:372.
18. Ibid., 7:381.

19. Ibid., 7:384.
20. Dostoevsky, "Status in statu. Sorok vekov bytiia" (*Status in statu*. Forty centuries of existence), *Diary of a Writer*, March 1877, in *Polnoe sobranie sochinenii* (Leningrad: "Nauka," 1972–1990), 25:81–85.
21. *Razsvet* (The Dawn), no. 46, November 13, 1881, 1798.
22. Houston Stewart Chamberlain, *Die Grundlagen des neunzehnten Jahrhunderts* (Munich: F. Bruckmann, 1899), 1:272; English translation in *Foundations of the Nineteenth Century*, trans. John Lees (New York: Lane, 1910), 1:269.
23. Chamberlain, *Grundlagen*, 1:273; *Foundations*, 1:271.
24. Chamberlain, *Grundlagen*, 1:290; *Foundations*, 1:292.
25. Chamberlain, *Grundlagen*, 1:294; *Foundations*, 1:295.
26. Bonnie S. Anderson, *Joyous Greetings: The First International Women's Movement, 1830–1860* (Oxford: Oxford University Press, 2000). See especially chapter 1, "Panorama," 7–27.
27. See the organization's website at http://www.antislavery.org/homepage/antislavery/history.htm.
28. As paraphrased in the *Times of London*, October 25, 1840, 14.
29. See Betty Fladeland, *Men and Brothers: Anglo-American Antislavery Cooperation* (Urbana: University of Illinois Press, 1972). For an account of the early stages of the antislavery movement, see 3–26.
30. For a list of travelers' accounts, see ibid., 171. As early as the final decade of the eighteenth century, one can find numerous newspaper stories about slavery in the *Times of London*.
31. Quoted in Michael Marrus, "Popular Anti-Semitism," in *The Dreyfus Affair: Art, Truth, and Justice*, ed. Norman L. Kleeblatt (Berkeley and Los Angeles: University of California Press, 1987), 59.
32. For an account of the American public's reaction to the Dreyfus Affair, see Egal Feldman, *The Dreyfus Affair and the American Conscience, 1895–1906* (Detroit: Wayne State University Press, 1981), 105–109.
33. Adam Hochschild, *King Leopold's Ghost: A Story of Greed, Terror, and Heroism in Colonial Africa* (Boston and New York: Houghton Mifflin, 1998), 2–3.
34. William Roger Louis and Jean Stengers, eds., *E. D. Morel's History of the Congo Reform Movement* (Oxford: Clarendon, 1968), 8–9.
35. Ibid., 10–11.
36. Booker T. Washington, "Cruelty in the Congo Country," *The Outlook*, no. 78, October 8, 1904, 375–377.
37. Mendel Beilis, *Di geshikhte fun mayne layden* (*The Story of My Sufferings*) (New York, 1931), 103. English translation: *The Story of My Sufferings*, trans. Harrison Goldberg (New York: Mendel Beilis Pub. Co., 1926), 109.
38. On the international reaction to the case, see Maurice Samuel, *Blood Accusation: The Strange History of the Beilis Case* (New York: Knopf, 1966), 231–45; Albert S. Lindemann, *The Jew Accused: Three Anti-Semitic Affairs (Dreyfus, Beilis, Frank) 1894–1915* (Cambridge: Cambridge University Press, 1991), 183–184, 190–193; and Ezekiel

Leikin, *The Beilis Transcripts: The Anti-Semitic Trial that Shook the World* (Northvale, NJ: Jason Aronson, 1993), 220–224.
39. Beilis, *Di geshikhte fun mayne layden*, 119; *The Story of My Sufferings*, 133.
40. *The Times of London*, *The New York Times*, and *Le Temps* in France provided especially thorough coverage.
41. Alain Locke, ed., *The New Negro* (New York, 1925; rept., New York: Touchstone, 1997), 411.
42. Ibid., 413.
43. Eleanor Roosevelt, "Race, Religion and Prejudice," *New Republic* 106 (May 11, 1942): 630.
44. Pacheco, *Los Derechos Humanos*, 53. English translation can be found in Brownlie, *Basic Documents on Human Rights*, 488.

8

Generating Uncertainty: Globalized Punishment and Crime

Thomas Siemsen

In the *Philosophical Investigations* Ludwig Wittgenstein writes, "A picture held us captive. And we could not get outside it, for it lay in our language and language seemed to repeat it to us inexorably."[1] At the midpoint of the seventeenth century Thomas Hobbes surveyed his world and found that the newly released economic forces had brought substantial disruption and disquiet in addition to substantial economic gain for some. In response to those disruptions, Hobbes sought to recreate the peace and quiet that preceded the rise of revolutionary economic and political forces. Now, at the beginning of the twenty-first century, we are again confronted with a world in which economic forces have brought disturbance and disquiet to many. But this time, the markets have chosen not to leave the reestablishment of peace and quiet to the philosophers or even to the political forces that may or may not listen to philosophers. Instead, the global markets themselves will impose their own order, their own discipline, and in their own way, as the governments and the peoples of Mexico, Argentina, Brazil, and the ASEAN block can attest. As a result of these developments and decisions, crime and punishment have taken on new meanings. In a context of growing uncertainty—in which the old rules of the game are no longer valid and in which players are not always sure what behavior will bring about punishment or reward—the meaning of crime and punishment has changed. But the picture of crime and punishment that our language has given us continues to hold us captive, despite the evidence that our picture is misleading. Beyond that, the picture of global relationships that the language of economic theory has given us is equally misleading. This essay is an attempt to suggest how we are misled by these language-pictures, the intellectual consequences of those misunderstandings, and, finally, an alternative understanding of "crime," "punishment," and "globalization" that better fits a context of growing uncertainty. This, I would argue, is especially important in less developed societies that have been forced to adjust to confusing rules of the game as a consequence of globalization and particularly the adoption of neoliberalism.

CRIME AND PUNISHMENT: ESTABLISHED PICTURES

The dictionary defines a "crime" as (1) an act or the commission of an act that is forbidden or the omission of a duty that is commanded by a public law and that makes the offender liable to punishment by that law, *especially* a gross violation of law; (2) a grave offense especially against morality; (3) criminal activity; and (4) something reprehensible, foolish, or disgraceful: "it's a crime to waste good food."[2] Similarly, the philosopher Warren Quinn tells us that a "crime" is something that warrants "civic punishment, in which one adult is made to suffer for his past wrongdoing by other adults who officially represent the community. . . ."[3] Note that, for both philosophy and common usage, there is the sense that a crime constitutes an exceptional act on the part of some individual or group that prompts official or community action. In all cases, punishment comes in response to an act that constitutes a violation of the law or accepted norm that is upheld or enforced by the state or those "who officially represent the community." This is our accepted picture of the crime/punishment relationship.

There is, of course, nothing surprising in these definitions and understandings. Even in the harshest of regimes, distinctions are made in the treatment of those who abide by the laws and those who do not.[4] Anthony Pereira, for example, documents the scrupulousness with which the Brazilian military, during the years 1964–1979, sought to legitimize that regime's suppression of dissent by its adherence to the appearance of due process, if not its practice, through the use of trials in military courts. In all instances the accused was charged with having committed some act that the state defined as "criminal."[5] Punishment, as opposed to, say, persecution, always follows the crime. Michel Foucault, however, offers an alternative understanding of punishment, one that serves to highlight the close ties between punishment and power. Briefly, Foucault suggests that if we start with what power *wishes* to punish, the thing against which a law is passed, rather than with an a priori law that is accepted by all as a standard that all must abide by and which is applied equally to all, crime takes on a new character. For one thing, it becomes the derivative of punishment rather than its stimulus or cause. In other words, as Thomas Dumm puts it, Foucault starts by asking: "What is a crime?"

> Foucault's answer is this: A crime is what is punished. With this answer Foucault refuses the conventions of liberal justice that have been used to claim that a crime is what violates a law.[6]

For most liberal thinkers the end or purpose of punishment is either retributive justice or some variant of utilitarian deterrence. The crime having been committed, the law having been violated, punishment seeks either to reestablish some preexisting arrangement through the imposition of an amount of pain on the perpetrator of the crime, or, at a minimum, to preclude a reoccurrence of disorder by demonstrating the consequences of a violation of the law to both the perpetrator and any others who might consider such behavior themselves. For Foucault, however, the modern aim of punishment is not justice, but discipline, the establishment of control, and ultimately the self-control of the one punished.[7] As such, discipline "may be identified neither with an institution nor with an apparatus; it is a type of power, a modality for its exercise, comprising a whole set of instruments, techniques, procedures, levels of application, targets . . . ."[8]

Here I want to suggest that the phenomenon known as globalization is best understood, not as a manifestation of (value-neutral) economic development, but as a new disciplinary capacity, as a set of relationships having the identification of "wrongs" or crimes and their punishment as one of its principal functions, and the aim of economic power as its end. In applying this notion to newly formed democracies under neoliberalism or to societies that, as those in Latin America, have gone through the aggressive privatization of public institutions (Argentina or Chile), we find that the identification of rights or wrongs becomes confusing. When citizens were told that the market was supposed to reward entrepreneurship and rationality, alarming unemployment told them otherwise. And while neoliberalism told national industry that the market was supposed to reward efficiency and competition, confusing rules of the game and unfair rivalry from abroad brought about uncertainty and diminishing returns. All of this contributed to discontent and frustration. The disciplinary side of globalization imposed rules that seemed both unjust and bewildering.

This view is obviously at odds with the accepted "picture" that is constituted by economic theory, and in the last part of this paper I will attempt to make clear the reasons for my own nonacceptance of that picture.[9] But first I want to offer some additional rationale by way of pointing to some examples of globalization punishments; then I want to consider what, if any, justification there is for such punishments. In other words, by what right, if any, do the global markets impose their discipline and punish those identified as (globalization) criminals?

Globalization As Punishment

For most of what we now think of as "the modern age" economic theory was dominated by some form of the idea of "comparative advantage." As Michael Porter wrote in 1990:

> Comparative advantage has a specific meaning to economists. Adam Smith is credited with the notion of absolute advantage, in which a nation exports an item if it is the world's low-cost producer. David Ricardo refined this notion to that of comparative advantage, recognizing that market forces will allocate a nation's resources to those industries where it is relatively most productive....
>
> .... The dominant version of comparative advantage theory, due initially to Heckscher and Ohlin, is based on the idea that nations all have equivalent technology but differ in their endowments of so-called factors of production such as land, labor, natural resources, and capital.[10]

But, as Porter explains, technology changes have forced economists to alter many of their theoretical assumptions regarding the nature of trade and the very idea of "comparative advantage." Indeed, in place of "comparative advantage," Porter offers the idea of "competitive advantage," which he develops at considerable length and which need not concern us here. The point, rather, is that

> [g]lobalization of industries decouples the firm from the factor endowment of a single nation. Raw materials, components, machinery, and many services are available globally on comparable terms. Transportation improvements have lowered the cost of exchanging factors or factor dependent goods among nations.[11]

Different writers have characterized the consequences of the globalization process in different ways, but virtually all acknowledge that there will be negative consequences for some. At the extreme, Hardt and Negri argue that we have already entered a period of "empire" in which nearly all must suffer; others envision widespread, if not universal, suffering.[12] Porter, for example, notes that the process of developing a competitive advantage means that "an upgrading economy is one which has the capability of competing successfully in entirely new and sophisticated industries. Doing so absorbs human resources freed up in the process of improving productivity in existing fields."[13] Those "human resources" that are, hopefully, "absorbed" by "new and sophisticated industries" are first "freed up" through the process that has become familiarly known in the United States and elsewhere as "downsizing." All too often, of course, those "freed up" resources are not absorbed at all, but instead are shifted into jobs that pay substantially less than those from which they have been freed.[14] Adrian Wood, for example, has estimated that "up to 1990 the changes in trade with the South had reduced the demand for unskilled relative to skilled labour in the North as a whole by something like 20 per cent."[15] Unskilled labor is, of course, the first kind of labor to be "freed up" by the processes that Porter describes, but it is not only unskilled labor that suffers. The Boeing Corporation, for example, has cut more than fifty thousand skilled jobs in the Seattle area alone since 1990, while at the same time it has built fabrication capacity outside the Unites States valued at nearly $1 billion.[16] Others are even more blunt in their characterizations of the globalizing process. Bryan and Farrell, two of globalization's staunchest advocates, note that, particularly in Europe,

> Generous unemployment benefits have protected individuals from economic hardship when jobs are lost. However, because these same restrictions and subsidies have led to lower productivity and soaring government deficits, they are unsustainable, and European nations have begun to dismantle them under the increasing pressure from the marketplace.
>
> This process will cause enormous disruption as governments cut entitlements, particularly pensions and health care, and as businesses dependent on government protection must restructure or perish. These changes, in turn, will lead to large job losses and enormous personal dislocation.[17]

These "losses and . . . dislocation[s]" will produce, according to Bryan and Farrell, "significant social unrest" in virtually all countries.[18] Looking at the experience of Latin America, losses and dislocations also produce uncertainty. It is only logical that job losses and personal transfers, changes in health care and the virtual abolition of welfare in some situations, would cause increasing uncertainty and confusion. Uncertainty breeds different notions of crime and punishment.

The suggestion here is that one of the "crimes" that globalizing forces have determined shall warrant punishment is the possession of a job that can be performed more efficiently by someone else in some other part of the globe.[19] This knowledge and its logic are not self-apparent. Yet the punishment for this crime is, of course, the loss of employment, the loss of one's way of "making a living," and perhaps even the experience of substantial social disruption that may follow such losses on a massive scale. Latin American nations, more than those in Europe, present a telling example. Unemployment was and still is the most severe punishment that globalization has imposed upon these societies.

Now, even in light of the comments above regarding the alternative way of thinking about crime and punishment, this characterization of economic inefficiency as a "crime" and the resulting loss of employment as globalized "punishment" are likely to jar the sensibilities of many. I therefore want to briefly reiterate the logic for the characterization I am offering before going on to suggest other globalized instantiations of these phenomena. "Punishment" is the authorized imposition of some kind of pain or loss in response to some act (or failure to act) on the part of one in a position of subordination to those (or the one) imposing the punishment. The possible ends of punishment may range from vengeance through retribution and/or deterrence to the moral education of the wrongdoer.[20] In any case, punishment is not an accidental or random occurrence of harm and it is certainly not a synonym for pain and suffering, per se. Argentina's recent financial crisis, for example, is not, I would argue, an instance of punishment by the international markets. Rather, it is a case of suffering as a result of the Argentine Government's refusal to break the link between the peso and the dollar until it was already too late.[21] Again, punishment is imposed by one on another; it is an intentional infliction of pain or loss.[22]

When such an imposition is committed without authority, it is not punishment but an unwarranted harm that may itself constitute a crime. And when it is done by one acting in a position of authority but without regard to the previous actions of the recipient of such harm, it is not punishment, but persecution. But when the imposition of harm on another is justified by the position of the one(s) imposing that harm, and when that harm comes as a response to an act (or a failure to perform a required act) on the part of the one receiving harm, the harm is termed punishment and the act warranting such harm is termed a wrong or, as Foucault suggests, a crime. Consequently, when a worker's relative inefficiency (or the inefficiency of an entire workforce) is viewed as something that is justifiably punishable, it satisfies Foucault's definition of a crime, i.e., "A crime is what is punished." Moreover, to suppose otherwise, to instead view the harm imposed as something other than a justified punishment, is likely to create for us even greater political difficulties. If, for example, we choose to think of the imposed harm as *unauthorized*, we must immediately concede the possibility that the act of imposing the unauthorized harm is itself a punishable offense, and that is a possibility that the defenders of globalization are even less likely to embrace. In the final part of this chapter we will consider the possibility of adopting just this view, but first we need to consider still another alternative view of the harm I have characterized as punishment.

This second alternative I want to consider is one that is likely to be offered by, among others, liberal economists. Indeed, the defenders of the global market system are likely to cry foul over most of what has been suggested to this point. We are likely to be told that the markets do not really "punish" and that inefficiency, while it is by definition wasteful, is not a "crime" by any stretch of the imagination. Markets are, we are reminded, natural or nearly natural phenomena that spontaneously evolve through the separate and independent actions of millions of individuals.[23] As such, they are liberating phenomena, not imposers of punishments. They reward efficiency, market proponents tell us, and leave the inefficient to their natural fate in a world of competition.

Now, in some respects this characterization is correct. There is, indeed, a great deal of spontaneity in market processes and certainly no one or some few individuals control(s) global markets. But markets, and certainly global markets, are anything but entirely spontaneous entities and there is a considerable amount of structuring and control that is consciously imposed on contemporary global markets. Michael Dreiling, for example, makes a compelling case for the argument that passage of the North American Free Trade Agreement (NAFTA) was championed principally by (and largely for the benefit of) business leaders who were members of the Business Roundtable and the Trade Advisory Committees (TACs) under the U.S. Trade Representative's office. In so doing, those business leaders sought to structure certain global markets along a specific set of lines and for a specific set of ends. Dreiling's point is that the campaign for the NAFTA's passage was a successful conscious effort by the members of a particular class to promote that class's interests at the expense of working-class Americans (Drieling 2000).[24] NAFTA, in other words, did not just "happen"; it was not an unintended consequence of spontaneous market actors. Rather, NAFTA was the result of a coordinated effort by the members of one class, crossing otherwise competitive business interests, at the expense of the members of another class. This is, however, but another way of saying that the *ability* to inflict the punishment of job loss on U.S. workers did not come about by happenstance, but was intentionally established through a political process. As of November 4, 2002, the U.S. Department of Labor had "certified" under its Trade Adjustment Assistance program 525,407 U.S. workers who had lost their jobs as a direct result of the NAFTA.[25] Moreover, 70 percent of the jobs lost were in manufacturing.[26] To suggest that these job losses (harms) were simply a consequence of the spontaneous activity of the market, that they were not consciously "imposed" by some on others (and for very specific reasons), is to ignore the actions of those who worked for the NAFTA's passage. Those who wish to view the harm of such job losses as "natural" or uncontrived are those who typically benefit most from such a view. Those on the receiving end of such harms, however, are far more likely to see them for the punishments that they are. But relative inefficiency is not the only crime of globalization, nor are job losses its only form of punishment.

On December 19, 1994, the Government of Mexico announced that it was raising the upper limit of the trading band within which the peso had been allowed to fluctuate against the U.S. dollar. This action occurred less than three weeks after Ernesto Zedillo was inaugurated president and was contrary to promises he had made during the campaign regarding devaluation of the peso. As Rogelio Ramirez de la O has pointed out, coming so early in the new administration's life, the action gave the appearance that Zedillo and his administration did not understand the Mexican economy and had entered office without a genuine economic plan; the currency markets therefore "mounted a massive speculative attack" on the peso.[27] Here Foucault's definition of a crime is particularly helpful. It was not, after all, the speculators who were guilty of globalization crimes; they were not the ones punished. Indeed, far from being punished for their having bet against the Mexican peso and having thereby assisted its decline in value, the currency speculators were substantially rewarded with massive profits for their foresight and boldness. No, the crime in this instance—the thing that was punished—was the crime of holding that currency once the speculators had begun their selling. Those who either could not or would not participate in the punishment of others through the devaluation of the currency they were holding, because they were paid their wages in that currency and because everything they owned or ever hoped to own was valued in that, their national currency, themselves became the punished. According to Miguel Ramirez, the actual drop in Mexico's gross domestic product (GDP) was 6.9 percent, resulting in the loss of between 800,000 and 1,000,000 jobs in the first ten months of 1995, and more than 20 percent of the nation's small businesses were projected to go out of business.[28]

Unfortunately, the harms resulting from the peso crisis were not confined to Mexico. As Sachs, Tornell and Velasco put it, "the *possibility* of a [currency] panic, which existed before December 1994, in several countries became the *fact* of a panic after December 1994" and that realization caused additional panics in Argentina, Brazil, and even the Philippines.[29] Although the consequences were less severe, substantial damage occurred in all three countries, with Argentine banks losing 18 percent of their deposits in just three months while economic output fell by 4.4 percent, resulting in substantial job losses. Needless to say, this created great uncertainty not only among the working class but also among the owners of industry and the middle sectors of the population. In the case of Argentina in particular, as the chapter by López-Alves in this volume shows, pessimism and uncertainty about the swings of the market has had a lasting effect.

Although it is now reasonably clear that Mexico's economy was never in a genuinely healthy state, we should not forget that it was neither the government officials who had mismanaged the privatization efforts of the Salinas de Gortari administration (1988–1994) nor the most wealthy Mexican investors, who were apparently informed of the impending devaluation prior to the government's official announcement, who were most severely punished by the market's reaction to the government's decision. Rather, it was those workers and peasants throughout Mexico and the other countries affected who failed to profit from the sharp decline in the peso's value and were instead punished for that failure.

Much of this capacity to inflict such punishing harm on others is a consequence of a "transfer" of power from public hands into private ones. As Bryan and Farrell put it, "Bad [government] policies will carry real penalties, and good policies will be quickly rewarded." Nations are no longer the sovereign entities they once were, dealing only with other sovereign nations, but are instead subject to disciplinary actions by the international currency and commodities markets.[30] This transfer of power has occurred, in large part, as a direct result of the growth and deregulation of the financial markets over the past decade and a half. In 1989 the global foreign exchange market averaged $590 billion per day; in 1997 (the year the "Asian crisis" began with Thailand's decision to float the baht) that average daily amount had grown to $1.54 trillion. That equates to $400 trillion in foreign exchange trades over the course of one year and that amount is approximately fifty times the roughly $8 trillion actually required to finance world trade and investment; the balance, as Richard Longworth puts it, is pure speculation.[31] The sheer size of this speculation means that small countries can no longer even influence their exchange rates and even large countries can no longer control them.[32] In such circumstances, individual citizens can only hope to endure the penalties or punishments that markets impose. And if this financial market capacity was not enough to force a realization of powerlessness, the citizen of a smaller nation need only take note of the fact that only 49 of the 100 largest economies in the world are actually *national* economies; the rest are private economies like the Mitsubishi Trading Company (#22 in size) or the General Motors Corporation (#26).[33] Indeed, 40 to 50 percent of all international "trade" is actually comprised of materiel and financial movements across international borders but within the confines of a single international corporation, making the control of such trade (and its consequences for any particular national economy) even more absolute than would otherwise be the case.[34]

Economic Theory And Globalized Irresponsibility

Leonard Orland notes that shortly after he became a member of the Connecticut Board of Parole he came to realize that his power to punish (by deciding not to grant a parole) as a member of the Board "was not limited by legislation, and that my decisions were not reviewable in the courts. I learned, in short, that I was not bound by the rule of law." Moreover, although his decisions were based loosely on the prisoner's obedience to the "rules of the prison," Orland himself and his fellow Board members had only a vague understanding of what those rules actually were and how they were enforced by prison authorities.[35] Orland and his associates on the Parole Board were, in other words, men and women possessing power over other men and women, but without any formal institutional obligations to them. Moreover, the Parole Board members were working under circumstances that were unlikely to give rise to even an informal sense of obligation to those people most affected by their decisions.

In this sense, the members of the Connecticut Board of Parole bear a marked similarity to the modern investors and traders participating in the global economy. Until fairly recently, capital has generally been compelled by circumstances to recognize some minimal obligations to workers and to the communities in which it has invested.[36] If not from any moral sense, the need to protect the investment in capital equipment and the dependence upon a skilled workforce, often protected through unionization and by the laws of (quasi-) democratic institutions and popularly elected officials, meant that the well-being of workers and their communities could not be entirely disregarded. Capital was materially, if not emotionally, tied to labor. But, as Zygmunt Bauman points out, capital has now been freed from virtually all such obligations:

> The mobility acquired by people who invest—those with capital, with money which the investment requires—means the new, indeed unprecedented in its radical unconditionality, disconnection of power from obligations: duties towards employees, but also towards the younger and weaker, towards yet unborn generations and towards the self-reproduction of the living conditions of all; in short, freedom from the duty to contribute to daily life and the perpetuation of the community.[37] (1998, 9)

This freedom of capital, provided by a technology that permits control of resources over vast distances and by the need for nations to compete for the attraction of capital through tax incentives that offset the cost of capital investment by global corporations, makes the infliction of punishments of the sort described above all the more easy, since one never need experience or even witness it firsthand.

The source of the Parole Board's authority, that which establishes the Board's right to inflict punishment on those already incarcerated, is the law. The Board serves as an extension of the state, specifically the judiciary, and, although the Board's decisions are in many ways more independent than those of the courts, the legitimacy of the Board's actions is established by the legitimacy of the judicial system, which is to say, again, the State. As Foucault (1980, 201) points out, "It's the characteristic of our Western societies that the language of power is law, not magic, religion, or anything else." But to say that "the language of power is law" is not to suggest that power itself is necessarily *legal* power, power created by the law. On the contrary, as Foucault has argued, modern disciplinary power is more often than not extralegal and independent of any need for legal support or enforcement:

> My problem is . . . this: what rules of right are implemented by the relations of power in the production of discourses of truth? Or alternatively, what type of power is susceptible of producing discourses of truth that in a society such as ours are endowed with such potent effects? . . . We are subjected to the production of truth through power and we cannot exercise power except through the production of truth. (Foucault 1980, 93)

The truth that attempts to make the power of global punishment "right" is the discourse (and truth) of economic theory; it is a critical element of the picture that holds us captive. In the absence of such truth, the infliction of the punishments described above would amount to unwarranted harms and would themselves be subject to the charge of being crimes. But the discipline of economics effectively transforms these harms into punishments of those guilty of global crimes.[38] "Economics," of course, does not speak of punishment and seldom refers to anything like the power that citizens in virtually every country of the world are being subjected to; but these absences from its discourse do not mean that the discipline is not capable of creating and sustaining power. On the contrary, economics is the most "scientific" of all the social sciences and, as such, it speaks with the authority, which is to say power, of a science. And, as Foucault asks, "What types of knowledge do you want to disqualify in the very instant of your demand: 'Is it a science?' Which speaking, discoursing subjects—which subjects of experience and knowledge—do you then want to 'diminish' when you say: 'I who conduct this discourse am conducting a scientific discourse, and I am a scientist'?" (Foucault 1980, 85).

The loss of employment possibilities, the evaporation of an entire people's buying power as a result of a currency devaluation, the despoliation of the environment and disruption of traditional social arrangements, again, are not crimes according to liberal economic theory. Neither is it considered a crime to create a context of uncertainty in which old players (individuals, small firms) lack the skills, the capital or the power to re-insert themselves as players into a new game. In their best light, these developments are, according to the truth of economics, manifestations of progress and market freedom; at worst, they are "externalities," consequences of actions that the market is unable to appropriately allocate. Air pollution generated by a factory, for example, affects everyone; those who do not work in the factory or purchase its products breathe the same air as the factory owner and those customers who buy from him/her. There is a cost, in other words, that everyone is forced to endure (in the case of a "negative externality") as a result of the factory's operation.[39] While the state can attempt to minimize the occurrence and extent of such negative externalities, economic theory treats such costs as inevitable and even "natural" byproducts of economic activity.

Zygmunt Bauman has suggested that the role of the intellectual has shifted over time from that of a "legislator" to the contemporary role of an "interpreter."[40] During the early modern period the consolidation of political power in centralized monarchies required the legitimizing services of the intellectuals and a kind of co-dependency developed between the ruling and intellectual classes. That relationship, however, proved to be relatively "short-lived" and intellectuals have increasingly taken on an interpreter role, the principal function of which "consists of translating statements, made by one communally-based tradition, so that they can be understood within a system of knowledge based on another tradition"(Bauman 1987, 5). In the case of economic theory, however, the function appears to have shifted back to legitimation and away from interpretation. Instead of relying on such things as "divine right" or "the will of the people" as the basis for legitimizing the political power of the sovereign state, economics relies on its status as a science and, by virtue of that, its ability to portray a kind of "natural order" in social life as a way of legitimizing the conditions of market economies. Certainly among the qualities or characteristics of that order are such things as "externalities." When these qualities or characteristics of the economic order are described as "natural" or "inevitable" the initial sense of injustice that these qualities are likely to convey to a non-economist is lessened or perhaps even eliminated altogether and the occurrence of the phenomena described above is thereby legitimated; crime and punishment, of course, have no place in this picture.

The suggestion here, however, is that it is a mistake to accept the picture that economic theory would have us accept of the globalization harms that have been described. Unlike such things as air pollution or neighborhood property values, the loss of employment resulting from jobs being transferred from high labor cost areas to low labor cost areas or the loss of purchasing power resulting from currency devaluations are not externalities of economic activity, but are instead the intended consequences, or punishments, inflicted by the global markets.[41] Air pollution, after all, is not the intended product of an industrial operation; rather it is the consequence of some other-directed production effort. This is not to say that air pollution is not an *intended consequence* of production; more often than not the polluter is fully aware of the fact that his/her operations will generate pollution, and he/she proceeds with production in spite of that knowledge. But the *aim* of production is not pollution. Pollution occurs and those otherwise unconcerned with the production are adversely affected by it; economic theory then legitimates this sequence of events by characterizing the harm inflicted on those others as a "negative externality."

In the case of the global phenomena described above, however, the aims of the harms inflicted are the harms themselves, or, rather, the disciplining effect that the infliction of such harms imposes. Hence, these harms are not appropriately characterized as "externalities," but instead as punishments, and, in the case of globalization, a number of writers outside of economics have argued along just such lines. William Greider, for example, points out that the earning power of U.S. workers has declined relative to those of most other industrialized nations since 1975, but adds that the same global forces that have forced Americans to accept lower wages are now "disciplining" the new (Japanese and West European) wage leaders through the same sort of job transfer process (Greider 1997, 66). Elsewhere in the same work, Greider characterizes global finance as the disciplinary force of the globalization process (229), and, in a discussion of the Mexican peso crisis of 1994–1995, he describes how the International Monetary Fund (IMF) and World Bank sought to "impose" an economic strategy on Mexico that forced unemployment to rise and wages to decline on the grounds that low wages constituted Mexico's competitive advantage vis-à-vis the Unites States and other developed economies (262, 274). Even more explicitly, Zygmunt Bauman has suggested that the global markets insist that governments take a "hands off" approach to economic matters and that "any attempt" to impinge upon the freedom of the markets to determine a state's economic condition "would be met with prompt and furious punitive action from the world markets," primarily in the form of currency devaluation (Bauman 1998, 66). And there is nothing in the less developed countries today that would create more uncertainty than currency devaluation.

If, however, higher rates of unemployment, lower wages, currency devaluations and the uncertainty they create, are not seen as externalities of economic activity, but are instead viewed as punishments imposed on nations and their governments, as argued here, then we are brought to the conclusion that liberal economic theory has effectively failed in its legitimating function. With the recognition of that failure, the "picture [that] held us captive" dissolves and it becomes clear that the relations established through globalization are as much relations of power as they are economic relationships and that the harms inflicted on some by others may not be justifiable.[42] That power, however, is not the sort of sovereign power that Hobbes sought to establish with *Leviathan* and that characterizes much contemporary thinking about the nature of power. It is instead a power that more closely resembles the description of Machiavellian power offered by Stewart Clegg, consisting of an effective "networking" of relationships and strategies that seek to restrict the ability of one's opponents to act, while at the same time maximizing one's own freedom to move about and seek to maximize one's own interests

(1989, 32). By this account, multinational corporations can inflict job losses on communities and currency speculators can inflict devaluations on entire nations as disciplinary punishments, but they are in turn subject to punishments by other multinationals, other speculators, and, at times, the governments of the very nations whose power they openly challenge. As alignments of relationships are shuffled and as one strategy of one participant or set of participants gives way to the strategies of others, power shifts and the punisher becomes the punished, subject to the discipline of another.

Conclusions

Like Machiavelli, we confront a world in flux. Indeed, an analogy might be suggested between the circumstances confronted by Machiavelli's Florence and other Italian city-states and those circumstances confronted by a growing number of countries today. The fifteenth century Italian peninsula witnessed remarkable developments in the arts and the sciences that we now refer to as "the Renaissance." At the same time, the independence of the various city–states that had given rise to those developments was lost as a result of their confrontation with the forces of centralized nation-states like France. Florence, Milan, Naples, Venice and other city–states had long contended with one another, with one gaining an upper (and even controlling) hand at times and at other times seeing another become the dominant force. Such domination by one city or another, however, had never been so complete and overwhelming as to extinguish altogether the hope for a return to independence and *virtù*. But it was clear to Machiavelli that, in the absence of some sort of unification of Italy, independence would no longer be a realistic possibility.

Similarly, nation–states today confront the forces of globalization described above and, as a result, they too have lost the independence that they have struggled for decades and even centuries to achieve. The colonialism of the nineteenth and early twentieth centuries is gone, but states and peoples everywhere are increasingly subject to the disciplinary punishments of globalization. They must witness and suffer changes in the rules of the game that respond to the interests of others, interests that are not always transparent and that create increasing confusion and uncertainty regarding the short- and long-term future. It is indeed unclear whether there is any way to escape such influence, or whether nations, organizations and peoples can only seek to maximize their own power vis-à-vis others through the establishment of new alliances and the adoption of superior strategies of cooperation and confrontation.

What is clear is that definitions do matter in the struggle for power. As Bauman puts it, "The essence of all power is the right to *define with authority*, and the major stake of the power struggle is the appropriation or retaining of the right to define and, no less importantly, of the right to invalidate and ignore the definitions coming from the adversary camp" (*italics* in original, 2001, 208). The condition of uncertainty is neither new nor, in and of itself, a punishment. However, the imposition of punishments to heighten uncertainty, and the cloaking of such punishments through definitions that make them appear to be inevitable and even natural occurrences, are very much matters of power and should be recognized as such. It is not a pretty world or a pleasant journey that we confront, but it will be, perhaps, less dangerous (and the dangers will be more equally spread) if we begin by recognizing the true character of the globalization phenomena that we face, if we see the punishments imposed on us for what they are, if we begin to escape, thereby, the picture painted by liberal economic theory that has held us captive.

Notes

1. Wittgenstein 1953, paragraph 115.
2. *Merriam Webster Collegiate Dictionary*, 1999.
3. Quinn 1995, 47.
4. The Nazi treatment of the Jews appears to be an exception to this in that their "punishment" was not prompted by any action(s) on their part. But, as Bauman (1989, 91) makes clear, Hitler's campaign against the Jews was conducted not as punishment at all, but rather for the purpose of elimination, as social engineering. The actual elimination was but the means to the altered society that Germany would become, once it had been "cleansed."
5. Pereira 1998, 52.
6. Dumm 1996, 84–85.
7. Foucault 1977, 202–203: "He who is subjected to a field of visibility, and who knows it, assumes responsibility for the constraints of power; he makes them play spontaneously upon himself; he inscribes in himself the power relation in which he simultaneously plays both roles. . . ."
8. Ibid., 215.
9. In "The Market as Prison," Charles E. Lindblom (1982, 329) argues for thinking of free market ideology as imprisoning policymakers who might otherwise make decisions that would mitigate the adverse impacts of market participants.
10. Porter 1990, 11.
11. Ibid., 14–15.
12. Hardt and Negri 2000, 43.

13. Porter 1990, 6–7.
14. Greider 1997, 197, cites "a Census Bureau survey [that] reported that American workers who had lost their jobs in the recessionary years of 1990–1992 suffered a 23% drop in wages, on average, when they found full-time work again." Of course, not all of those who lost their jobs have been able to return to full-time work.
15. Wood 1994, 11.
16. Greider 1997, 123–125.
17. Bryan and Farrell 1996, 12.
18. It is interesting to note that the social disruption usually stops short of a complete breakdown of the order that international markets require for their effective functioning. See Remmer's (1991) discussion of electoral dislocations resulting from economic "crises" in Latin America during the 1980s.
19. Here I refer to any wrongdoing that justifies punishment in the eyes of an authority as a "crime." Obviously, there are numerous "wrongs" involving personal culpability that warrant punishment that are not normally thought of as being "crimes;" parents punish children and teachers punish classroom infractions, for example. These do, however, fit Foucault's definition of a crime, since the decision to punish any particular infraction, indeed, the decision to designate a particular act as a "wrong" may be entirely arbitrary on the part of the decision-maker.
20. Hampton 1995, 112–142, argues that all punishment, if it is to be legitimate, must have as its end the moral education of the one being punished.
21. Pastor and Wise 2001, 63–64. It can be argued, however, that recent developments in Brazil, Colombia, and Uruguay are, indeed, more recent instances of punishments imposed by the international markets. In the case of Brazil, international investors appeared to be punishing the *real* as a way of expressing their displeasure over the prospect of a leftist government, given the polls taken in anticipation of the presidential election in 2002.
22. Such impositions closely resemble the "normalization" process that Foucault writes of, although there is clearly a difference between them since Foucault's normalization is explicitly directed at the bodies of individuals. As David Garland (1990, 145) points out, normalization "is essentially corrective rather than punitive in orientation, concerned to induce conformity rather than to exact retribution or expiation"; so too with the punishments imposed by the globalized economic system.
23. Bryan and Farrell 1996, 10.
24. Dreiling 2000, 21–48.
25. U.S. Department of Labor NAFTA–TAA data, as of November 4, 2002. http://www.doleta.gov/tradeact/nafta_certs.cfm. The Department of Labor stopped accepting petitions for NAFTA-TAA on November 2, 2002.
26. Rothstein and Scott 1997.
27. Ramirez de la O 1996, 17.
28. Ramirez 1996, 141–142.

29. Sachs, Tornell, and Velasco 1996, 147–198.
30. Bryan and Farrell 1996, 1, 8. This is not to suggest that the "privatization" of power is as pure as some market advocates would like to suggest. State power continues to be called upon to assist market power in a variety of ways. In an article devoted to the recommendation of the expansion of free markets, Brown 1998, 46–47, notes that "[n]o country should enjoy unhampered commodity trade with the U.S. that uses NTB [non-tariff trade barriers] to subvert the impact of tariff reductions, closes its doors to American banks, insurance companies and other financial entities or fails to treat them on a national basis."
31. Longworth 1998, 7–8.
32. Bryan and Farrell 1996, 4.
33. Longworth 1998, 32–33.
34. Ibid., 31; and Greider 1997, 23. See also Hummels, Rapoport, and Kei-Mu Yi 1998, 79–99, who point out, e.g., that such "vertical specialization" (intra-firm cross border trade) increased 900% between 1986 and 1995 in the Japanese-Asia electronics trade.
35. Orland 1975, xiv.
36. While generally true, there have always been exceptions to this rule. For example, Gaventa (1980, 52–55) writes of how in the late 1880s the American Association, Ltd., a British-based firm, acquired in excess of 80,000 acres of coal-bearing land and established itself as an absentee colonizer of the Cumberland Gap region of Appalachia. As such, it functioned without any sense of obligation to either the land or people of the region.
37. Bauman 1998, 9.
38. Ibid., 123, writes that "[r]obbing whole nations of their resources is called 'promotion of free trade'; robbing whole families and communities of their livelihood is called 'downsizing' or just 'rationalization.' Neither of the two has been ever listed among criminal and punishable deeds."
39. There are, of course, positive externalities as well. If I improve the appearance of my house at my own expense, the value of my neighbor's house may increase somewhat by virtue of the fact that he/she lives in a "better" neighborhood.
40. This shift in function is a recurring theme in Bauman's work. See, e.g., Bauman 1987, 1991, 1992.
41. It remains an open question as to whether the negative consequences of economic decisions should ever be treated as mere externalities. Andrew Schmookler (1993, 53) describes the treatment of externalities as a manifestation of "the key to a fundamental fallacy at the root of the free-market ideology. It is the notion that the interests of the buyer and the seller are the only interests at stake in their exchange." For a critique of the overall approach of modern economics, see McCloskey (1996); for a debunking of many of the widely accepted interpretations of economic history, see Bairoch (1993).

42. The question of to what extent all economic relationships are relationships of power is clearly beyond the scope of this paper. Liberal economics, however, makes a clear distinction between economic relations, governed by free labor, legal contract and market competition, and relations of power.

BIBLIOGRAPHY

Anderson, Sarah, and John Cavanagh. 2000. "Bearing the Burden: The Impact of Global Financial Crisis on Workers and Alternative Agendas for the IMF and Other Institutions." Institute for Policy Studies, Washington, DC, April.

Bairoch, Paul. 1993. *Economics and World History: Myths and Paradoxes.* Chicago: University of Chicago Press.

Bauman, Zygmunt. 1987. *Legislators and Interpreters: On Modernity, Post-Modernity, and Intellectuals.* Ithaca, NY: Cornell University Press.

———. 1989. *Modernity and the Holocaust.* Ithaca, NY: Cornell University Press.

———. 1991. "Ideology and the Weltanschauung of the Intellectuals." *Canadian Journal of Political and Social Theory* 15 (1, 2 and 3):107–130.

———. 1992. *Intimations of Postmodernity.* London: Routledge.

———. 1998. *Globalization: The Human Consequences.* New York: Columbia University Press.

———. 2001. *The Individualized Society.* Oxford: Blackwell Press.

Brown, Timothy. 1998. "Realist Revolutions: Free Trade, Open Economies, Participatory Democracy and Their Impact on Latin American Politics." *Policy Studies Review* 15 (2/3): 35–51.

Bryan, Lowell, and Diana Farrell. 1996. *Market Unbound: Unleashing Global Capitalism.* New York: John Wiley & Sons.

Clegg, Stewart. 1989. *Frameworks of Power.* Newbury Park, CA: Sage Publications.

Dreiling, Michael C. 2000. "The Class Embeddedness of Corporate Political Action: Leadership in Defense of NAFTA." *Social Problems* 47 (1) (February): 21–48.

Dumm, Thomas L. 1996. *Michel Foucault and the Politics of Freedom.* Thousand Oaks, CA: Sage Publications.

Foucault, Michel. 1977. *Discipline and Punish: The Birth of the Prison*, translated by Alan Sheridan. New York: Vintage Books.

Garland, David. 1990. *Punishment and Modern Society.* Chicago: University of Chicago Press.

Gaventa, John. 1980. *Power and Powerlessness: Quiescence and Rebellion in an Appalachian Valley.* Urbana: University of Illinois Press.

Greider, William. 1997. *One World, Ready or Not: The Manic Logic of Global Capitalism.* New York: Simon & Schuster.

Hampton, Jean. 1995. "The Moral Education Theory of Punishment." In *Punishment*, edited by A. John Simmons, Marshall Cohen, Joshua Cohen, and Charles Beitz. Princeton, NJ: Princeton University Press, 112–142.

Hardt, Michael, and Antonio Negri. 2000. *Empire*. Cambridge, MA: Harvard University Press.
Hummels, David, Dana Rapoport, and Kei-Mu Yi. 1998. "Vertical Specialization and the Changing Nature of World Trade." *Federal Reserve Bank of New York Economic Policy Review* 4 (2) (June): 79–99.
———. 1999. *The Return of Depression Economics*. New York: W. W. Norton & Co.
Lindblom, Charles E. 1982. "The Market as Prison." *The Journal of Politics* 44 (2): 324–336.
Little, Jane. 1997. "Anatomy of a Currency Crisis." *Regional Review of the Federal Reserve Bank of Boston* 7 (4) (Fall).
Longworth, Richard C. 1998. *Global Squeeze: The Coming Crisis for First-World Nations*. Chicago: Contemporary Books.
McCloskey, Deirdre N. 1996. *The Vices of Economists—The Virtues of the Bourgeoisie*. Amsterdam: Amsterdam University Press.
Merriam Webster Collegiate Dictionary, 1999.
Mussa, Michael. 2002. "Argentina and the Fund: From Triumph to Tragedy." Institute for International Economics Policy Paper, March 25, 2002.
Orland, Leonard. 1975. *Prisons: Houses of Darkness*. New York: Free Press.
Pastor, Manuel, and Carol Wise. 2001. "From Poster Child to Basket Case." *Foreign Affairs* 80 (6) (November/December): 60–72.
Pereira, Anthony W. 1998. " 'Persecution and Farce': The Origins and Transformation of Brazil's Political Trials, 1964–1979." *Latin American Research Review* 33 (1): 43–66.
Pomerleano, Michael. 1998. "The East Asia Crisis and Corporate Finances: The Untold Story." World Bank Policy Research Working Papers, October.
Porter, Michael E. 1990. *The Competitive Advantage of Nations*. New York: Free Press.
Quinn, Warren. 1995. "The Right to Threaten and the Right to Punish." In *Punishment*, edited by A. John Simmons, Marshall Cohen, Joshua Cohen, and Charles Beitz. Princeton, NJ: Princeton University Press, 47–93.
Ramirez, Miguel. 1996. "The Latest IMF-Sponsored Stabilization Program: Does It Represent a Long-Term Solution for Mexico's Economy?" *Journal of Interamerican Studies and World Affairs* 38 (4) (Winter): 129–156.
Ramirez de la O, Rogelio. 1996. "The Mexican Peso Crisis and Recession of 1994–1995: Preventable Then, Avoidable in the Future?" In *The Mexican Peso Crisis*, edited by Riordan Roett. Boulder, CO: Lynne Rienner Publishers.
Remmer, Karen. 1991. "The Political Impact of Economic Crisis in Latin America in the 1980s." *American Political Science Review* 85 (3): 777–800.
Rothstein, Jesse, and Rob Scott. 1997. "NAFTA's Casualties." Economic Policy Institute Study, Washington, DC, September 19.
Sachs, Jeffrey D., Aaron Tornell, and Andres Velasco. 1996. "Financial Crises in Emerging Markets: The Lessons from 1995." *Brookings Papers on Economic Activity* 1, 147–198.

Schmooker, Andrew B. 1993. *The Illusion of Choice: How the Market Economy Shapes Our Destiny.* Albany: State University of New York Press.

Wittgenstein, Ludwig. 1953. *Philosophical Investigations.* 3rd ed. Translated by G. E. M. Anscombe. New York: Macmillan Co.

Wood, Adrian. 1994. *North–South Trade, Employment and Inequality.* Oxford: Oxford University Press.

Conclusion

Diane E. Johnson and Fernando López-Alves

In an old-fashioned and venerable tradition, we believe that to conclude is not to restate what was said in the introduction. In our conclusion, we wish to offer a brief overview of the contributions made by the authors in this volume, and to connect them with the overall theme of the book.

Explicit or implicit in much of the early globalization literature was the belief that after an unspecified period of adjustment, the changes taking place throughout much of the world would usher in a period of stability and growth. Moreover, this would be accompanied by a greater sense of predictability for developing regions that had long lacked such certainty. During much of the 1980s and part of the 1990s, the promise of globalization's benefits appealed to both governing elites and regular citizens in Latin America. The elites appeared to accept the view that the set of structural reforms prescribed by the so-called Washington Consensus, international financial organizations, and economic advisers would allow the region to join the exclusive club previously reserved mainly for North Americans and Western Europeans. The bulk of the population, meanwhile, longed for stability and some degree of predictability following the breakdown of democracy throughout most of the region from the 1960s through the mid-1980s.[1] The military-led regimes during that period attempted to provide some political stability by repressing the opposition; by the end of their tenure, however, this had created the opposite effect. And while in some cases these military governments were able to create a more stable economic climate, in most of the region these regimes remained unable to provide a reasonable degree of economic certainty. By the time democracy was restored, especially in the Southern Cone, the bulk of the population expected not only more political freedom but the ability to plan for a future that looked brighter in a context of stability and greater certitude.

More than two decades have passed, however, and according to evidence presented in this book, many of the early expectations about globalization—whether economic, political, or cultural—have failed to materialize. In some cases, the results have indeed been quite different than what was predicted. We believe that this is of critical importance today, both to academics and to policymakers in Latin America and elsewhere. The chapters by Fernando López-Alves and Miguel Centeno indicate, for example, that the neoliberal society envisioned by elites in both North and South in the 1980s and early 1990s has failed to take root in Latin America. Neoliberalism did not open opportunities as much as our theories predicted it would, and this has generated a negative response among elites and citizens throughout much of the region.

López-Alves argued in chapter 2 that while terrorism, internal war, and war among states has been the main cause of uncertainty in other regions, neoliberalism in general—and second-generation liberal reforms in particular—has been the main cause of rising levels of uncertainty affecting most Argentines. Based on a number of opinion polls and interviews, he contended that this has created a popular sense of pessimism, mistrust in government, and a serious weakening of political obligation. Focusing on urban Argentina, especially in the city of Buenos Aires, he showed that neoliberal reform may lead to the erosion of obligation and to a growing "divorce" between citizens and the state that threatens the very foundation of democracy and contributes to further instability. He suggested that, in particular, blurred images of what lies ahead have weakened the legitimacy of government; while globalization created wonderful new opportunities, it simultaneously fostered societies that looked at a future with less hope and greater uncertainty. The author presents stunning figures regarding growing mistrust in government among the population of Buenos Aires (regardless of age and gender), and the inability of political parties and the state to regain the support of constituencies. According to López-Alves, the government's lack of a clear project for the future has weakened the citizens' sense of obligation and responsibility to the state. Moreover, citizens believe that real political power seems to be in the hands of external forces or nongovernmental organizations. In sum, the weakening of state authority in addition to the negative image of politicians, combined with growing mistrust in the future, increases the already existing gap between governors and governed. López-Alves argued that the case of Argentina is particularly telling, because for most of the 1990s this was the "poster child" of neoliberal economic reforms. By the end of the decade, however, Argentines faced a deep and persistent recession, soaring unemployment, and a dramatic increase in poverty. Uncertainty—among other things—has eroded the deeply rooted notion of progress that is so characteristic of an immigrant's society such as Argentina's. According to López-Alves, many Argentines believe that some sense of certainty about the future is a necessary precondition for development.

In chapter 3, Centeno argued for a novel and refreshing view of the uncertainties created by markets and their effects. He suggested that beyond a set of policy prescriptions, neoliberalism represents a shift in both the logics and intended audience of policymaking. Macroeconomic goals have replaced political reasoning in the formation of policy, and the audience has become internationalized. The victory of neoliberalism is not necessarily attributable to its virtues or benefits; rather, it represents the triumph of an "imperial vision" spread through networks of individuals and institutions whose power is asymmetrically distributed. The early confidence in the efficiency of the markets has today largely given way to uncertainty. Centeno demonstrated the significant growth of economic inequality in Latin America as "market forces" have become more prevalent, and as the uncertainty of outcomes has become commonplace in people's thinking and behavior. Early globalization theorists did not anticipate such inequality and uncertainty—at least to its current degree and persistence. One of Centeno's core arguments was that geopolitical position helps to explain the sometimes puzzling adherence to neoliberal economic doctrine. Neoliberalism gained strength due to the increasing importance of global financial flows and the growing dependence on the approval of a few players espousing a dominant political and economic paradigm. In short, despite the uncertainties it created, Latin American policymakers felt they must adopt neoliberalism in order to be taken seriously in the international community.

The changing of rules and institutional certainties as a result of liberal reform and globalization constitute another theme that arises in a number of chapters in this volume, notably those by Tom Siemsen (chapter 8) and Steven Cassedy (chapter 7). Siemsen and Cassedy showed that the rules of the game are changing as a result of globalization, but these changes are not always clear to the actors involved, and the rewards and punishments are often uncertain. In this sense, the future in Latin America has in many ways become *less* predictable rather than more so in recent years. This is true for the political elites as well as the general citizenry.

In chapter 7, Cassedy critiqued accepted uses of language over time in the context of human rights. The conception of human rights, and the links between notions of human rights and nationalism, are critical to Latin America's integration into global society. Following decades of authoritarian rule throughout much of the region, it is perhaps not surprising that uncertainty surrounded the discussion of human rights in the 1980s; moreover, the market imposed its own agenda upon these debates. Cassedy asserted that new conceptions and norms have shaped the understanding of human rights. Specifically, claims about the universality of human rights have evolved over the past century from being merely implicit to explicit. Cassedy tied this trend to globalization. For example, improvements in communication technology in the nineteenth century meant that human rights movements could become truly international, both in their membership and in their impact. The question of human rights in Latin America is closely connected with issues of nationality in general. The status of groups excluded from "the nation" by the elites form a natural part of the story of globalization. Cassedy notes that the evolution of human rights in relation to the building of the nation marks one of Latin America's contributions to globalization theory. Cassedy's chapter reinforces the notion that globalization and the uncertainty it brings with it challenges conceptions in often unexpected ways. This is true not only of the current period of globalization but also in its nineteenth-century manifestation.

Siemsen also focused on the evolving meanings of language. In chapter 8, he offered a provocative essay on globalized crime and punishment. Siemsen claimed that in the current climate of uncertainty, these terms have taken on new meanings. He used as a starting point Michel Foucault's conception of punishment as it relates to power. Foucault essentially reverses the liberal idea that a crime is what violates the law, by stating that a crime is "what is punished." Moreover, the modern aim of punishment is to impose discipline and control, rather than justice. Siemsen challenged the notion of globalization as a "manifestation of (value-neutral) economic development," suggesting instead that global markets seek to exert a disciplinary function by identifying "crimes" and punishing offenders. Shifts in notions of punishment and crime foster higher levels of uncertainty at the societal and individual levels. Latin America, Siemsen argues, is an excellent example. In addition to coping with the uncertainty about meanings, individuals and governments must create new norms that adjust to the changing understanding of punishment and crime that apply to most manifestations of cultural, economic, and social life. Siemsen asserted that globalizing forces have deemed "crimes" things such as the possession of a job that can be performed more efficiently by someone else, somewhere else.

These "crimes" then warrant "punishment"; in this case, the loss of employment (or perhaps social instability, if the losses are large-scale). Job loss and changing rules regarding performance at the workplace of course increase uncertainty. Siemsen's work supported López-Alves's contention that the loss of employment and social benefits in the Southern Cone has created high levels of uncertainty under newly restored democratic rule, which in turn is seen as a punishment for not fully complying with global norms. The connection between the benefits of democratic reform and compliance with global rules becomes fuzzy. The author made the normative claim that globalization will be less harmful and less dangerous if we can begin to get beyond the traditional views (mostly borrowed from economics) that have until now held us captive.

As we acknowledged in the introduction, it is not particularly surprising that a period of widespread and rapid change would bring with it some level of uncertainty; in fact, it would have been startling if it had not. But whether they were proponents or opponents of globalization, few observers seemed to anticipate that the uncertainty would linger as long, or be as pervasive, as it has. Nor did our theories prepare us for the kinds of popular challenges to the neoliberal model, and even to Schumpeterian democracy, that have arisen throughout much of Latin America in the last half decade.[2] The election of left-leaning presidents in Venezuela, Chile, Argentina, Brazil, Uruguay, and Bolivia is just one indication. Is this a short-term shift, or a sign that globalization is receding as it did in the aftermath of World War I? Are we seeing a particularly Latin American response to global changes that will distinguish it from other developing regions in the long term? The answers to these questions are still speculative, but we think that they are important for future research. Chapter 4 in this volume by Benjamin Cohen, for example, suggested that the current backlash against economic globalization in Latin America could be contained as a result of policy changes.

Like López-Alves and Centeno, Cohen examined the impact of global markets on Latin America. A crucial question is whether economic globalization can be halted, and the lack of a clear answer is partially responsible for the uncertainty that globalization has wrought. If globalization were to slow or even reverse, what would happen in the aftermath? Contrary to much of the current economic thinking, Cohen argued that globalization is a process that could be brought to an end. In fact, he contended that a backlash is mounting against globalization. Economic change, income inequality, environmental decay, and cultural degradation have created "losers" with a loud and clear voice. These voices are becoming louder as uncertainty increases. Cohen worried that these challenges to global capital, and the entrenched resistance on the part of the discontented, risk the benefits of globalization. How can we then reach a wise balance in which benefits are kept and the discontented are satisfied? Cohen argued that we must respond effectively to uncertainty in the spheres of trade and finance. This means addressing the legitimate concerns of globalization's critics regarding the effects of open markets. If policymakers fail to heed these warnings, Cohen fears that we may return to "an earlier era of rampant protectionism and economic nationalism," which would represent a loss for all.

An important idea that emerges in this volume is the fruitlessness of trying to characterize the effects of globalization as either good or bad. It is clear, as many observers have noted in this volume and elsewhere, that globalization has created both winners and losers. Cohen's chapter made the case that economic globalization is largely positive for the developing world, with some modifications to mitigate the pain imposed on the economic losers. Others saw the effects of global developments in less glowing terms. Most, however, suggested that the results of globalization are often conflicting. It also affects different sectors in society in different ways. What this volume has emphasized, however, is that despite all these different perspectives it can be argued that globalization and uncertainty have gone hand in hand, and that any observer trying to describe and study the effects of globalization on Latin America would have to acknowledge this connection.

Some of the evidence in the volume suggests that the connection between globalization and uncertainty has historical precedent. There is no obvious theoretical or historical reason to expect that uncertainty would be absent prior to the second wave of globalization examined in some chapters in this volume. Likewise, globalization is not a new phenomenon. It is common in the historical literature to see references to the development of a "global economy,"[3] or a "world economy"[4] in the period between the mid- to late nineteenth century and the onset of World War I. These terms generally refer to the dramatic expansion of markets, new technologies, overseas trade and investment, levels of immigration (especially from Europe), and colonization.[5] We felt that some reference to Latin America's first experiences with globalization had to be made in order to contribute a more complete picture of how global change and rising uncertainty have been connected. Thus, we included the chapters by David Rock and Steven Cassedy that address the impact of nineteenth-century globalization. These two chapters offer an indication that the wave of globalization that began in the late nineteenth century also changed the world in unpredictable and uncertain ways.

In chapter 1, Rock offered a fascinating historical account of the widening world of the late 1800s. In his analysis of the life of Jabez Spencer Balfour, a minor British politician but fascinating businessman and adventurer, Rock demonstrated some of the uncertainties unleashed or exacerbated by the first wave of globalization. The chapter provided an example of how individuals are forced to cope with uncertainty, and how they adapt their practices as society changes. In the 1880s, Balfour found that he could be anonymous, isolated, and unreachable in Argentina. Uncertainty was minimal; he had found a safe heaven. Only a decade later, Balfour could no longer escape his pursuers thanks to transformations in communications and transportation. Rock also addressed the theme of collective uncertainty. In the late 1870s, Argentina stood at the fringes of the Atlantic world, relatively untouched by globalization. By the late 1890s, however, the situation had radically changed. Rock added rich evidence to suggest that many nineteenth-century Argentines conceptualized globalization in terms very similar to today's. A subsequent generation of Latin American leaders responded far differently. By the 1930s, many had turned inward and had adopted highly nationalistic and protectionist economic programs. It is unlikely that Balfour or his contemporaries could have imagined such a reversal. Such are the uncertain outcomes of globalization. Rock's work showed that advances in global communication and transportation can lead to profound changes and unpredicted responses at both the individual and societal levels, while other social and cultural areas remain relatively unaffected. This is still the case today, as evidenced by the persistence of diverse values and practices; moreover, it is often difficult to predict which aspects of individual and social life will be altered by global trends and which will not.

We believe that the varied approaches and concerns of the chapters contained here strengthen our argument that uncertainty has accompanied the global changes sweeping Latin America and elsewhere since the late twentieth century. While much of the existing literature focuses fairly narrowly on a particular aspect of globalization, we seek to show how broadly it has affected Latin American societies. One clear concern is how the adoption of the neoliberal economic model has affected the region, and deservedly so. The chapters by Rock, López-Alves, and Cohen addressed this very important issue. But globalization also has implications for the relations between the state and civil society, as we see in the chapters by Diane Johnson, and

Jonathan Rosenberg. This ranges from the strategies that organizations adopt in presenting their goals to governments, to the formulation of public policy in a wide range of areas.

One of the early expectations of globalization theory was that for better or worse, we would see a growing homogenization of public policy as states became ever-more interconnected and subject to the norms and regulations of international organizations. In chapter 5, Johnson took up this issue with a focus on communication policy in Latin America, specifically government policies regarding ownership of the mass media. One can observe a great deal of popular and academic consternation about the emergence of global media empires, which have profound implications for the range of views presented in the media and challenge long-held assumptions regarding a "free press" in a liberal democratic society. A parallel concern is that Western culture is being imposed on developing regions, particularly through the broadcast media and film. On the other hand are the globalization optimists, who believe that greater reliance on markets will allow the entrance of new players, and see opportunities for extended communication and cultural exchange through the development of new technologies such as the Internet. Since the 1980s, deregulation and internationalization swept both policymakers and the media who are regulated (or not) by state policy into unfamiliar and uncertain territory. The situation was exacerbated by the dramatic growth of "new media" such as cable and satellite television and the Internet. Policymakers who were uncertain of the potential of the new media thus fell behind the technological curve, leading to variance among national policies and in some cases neglect of important issues. While some aspects of communication policy have responded to globalization along expected lines, others have not. Johnson argues that we need a more nuanced account of how globalization affects domestic political relationships than was offered by early theorists. Economic liberalization may exert similar pressures, but the outcome varies from state to state.

We can observe the uncertainty created by globalization in other policy areas as well. In chapter 6, Rosenberg examined the effects of globalization on environmental policy. He asserted that the need for loans and a focus on growth-oriented projects has been antithetical to environmental sustainability and substantive participation by grassroots actors in both authoritarian and democratic states. Stressing the unexpected outcomes of globalization and the uncertain consequences for environmental policy, Rosenberg observed an increased attention to environmental preservation and stakeholder participation in development financing in recent years. This is related to changes in civil society, state governments, and international institutions. Environmentally oriented nongovernmental organizations (NGOs) have increased their activities with direct action and the application of pressure on governments and international organizations. Latin American governments have established environmental ministries and regulatory agencies. Moreover, World Bank operational directives for development projects now include guidelines for environmental assessment and prescribed participation by the affected populations. Recipient governments and communities find themselves faced with a new set of conditions that could affect economic growth and empower new groups. In some respects, this builds on the processes of globalization originating in the 1970s. In other respects it is novel, reflecting the uncertain course of a rapidly changing world.

In conclusion, the evidence presented in the chapters asked for the inclusion of *uncertainty* as a variable in globalization literature, and strongly pointed to the importance of Latin America in reshaping theories of globalization and the evolution of the current debate. Perhaps not surprisingly, the chapters in this collection strongly defied the simplistic notion advanced by many people that globalization will lead to economic, political, and cultural homogenization. We have argued that we need much more comparative research involving Latin America for the formulation of a richer theory of globalization. We hoped to encourage this by stressing that neoliberalism has not been able to offer a promising image of the future, by suggesting that the rules of the game are still blurred and unsettled, by submitting that state-societal relations are often evolving and taking unpredictable directions, and by insinuating that despite the great gap that separates the first and second waves of globalization, rising uncertainty was a common feature of both.

Notes

1. The exceptions were Colombia, Venezuela, and Costa Rica.
2. Joseph Schumpeter's procedural definition has been the springboard for most discussions of democracy among political scientists for the last several decades. He defines democracy minimally as "that institutional arrangement for arriving at political decisions in which individuals acquire the power to decide by means of a competitive struggle for the people's vote" (1947, 269).
3. See, e.g., Perry et al. 1996, chapter 27.
4. See, e.g., Cameron 1997.
5. Specifically, O'Rourke and Williamson (1999) argue that the world economy has experienced two long phases of globalization: the period

from 1850 to 1914, and the current period. Their findings are based on data such as the convergence of real wages, and increasing levels of foreign trade and labor migration. Most contemporary scholars suggest that the current period has been the most intense, based on the phenomenal recent growth of things like foreign exchange transactions, world trade, foreign direct investment, and portfolio flows. But this has been strongly challenged by Hirst and Thompson (1999, 2) on the basis of data going back to the nineteenth century. In fact, both Hirst and Thompson, and O'Rourke and Williamson, conclude that in some ways the current international economy is *less* integrated than it was in the earlier period from approximately 1870 to 1914. Rock's work on Argentina and Britain in the 1880s and 1890s shows, for instance, that advances in global communication and transportation can lead to profound changes and unpredicted responses at both the individual and societal levels, while other social and cultural areas remain relatively unaffected. This is still the case today, as evidenced by the persistence of diverse values and practices; moreover, it is often difficult to predict which aspects of individual and social life will be altered by global trends and which will not.

References

Cameron, Rondo. 1997. *A Concise Economic History of the World.* 3rd ed. New York: Oxford University Press.

Hirst, Paul, and Grahame Thompson. 1999. *Globalization in Question: The International Economy and the Possibilities of Governance.* 2nd ed. Cambridge, UK: Polity Press.

O'Rourke, Kevin H., and Jeffrey G. Williamson. 1999. *Globalization and History: The Evolution of a Nineteenth-Century Atlantic Economy.* Cambridge, MA: MIT Press.

Perry, Marvin, Myrna Chase, James R. Jacob, Margaret C. Jacob, and Theodore H. Von Laue. 1996. *Western Civilization: Ideas, Politics and Society, From the 1400s.* 5th ed. Boston and Toronto: Houghton Mifflin Company.

Schumpeter, Joseph. 1947. *Capitalism, Socialism and Democracy.* New York: Harper and Brothers.

Index

Africa 8, 16, 49, 52, 74, 83, 120, 123, 147, 190–1, 194–6, 198–9, 203
agriculture 103–5, 152, 155, 158–9, 171, 173
Andean Pact 181, 200
Argentina 3–9, 11–15, 17–18, 21–25, 27–43, 48–9, 52, 54–63, 65, 67–9, 71–5, 81, 86, 93, 103, 108–9, 118, 127–9, 131–42, 144, 205, 207, 210, 213, 224, 228–9, 231, 233, 236
Asia 11, 12, 16, 51–3, 83–4, 87, 98, 104–5, 108–10, 113, 123, 147, 213, 222, 224

Bolivia 7, 8, 11, 14, 21, 23, 37, 51–2, 93, 103, 231
Brazil 3, 7, 8, 11–14, 17, 21–3, 48, 52, 55, 60, 74, 92–3, 95, 103, 105, 109, 118, 120, 128–34, 138, 141, 143, 205–6, 213, 221, 224, 231
Bush, George W. 51, 169

Canada 30, 101, 103, 112, 120, 125, 132, 152, 159, 170
capital flows and mobility 3, 5, 11, 16, 78, 90, 92, 98–100, 107–12, 145, 148, 214–16, 232
Caribbean 146–71
Central American Common Market 13, 23
Chile 3, 6, 8, 11, 14, 16–17, 21–4, 52, 55, 74, 82, 92–3, 103, 110, 126, 128–34, 140, 207, 231

China 11, 13, 17, 24, 52, 69, 74, 93, 105
civil rights 186, 191, 195, 197
civil society 15–16, 19–20, 115, 127, 169, 175, 179, 185–7, 233, 235
cold war 51, 68, 73, 101, 105, 145, 147, 171
Colombia 15, 21, 23, 92–3, 118, 128–32, 141, 181, 221, 235
communication policy 9, 117, 119, 121–5, 129–31, 134, 136, 138, 160, 234
communication technology 16, 28, 36, 103–4, 106, 179, 190–1, 193, 230, 233–4, 236
conditionality 19, 109, 111, 145–50, 153, 162–6, 168–71, 235
Congo 191–203
crises, economic 3, 5, 11, 14, 55–6, 58, 60, 63–5, 68–9, 77, 107–11, 135, 148, 210, 213, 218
crises, political 38, 60, 63–4, 68
Cuba 118, 147, 183
culture and globalization 9–11, 15–17, 19, 53, 61, 89, 94, 97, 99, 100–1, 103–6, 111, 121, 124, 139, 147, 152–3, 170–1, 180, 182–4, 199, 228, 230–1, 233–6

democracy and globalization 2, 7, 8, 10, 13–15, 19, 48–51, 54, 57, 59–61, 65, 68, 70–2, 80, 115, 117, 120–3, 125, 127, 135, 148, 150–1, 169–71, 207, 227–8, 231, 234

dependency theory/approach 23, 50, 79, 122–4, 140
deregulation and globalization 5, 19, 97–8, 118, 122, 125–7, 131, 135, 138, 213, 234
Dominica 146–7, 152, 154, 159–63, 166–7, 169

Ecuador 7, 11, 15, 21, 23, 93
education 29, 48, 69, 117, 154, 158–63, 166–7, 169, 182–5, 201, 210
environmental issues 97, 100–1, 103–6, 111, 117, 145–71
Europe 11–12, 16, 39, 49, 52, 77, 82, 87, 89, 98, 119–20, 123, 125, 127, 135, 137–9, 147, 188, 190, 192, 195, 209–10, 218, 227, 232
European Union 17, 60, 104, 108, 120

first wave of globalization 9, 19, 25, 27–43, 119, 179, 180, 233
fiscal policy and globalization 79, 91, 99, 109, 111
Foucault, Michel 9, 21, 206–7, 210, 212, 215, 216, 221, 230
France 61, 74, 101, 147, 152, 159, 163, 169, 181, 191–6, 199, 204, 219
FTAA (Free Trade Area of the Americas) 12, 13, 52, 104, 105

GATT (General Agreement on Tariffs and Trade) 103–4, 107
Germany 74, 126, 186, 187–9, 199, 220
Great Britain 17, 18, 27–43, 112, 120, 126, 147–8, 152, 156, 169–70, 191–2, 194, 197–8, 222, 236
Grenada 146–7, 152, 154–8, 164–71

Hobbes, Thomas 185–6, 205, 218
human rights 9, 18–20, 177, 179–201, 229–30

IMF (International Monetary Fund) 2, 12, 47, 49, 55–6, 65, 67, 97, 101–2, 108–11, 131, 145, 169, 218, 223–4
immigration and globalization 117, 192, 232
imperialism 11, 12, 16–18, 29, 50–2, 78, 147, 194, 208, 229
India 81, 92, 119
Indonesia 55, 91, 109
inequality and globalization 56, 82, 84, 97, 105, 111, 229, 231
inflation 33, 48, 57, 79, 81–2, 85
institutionalism as an approach 88, 124–5, 134, 138
international finance 78, 98–9, 102, 107–9, 111, 218, 232
international trade 12, 13, 17, 28, 33–4, 52, 70, 79, 84, 86, 89, 97–111, 117, 125, 139, 147, 171, 191, 208–9, 211–14, 232, 236
investment in Latin America 2–4, 28, 33, 48, 52, 55–6, 59, 80, 91–2, 94, 97–9, 101, 103, 108, 118–21, 123, 129, 130, 132, 134–6, 138–41, 148, 170–1, 214–5, 232, 236

Japan 52, 98, 101, 105, 112, 138, 218

labor and globalization 31, 37, 101, 104, 106, 183–5, 194, 198–9, 208–9, 212, 215, 217, 221, 223, 236

Malaysia 92, 109
mass media 16, 18, 19, 56, 117–39, 166, 192, 234

Index

MERCOSUR 11–13, 17, 22, 52, 60, 72, 75, 103, 105
Mexico 3, 14, 21, 55, 81–6, 88, 91–3, 103, 108, 117–18, 124, 128–34, 137, 138, 183–5, 192, 201, 205, 212–13, 218, 224
Middle East 8, 16, 49, 87
military regimes in Latin America 49, 60, 68, 129, 131, 135, 206, 227
MNCs (multinational corporations) 100, 118, 121–2, 124, 135, 219
modernization theory 16, 122
monetary policy 47, 79, 89, 91, 99, 109, 110

NAFTA (North American Free Trade Agreement) 11–14, 21, 103, 105, 211–12
nationalism 20, 38, 97, 100, 111, 179, 181, 187–90, 198, 230, 232
New Trade Agenda 104–6, 110
NGOs (non-governmental organizations) 101, 115, 149–51, 153–4, 157–8, 164–8, 173, 228, 235

Organisation for Economic Cooperation and Development (OECD) 80, 82–4, 87, 89

Paraguay 22, 93, 103, 128, 131–2
Peru 7, 11, 15, 21, 23, 52, 86, 92–3, 118, 128–9, 131–2, 143
Philippines 92, 213
piqueterismo 61–2
political left 5, 6, 8, 11, 13, 16, 21, 52, 60, 139, 183, 221, 231
policy, domestic 115, 117–39, 229, 231–2, 234
policy, environmental 145–76
policy, foreign 145, 147
poverty in Latin America 15, 56–7, 69, 82, 84, 229

privatization 2, 56, 59, 81, 97, 101, 118, 121, 126–7, 131, 134–6, 207, 213, 222
protectionism 97, 101–3, 105–7, 111, 232
punishment and globalization 2, 9, 15, 18, 20, 80, 186, 201, 205–20, 229–31

race 7, 179–82, 186–201
Russia 11, 93, 120, 184, 188–9, 192, 196–8

social mobilization in Latin America 8, 16, 18, 19, 61–2, 70, 146
social welfare state in Latin America 5, 53, 81, 83, 106, 109, 209
socialism in Latin America 11, 14, 16, 72, 87, 147, 183–5, 190, 192, 197–8, 201
South Korea 52, 55, 109
St. Lucia 146–7, 154, 163, 165, 167, 169
state sovereignty 47, 100, 103, 105, 107, 110–11, 123, 148, 188, 190–1, 195

tequila crisis (Mexico) 3, 55, 108
terrorism and Latin America 8, 47, 49–50, 52–3, 228
Thailand 109, 213

unemployment 5, 15, 48, 54, 56–8, 62, 69, 79, 82, 85, 106, 109, 207, 209–10, 218, 229
Union of Soviet Socialist Republics 78, 81, 87, 93, 101, 126
United Nations 80, 148, 151, 154–5, 179–81, 183
United States, policy in Latin America 8, 9, 11, 13–14, 17, 39, 42, 49, 50–2, 56, 60, 68, 73–4, 78, 82, 89, 90, 93, 101–5, 108–9, 111–13, 117, 119–21, 123–5, 127–9, 132,

United States, policy in Latin America—*continued*
    136–9, 148, 169, 170, 190–2, 194, 196–7, 199, 209, 211–12, 221–2
Universal Declaration of Human Rights   179–84, 191, 200–2
Uruguay   3, 7–8, 13–15, 17, 48, 52, 55, 60, 93, 103, 128, 131–2, 134, 231

Venezuela   8, 11–12, 14–15, 17, 51, 93, 118, 128–9, 131–4

Washington Consensus   79, 97, 111, 148, 227
welfare state in Latin America   5, 53, 81, 83, 106, 109, 209
World Bank   2, 12, 47, 49, 55, 65, 67, 97, 101–2, 131, 145, 148, 169, 218, 235
world wars   18, 52, 99, 109, 119, 145, 182, 192, 231, 232
WTO (World Trade Organization)   101, 102–5, 107

FERNANDO LÓPEZ-ALVES is Professor of Sociology and Global and International Studies at the University of California, Santa Barbara. His books include: *Between the Economy and the Polity in the River Plate* (1993); *State Formation and Democracy in Latin America* (2000); and *Societies without Future* (2002), now in its third edition. He is co-author (with Miguel A. Centeno) of *The Other Mirror: Grand Theory in the Lens of Latin America* (2001), and also the editor of *Seven Scenarios for the 21st Century* (2004). His articles on globalization, Latin America, and comparative politics have appeared in *Past & Present*, *Latin American Research Review*, and other journals and edited collections. He is presently working on another book manuscript entitled *Futures, States, and Nations*.

DIANE E. JOHNSON is Assistant Professor of Political Science at Lebanon Valley College, Pennsylvania. She has published book chapters on the relationship between interest groups and political parties in Argentina, and the democratic impact of the Internet in the U.S. She has also presented numerous papers on the effects of globalization on media–state relations in Latin America, the impact of neoliberal economic reforms on democracy in Argentina, and issues related to the freedom of the press in the Southern Cone. She is currently doing research on the reemergence of the left in recent South American elections, and the relationship between neopopulist leaders and the mass media.